THE
TOBIAS
MATERIALS

the Creator Series

New Tools for
Our New Spiritual Journey

THE TOBIAS MATERIALS
the Creator Series
New Tools for Our New Spiritual Journey

Copyright © 2002 by Geoffrey A. Hoppe

Published by Sundance Group, Inc.
P.O. Box 7328, Golden, Colorado 80403
Voice: 303-642-1678
Fax: 303-642-1696
Email: SundanceGroup@aol.com

All rights reserved. Up to 250 words from this book may be quoted or reprinted without permission, with proper credit given to *The Tobias Materials - The Creator Series: New Tools for Our New Spiritual Journey* by Geoffrey Hoppe. Do not reproduce by any mechanical, photographic or electronic process.

The Crimson Circle™ and The Tobias Materials™ are trademarks of Geoffrey Hoppe, Golden, Colorado. All rights reserved.

Library of Congress Control Number: 2002108294

ISBN 1-59231-002-8

First Printing, July 2002

Printed in the United States of America

To Shaumbra

for all that you do.

And to Tobias

for your love and compassion.

We are never alone.

CREDITS

Cover illustration:
Tobias and the Angel (Raphael) by
Verrochio/National Gallery, London
circa 1470-80
Egg tempera on poplar, 84.4 x 66.2 cm

Pen and ink rendering of *Tobias and the Angel* by Cory Fowler, Arvada, Colorado, 2002

World Angel artwork (page 15) by Kathy Hawke

Transcribed by Dr. Mindy Reynolds

Editing and proofreading by Lora Barlow and Linda Lonnecker

Cover and page design by
Geoffrey Hoppe

For a witty and inspired novel about the life and times of Tobias, read *On the Road with the Archangel* by Frederick Buechner, HarperSanFrancisco

Contents

Acknowledgments 7
To the Reader 8
About the Author 9
About Tobias 11
The Crimson Circle 15
Channeling Tobias 17
About the Creator Series 19
Glossary 21
Introduction 23

Lesson One *Accept All Things As They Are* 35
Lesson Two *Accept Your Human Self* 49
Lesson Three *Live In The Divine Moment* 61
Lesson Four *Create In Grace* 73
Lesson Five *Expect Changes and Bless Them* 87
Lesson Six *Within You Is Divine Balance* 99
Lesson Seven *Create In Broad Strokes* 113
Lesson Eight *Receive The Fruit Of The Rose* 129
Lesson Nine *Dance With What Comes*
To Your Front Door 147
Lesson Ten *Step Into Your Divine Will* 161
Lesson Eleven *Give Thanks To Yourself* 177
Lesson Twelve *Your New Relationship With Spirit* ... 193
Tobias Questions & Answers 205

www.crimsoncircle.com

Acknowledgments

The contents of this book are only words on paper. What is important is the journey that brought us to this place. I have endless thanks for the humans and angels who guided me and blessed my life these past six years. The journey would not have been possible without the awakening from Kryon, and the friendship and support of Lee Carroll and Jan Tober. Their work broke new ground in the New Age.

My deepest appreciation to those who helped me get started and have been loyal supporters throughout the years: Bonnie Capelle, Pete Cascio, Azaya Deuel, James Deuel, Emily Green, John Kuderka, Michelle MacHale, Dr. Mindy Reynolds, Joe Schmidt, Katie Vaspra, Woody Vaspra and Dr. Melanie Wolf.

Special thanks to those who have been my mentors and guides; I could feel your energetic support even when you weren't present: Dr. Garret Annofsky, Zehria Boccia, Dr. Doug Davies, Dr. Norma Delaney, Peggy and Steve Dubro, Ronna Herman, Nicholas Mamak, Dr. Todd Ovokaitys, Barbara Rother and Steve Rother.

I am blessed by those who continue to hold the energy for the Crimson Circle including Judy Anderson, Rick Anderson, Kathy Hawke, Mark Jamison, Christine L'Heureux, Casey Lesko, Steve Lesko, Karen McCoy, Nick McCoy, David McMaster, Robihynn Roberts, Yossi Ronen, Jeff Rumsey, Ron Schipae, Pril Snyder, Mira Stanley and Jim von Gesjen.

The success of the Crimson Circle has been made possible by the financial support of many who wish to remain anonymous but share their energy in such an important way. I know who you are, and I appreciate you immensely.

The support of the "unseen" entities on the other side has been invaluable. I know you told me not to include you – rather to focus on the humans – but I'm going to away: Yeshua ben Joseph, Metatron, Archangel Michael, Archangel Raphael, Archangel Amiel, Archangel Uriel, Gautama and the Crimson Council.

And to all of you who have helped make the Crimson Circle and the Tobias Materials a reality: You know who you are, and I thank you for touching my life.

Finally, my most heartfelt appreciation and love to my wife Linda. You have been my biggest supporter and fan. Thank you for sharing this incredible journey with me. Thank you for the love it took to agree to this spiritual contract, and the strength and wisdom it took to release it.

TO THE READER

The author of this book does not dispense medical or psychological advice or recommend the use of any technique or treatment without the advice of a physician, certified spiritual counselor and/or a mental health professional. The information contained herein is of a spiritual nature only. In the event you use the information in this book for yourself, the author and publisher do not assume responsibility for your actions. It is your journey, and the outcome is your responsibility and blessing.

About the Author

Geoffrey A. Hoppe was born in Appleton, Wisconsin, the third of seven children in a Catholic family.

He enlisted in the U.S. Army after graduating from high school in 1973. He was assigned to the National Aeronautical and Space Administration, where he spent 2-1/2 years as a Public Information Specialist at NASA/Ames Research Center, Mountain View, California. His interest in spirituality and metaphysics started here when he hypnotized a friend for "fun." While in a trance state the friend began to recount a series of previous lifetimes. Geoff immersed himself into the study of metaphysics and religion for the next several years.

His spiritual journey was all but forgotten for nearly 20 years with the demands of his business career. Geoff worked for several advertising agencies and manufacturing companies in the Midwest and Texas in senior marketing positions. At age 28 he started a marketing consulting company in Dallas, Texas, operating it for 12 years with industrial and high tech clients throughout the United States. In addition to the marketing agency, he cofounded several other business ventures including an aviation telecommunications company where he served as Vice President of Sales and Marketing until 2001. Geoff holds two U.S. patents and one international patent for telecommunications technologies, and numerous trademarks and copyrights.

His spiritual journey was renewed in 1995 when an acquaintance gave him a copy of *Kryon Book I: The End Times* by Lee Carroll. After experiencing several mystical insights, Geoff contacted Lee and soon the two became friends and business associates.

Tobias first presented himself to Geoff in 1997 while on an airplane flight. Having never studied the Bible, Geoff was not familiar with Tobias or the apocryphal Book of Tobit. He learned later of the biblical story of Tobias. The two "talked" for nearly a year before Geoff brought Tobias through for another person. For the next year and a half, he worked with a psychologist conducting private sessions for clients who were open to new spiritual potentials. Tobias provided deep insights into their past lives and current challenges. Through the experience of working with many clients Geoff became familiar and comfortable with the energy and presence of Tobias.

Geoff founded the Crimson Circle in 1999. It has rapidly developed an international audience, with hundreds of local study groups and thousands of visitors each day to the web site.

Geoff began dating Linda Benyo in high school, and they were married in 1977. They have been partners in life and business ever since. They live in the mountains outside of Golden, Colorado, where they manage the Crimson Circle as well as a publishing and marketing consulting business.

About Tobias

I had never heard of Tobias when he first appeared to me on an airline flight in 1997. It wasn't until many months later that I learned who he was and where he came from.

In the early days of talking with Tobias, the communications were sometimes hazy. Just like a distant radio station, the messages were garbled or subject to interference from my intellect. One day I asked, "Tobias, who are you anyway?" His answer was simple, but it confused me. "You'll find me in the Bible," he said. Even with my limited knowledge of the Bible, I didn't recall reading or hearing of Tobias.

I paged through the Old and New Testaments of Gideon's Bibles in hotel rooms during my business travels in search of Tobias. No luck. I even asked a friend to do a search for Tobias on his laptop bible program. Still no luck. I was beginning to wonder about the existence of Tobias, and who this voice in my head really was.

At the height of my frustration, I discovered the story of Tobias. He forgot to mention that he *had* been in the Bible, but got kicked out. The Book of Tobit is in the Apocrypha, or the "lost books" of the Bible, that were removed by the church in 1546 during the Council of Trent. I discovered later that some of the older Catholic bibles still contain the Book of Tobit. I was delighted to have found Tobias, and amused that I had the distinction of talking to someone who had been throw out of the Bible.

Tobias is one of the main characters in the Book of Tobit. The historical period was somewhere between 700 BC - 600 BC. Tobit (or Tobias Sr.) was from the Hebrew tribe of Naphtali and lived as an exile in Nineveh. Obeying the tenets of Jewish piety, Tobias buried the corpses of his fellow Israelites who had been executed. One day, when he buried a dead man, the warm dung of sparrows fell in his eyes and blinded him.

On the verge of poverty, Tobias remembered that he had once left a deposit of silver at Rages in Media. He sent his son Tobias Jr. along with a companion, who was in reality the Archangel Raphael under the guise of an Israelite, to retrieve the deposit.

During the journey, while Tobias Jr. was washing in the Tigris, a large fish nearly devoured him. Raphael instructed Tobias to catch the fish and remove its gall, heart, and liver. He told young Tobias that the smoke from the heart and liver had the power to exorcise demons and that ointment made from the gall would cure blindness.

On the way, Raphael and young Tobias stopped at Ecbatana (in Persia), where Raguel, a member of Tobias' family, lived. His daughter Sarah had been married seven times, but the men had been slain by the demon Asmodeus on the wedding night, before they had lain with her. On the counsel of Raphael, Tobias asked to marry Raguel's daughter. True to form, Asmodeus came to kill Tobias Jr. on his wedding night, for this demon had fallen in love with Sarah and Sarah was in love with him. But young and courageous Tobias put Asmodeus to flight through the stench of the burning liver and heart of the fish.

Raphael went to Rages and returned with the deposit. When he returned with his young wife and Raphael to Nineveh, Tobias restored his father's sight by applying the gall of the fish to his eyes. Raphael then disclosed that he was one of God's seven angels and ascended into heaven.

After reading the apocryphal Book of Tobit, and later the novelized version in Frederick Buechner's *On the Road with the Archangel*, I asked Tobias if the story was true. "Not really," was his reply. "Parts of it actually occurred," he continued, "but it is a parable more than anything. It is a story about fear... and overcoming fear."

In a workshop several years later, Tobias decoded this story of fear, and told the audience that Archangel Raphael was the Angel of Fear. The energy of Archangel Raphael is available to all who are faced with fear and attempting to walk through it with the virtues of love, integrity and courage. Therefore it was most appropriate that Archangel Raphael was a key player in the Book of Tobit, a story of many people faced with inner and outer fears.

Tobias, the delightful and loving entity I converse with, said that he was Tobias Sr., and that he knew me in that lifetime as his son, the young Tobias. He likes to remind me, in private as well as in public, that I was a bit of a bemused son in that lifetime with him.

Tobias said his last lifetime on Earth was shortly before the time of Jesus. He was a landowner and merchant at the time. A greedy neighbor who had the favor of local government officials had him thrown in prison where he spent the rest of his life. According to Tobias, this was one of the most painful yet enlightening lifetimes for him. In prison he learned to release the human bars and walls that held his spirit hostage.

As Tobias tells the story, a beautiful bird would come to his prison cell window each morning to sing the praises of freedom and life. At first Tobias resented the bird, shooing it away so he could lay in suffering by himself. One day shortly before his death, the bird perched on his window to sing, and Tobias realized it was much more than a song bird. It was Archangel Michael coming to ask him to return to the "other side." The Archangel told Tobias that great changes were coming to Earth. He said that wise and holy souls who had walked the human path were needed on the other side to assist the humans who stayed on Earth.

Tobias chose to leave the human form and has not returned to Earth since then. The event Archangel Michael referred to was the awakening of the Christ consciousness within us, a process that started with Siddhartha, intensified with Jesus, and continued with Mohammed as well as many other prophets and holy ones.

Today, Tobias and those in the angelic realms continue to counsel and assist us. Tobias says they cannot do it for us – we have to take responsibility for our own journey and divinity – but they are always available for guidance, friendship and support. In the classic words of Tobias, "You are never alone."

The Crimson Circle

In August 1999 a small group of friends gathered in a tepee in rural Woodland Park, Colorado to listen to Tobias. This was the first "lesson" delivered by Tobias, and the official beginning of the Crimson Circle. Tobias informed the small group that their Spirit Guides were leaving. Tobias' message shocked and dismayed many of the people, but in a loving and gentle way he explained that it was time for humans to accept the responsibility for their own divinity. Tobias said that the time had come for humans to become Angels-on-Earth and that by releasing our guides – and most of the other old beliefs and rituals – we could begin to take ownership of our divinity.

Tobias has noted that crimson is the vibrational color of teaching, and that those involved in this work are "draped in the light of crimson." The Crimson Circle is the group of humans among the first to walk into the New Energy in order to personally experience the path and later to become the teachers.

In early 2000, the Crimson Circle started an Internet web site (www.crimsoncircle.com) where all of the Tobias lessons are now available in print or audio versions. The web site attracts thousands of people each day from all corners of the world. Monthly meetings are held in Denver, Colorado where Tobias delivers the latest lessons and answers audience questions. These meetings are also broadcast live on the Internet. Tobias refers to this as "The Classroom of the New Spiritual Energy of Earth."

The purpose of the Crimson Circle is to provide a consciousness gathering place for humans who are going through a spiritual awakening process. These same people may then choose to serve as guides and teachers to other humans as they begin their awakening. According to Tobias, the most powerful and credible guide is not a celestial angel, but rather a human angel who has already walked the path.

The Crimson Circle also sponsors "The Higher Learning" workshops and seminars. This venue is designed to encourage Crimson Circle members to begin guiding and teaching others who are going through the challenges of the spiritual awakening process.

The Crimson Circle Foundation provides financial, business and marketing support for people with ideas, technologies and projects related to the new spiritual energy. Projects the Foundation will consider and support include books, music CDs, healing techniques, artwork, web sites, experiential workshops, nutrition, and spiritually-related products.

The Crimson Circle is a nonprofit (and non-prophet) organization that receives its abundance through the blessings and financial support of people throughout the world. While it is called an organization, there is nothing to join, no dues to pay and no rules to adhere to. The Crimson Circle is a volunteer organization guided by Geoffrey and Linda Hoppe, and managed by a group of volunteer coordinators.

www.crimsoncircle.com

Channeling Tobias

The lessons in this book are channeled from Tobias, a dear soul who was once in human body and now makes his home on the nonphysical side of the veil. His messages come through me to the people in the audience. More about that in a moment. It's a simple process, yet when I think about the dynamics it suddenly becomes very complex. That in itself should tell you something about channeling. It's relatively easy to do as long as the intellect doesn't grab control. But it's extremely difficult and fearful for most humans to release their intellectual control and allow their divinity to manage things. It takes courage and practice.

If you're reading this book, you probably already accept the presence of angels, afterlife, a spiritual life-force, and multiple soul-experiences (reincarnation). You've gone beyond the intellectual struggle with these concepts. There were just too many experiences and events in your life that, while not providing conclusive scientific proof, provided you with deep inner trust and knowingness that transcended the need for proof-on-paper.

My relationship with Tobias started with casual conversations between the two of us. In those early days, I thought entities on the Other Side *knew all* and *saw all*. I quickly learned otherwise. Tobias told me that the future has not yet been created, so how could "they" possibly predict what was going to happen tomorrow. From their vantage point they can see "potentials" better than we can, just like a man standing on top of a tall building can see the activity on the street below better than the man driving down a narrow street. But on the Other Side they still don't know which way the car will turn until the driver makes the final choice.

Our casual conversations developed into a close and trusting relationship. Tobias became a good friend, sharing laughs and tears with me on a regular basis. One day he asked me to invite some friends to my house – he had a message for them. "Good lord," I thought, "Tobias is asking me to CHANNEL!" His response, heard inside my head, was a simple, "And?"

It took me a while to get over the fear of channeling. I had no problem chatting with Tobias by myself, but the thought of channeling him for others terrified me. I look back now and know that my real fears were about: (1) my own human filters getting in the way, (2) how other people would view me (I was a business executive, not a meta-flake) and, (3) at the deepest level, was all of this talk with Tobias simply the creation of "a beautiful mind" (as in the movie)?

One of the early challenges of channeling (or talking to any entity on the Other Side) is that "they" sound like "you." Their thoughts come in through your brain processors, bypassing the ears which are the normal receivers of information. There is no physical mechanism to put a unique auditory vibration to their communications. So yes, at first "you" will "think" it is just you. With a little practice, you'll begin to differentiate between that little voice in your head and the voices of those on the Other Side. Suddenly the internal receiver within you will burst to life and you're on your way to spirit-based communications! Realize that there are many layers of filters in place for your protection. Otherwise you'd hear thoughts and voices from both sides of the veil and eventually go crazy. But just like a radio receiver, you can learn to tune into the stations you want, when you want.

I am a conscious channel. That means I'm aware of what's going on both in and around me. Tobias doesn't come into my body or take over my mind. Rather, I can sense his energy come in on the right side of my head, slightly above my shoulder. It takes a few minutes for us to synchronize the gears. I have to take his incoming thoughts and rapidly translate these into human English words. Once the alignment takes place, we're off and running – at times it seems like Tobias won't ever stop talking!

Tobias is a bit unique in that he says he is channeling *us*. When I sit down in front of a group to deliver a lesson, Tobias says I'm really not channeling him. He and his entourage are channeling us. They gather the consciousness and enlightenment of the group, then relay it back from Tobias through me to the audience. Perhaps that is why the single most frequent comment I get is, "I felt like I already knew the information, I just didn't *know* I knew it." The information was already part of them, but it hadn't surfaced to the conscious level.

Tobias and Company help us see ourselves in the mirror. They give us a snapshot of where we are on the street down below. His messages help us confirm what is going on at our deep spiritual levels... levels that are difficult for us to comprehend in the human mind. Tobias doesn't deliver new information. He simply delivers the divine *us*. If you resonate with the materials in this book, it's probably because Tobias is also channeling you.

✤ ✤ ✤ ✤

The Creator Series
Lessons 1 - 12

The Creator Series lessons were presented by Tobias from August 2000 - July 2001 before a live audience. Most of the meetings were held at the rustic Coal Creek Canyon Community Center, Golden, Colorado, in the mountains outside of Denver. As many as 220 people packed the tiny hall to listen to Tobias and take part in the Crimson Circle activities. People traveled from as far away as Australia, South Africa, Mexico, Israel, Ireland, Hawaii, Canada and all parts of the United States to attend the meetings. Lesson Twelve was delivered in July 2001 at the Midsummer Light Conference in Breckenridge, Colorado to a group of more than 400 people.

This is the second set of Tobias lessons and channels. The first set, called the New Earth series, was delivered from August 1999 - July 2000. These lessons will constitute The Tobias Materials Book I which will be available in early 2003. The third set, titled the Ascension Series, was delivered from August 2001 - July 2002. This material will also be available in Book III in early 2003.

Tobias' lessons are transcribed by Dr. Mindy Reynolds and posted on the Crimson Circle web site (www.crimsoncircle.com) within two weeks. The lessons are digitally recorded by John Kuderka and made available for download off the web site within two days.

Tobias brings in "invited guests" from the celestial realms to the meetings. According to Tobias, there is even a waiting list on the "other side" to come into the "second circle" of the meeting (the humans are in the "first circle"). Their presence is directly relevant to the lesson of the day, and their distinctive energies can be felt by the audience.

The lessons generally last 60 - 90 minutes. According to Tobias, that's about the amount of time needed to deliver the energy – not the words – to the human audience. And 90 minutes is about the maximum time this author/channeler can physically and energetically handle. After that, the flow of energy between the channeler and Tobias begins to degrade, and the translation of Tobias' thoughts into human words gets sloppy.

Although you may be reading these words years after the actual lesson was delivered, Tobias says that you will receive the full and appropriate amount of spiritual energy for your personal journey.

Glossary

There are several terms used by Tobias that will be helpful to know before you begin reading the lessons. These include:

Ascension - The process of going from one lifetime to the next while staying in the same physical body, and birthing the divine seed within.

Cauldre - The name Tobias calls Geoffrey Hoppe. This is not his "spirit name," rather a nickname Tobias uses. It's pronounced Ka-ool-dra.

Channeling - When a nonphysical entity or angel speaks through a human. The human translates the entity's "thought packets" into words for others to hear or read.

Crimson Circle - The group of humans involved in this spiritual journey, preparing to become teachers to others on the journey.

Crimson Council - A celestial teaching order, including Tobias and other angels, assisting us on our journey.

First Circle - Home, the original creation of God. Also referred to as the First Creation. Where we came from before embarking on this journey for Spirit.

New Energy - The new consciousness and vibration of Earth that allows the integration of our divine nature into our human nature. Also, the transition from the physics of "duality" or "2" into the "quad physics" or energy of "4."

New House - Tobias uses this term to refer to the vessel of our new divinity, including the body, mind, consciousness and spirit.

Second Circle - Everything outside of the First Circle. The realm in which we as humans live. The consciousness we are responsible for creating and shaping. Also referred to as the Second Creation.

Shaumbra - The name Tobias uses for the group of humans going through the awakening process. Tobias claims the term originated during the times of Yeshua ben Joseph, when people – many of them Essenes – would gather for secret spiritual meetings. Loosely translated in old Hebrew, the first portion of the word Shaumbra is pronounced "shau-home."

"Shau-home" means home or family. The second portion of the term is "ba-rah," which means journey and mission. When these terms are put together, it is "shau-home-ba-rah" which means family that is on a journey and experiencing together. Tobias says that in the biblical times, a "shaumbra" was also a scarf or shawl that was worn by either male or female. It was a distinctive crimson color that let the others know it was time to meet. Pronounced "Shom-bra."

The Kingdom - Home, the center of All That Is. The pure energy and essence of Spirit. Also referred to as the Kingdom of the First Creation.

The Void - The nothingness outside of the Kingdom, or First Creation. The consciousness we ventured into to discover something new for Spirit that could not be known within the First Creation.

Tobias - Popularized in the apocryphal (biblical) Book of Tobit. Tobias spent many lifetimes on Earth and is now part of the celestial Crimson Council. He speaks through Geoffrey Hoppe to encourage humans to accept their inner divine essence.

True Self or Higher Self - Our divine essence which is now awakening within us. The "divine angel within."

Wall of Fire - A metaphor for "doorway" leading from Home into the Void, which is now our universe. The zone we crossed through going from the First Circle to the Second Circle.

Yeshua ben Joseph - According to Tobias this was one of the actual names for Jesus, appropriate for the biblical times in which he lived.

Introduction

It had been a long day of business meetings, complete with the typical dull presentations, analytical charts and promises of better sales in the future. I had been in the business world for 20 years, and I wished that someone would create a better way to do meetings.

I would be happy to get back home to the mountains in Colorado later that night. In the meantime, I had several hours of sitting time aboard the United Airlines flight and then a long drive from the new Denver airport to home. The airplane was dark and relatively quiet, and I wasn't in a mood for office work on my laptop. I was sitting in a relatively comfortable window seat in an emergency exit row, so I was able to stretch my feet with some ease. Being 6'2" and traveling on airplanes nearly every week didn't always mix well. Thank God for emergency rows and first class seats when they were available.

I closed my eyes and laid my head back to rest. Within a few minutes I was in that zone somewhere between sleep and meditation. Although I had overcome my fear of flying – somewhat of a necessity since I was in the aviation business and traveled for a living – I could never fall fully asleep on flights.

Eighteen months prior to this, I would have been an ordinary businessman, who didn't like flying, trying to get a little rest after a long day. But in April 1995, an acquaintance had given me a box of books to read. One night I dug into the box and picked out a book titled *Kryon Book I: The End Times* by Lee Carroll. I wasn't consciously spiritual at the time. I had done some interesting work with hypnotic past-life regressions more than 20 years earlier, but later on it seemed like just a phase I was going through.

The aircraft bumped with some evening air turbulence and my stomach turned a few knots. We smoothed out almost immediately and I returned to my nap. I didn't think I'd ever get used to flying, especially when I realized I was still white-knuckling the armrest.

The Kryon book had changed my life. There were days when I wasn't sure if that was a good thing or not. Prior to Kryon, I had my share of struggles and problems. After reading the books, it seemed as though I had less challenges in my life, but I was more acutely aware of the ones that were there. Such is the story of our spiritual awakening. Everything is intensified.

The night I picked up the Kryon book changed everything. I had an incredible, almost indescribable "journey" to places in the universe I could have never imagined. I had a similar experience exactly one week later. At the time I felt like I was going to burst from within because I couldn't share the experiences with anyone. The experiences seemed so incredibly real – more real than this reality – yet I struggled in vain to relate the experiences to my everyday life. I felt like I was two separate people living in the same moment of time.

I learned later that this was my spiritual awakening. I was struggling to analyze it in my mind, but it was happening in my soul. If I had it to do all over again, I would put my mind on hold while I basked in the joy of the awakening. It would have been easier and rewarding that way.

Not knowing where to turn, I wrote a letter to Lee Carroll asking for guidance. Much to my surprise, I received a personal, four-page reply from him within a few weeks. The letter helped validate what I was going through, and put me at ease.

Within a short period of time, Lee and I became friends and casual business associates. He allowed me to help him with some of the marketing and workshop issues, and together with Rob and Barb Harris from Los Angeles, we started the *Kryon Quarterly* magazine. I was in heaven, getting to use my marketing experience in the New Age arena.

This was all quite unusual for me, as well as my wife Linda. We were raised in Midwest Catholic families, and stopped going to church as soon our parents got tired of inflicting it on us. In all of the years of kneeling and saying Hail Mary's, I never had an inspiring moment. I didn't have anything against the church – any church – I simple could not relate to anything they were saying. So I opted out at the earliest possible age.

Now, here I was on an airplane flight, a year and a half after my life had been turned inside out by a spiritual awakening. In that short period of time, Linda and I had moved from the heat of Texas to the mountains of Colorado. The aviation business I cofounded was, as they say, beginning to take off. Linda and I were heavy into the business and marketing end of the Kryon work.

Now if I could just learn to sleep on airplanes.

✧ ✧ ✧ ✧

Suddenly I felt a strong and intense presence directly in front of me. My eyes didn't open because I didn't want to break the quasi-sleep state I

was in. At first I thought someone was trying to get by to use the bathroom. Then I remembered I was sitting at the window seat.
My limited metaphysical training leapt to the front of my mind. "Who are you!" I demanded, speaking through my mind, not my mouth. The last thing I wanted was the lady in the seat next to me to answer the question. I was holding a conversation in a totally different realm at this moment.
"I AM TOBIAS," was the powerful and direct answer. No mincing words here.
I wasn't sure where to go with the conversation. I was somewhat alarmed, somewhat excited and somewhat questioning my sanity. "How ya doing today?" just didn't seem like the appropriate thing to ask under the circumstances.
"Why are you here?" was all I could muster.
"I'm here to work with you." Again, short and sweet.
In spite of this bizarre situation, I chuckled at the very idea. "I'm too busy for more work," I thought to myself, like he couldn't hear me.
"It's time for our work to begin," he restated, probably in direct response to my inner thoughts.
Whoa! I had heard about this phenomenon in my recent New Age reading. This was an entity from the "Other Side." And he was right in front of me, talking to me. Get a grip, I thought to myself. Use white light. Surround yourself. I had never had a psychic experience before. Now what happens?
"ARE YOU FROM THE LIGHT ... OR FROM THE DARK?" I demanded of this Tobias, with all of the inflated strength and power I could conjure. Perhaps he would think I really knew my stuff.
"You figure it out," Tobias said nonchalantly.
Why can't they just answer the question, I thought. And I've thought it a thousand times since then when I'm talking to Tobias or others. Just answer the question, any question!
Tobias must have been reading my mind. He asked me to "feel" his energy. He asked me to "feel" how I was feeling. He told me not to rely on what he said, but to go within for the answer. Very wise, Tobias. Very wise.
I calmed down a bit, realizing that this was indeed a good thing. Other than the fact that I was talking to a spirit standing in front of me on the airplane, and he was talking back, everything felt right.
Tobias and I talked for the next hour. I was fully conscious of everything else happening around me in the aircraft. Yet at the same time I was fully engaged in a conversation with Tobias.
Tobias told me that we had a mutual agreement going back many

thousands of years. The agreement stated that when the consciousness of Earth was at the appropriate vibration, we would work together again. He didn't exactly say what we would do, just that there was plenty of work for both of us.

In that conversation on the airplane, we talked about life and death, the universal order of nature, why humans were faced with so many challenges, the upcoming Millennium, and oddly enough, some of the things I was going through in my business and personal life. After an hour, Tobias began fading out, and I started coming back into this reality. I was in awe, I was overwhelmed, and I was questioning my sanity. The lady next to me was typing away on her laptop. She didn't have a clue about the monumental life-altering experience I just went through. And neither did I at the time.

During the next year, Tobias and I chatted on a frequent basis. It happened while I was driving to work, in the shower, on airplanes and just before I fell asleep at night. One of his favorite times was during an otherwise boring business meeting. We talked about a wide variety of subjects, sometimes at great length and other times for only brief periods. Most of the time I enjoyed our discussions; at other times Tobias angered and frustrated me.

One day shortly after our initial meeting, I asked Tobias, "Who are you, anyway?" He responded in his typical simple and direct manner, "I am your father." I was shocked, confused and angered at his answer. My biological father has passed away only months before, but was still alive when I began my conversations with Tobias. The anger caused me to lose connection with Tobias. "My father, as in heavenly Father?" I wondered. "Or an aspect of my biological father?" What exactly did Tobias mean, and why didn't he give me more details. I was furious.

Shortly afterwards, he popped in again. When I questioned him further about his identity, he added, "You'll find me in the Bible." It took several weeks of searching to find him. It wasn't easy because Tobias forgot to mention that it wasn't in the current, popular Bible. I found him in the Apocrypha, or the "Lost Books" of the Bible. He was one of the main characters in the Book of Tobit, a magical story of two families and Archangel Raphael. In the biblical account, Tobias Sr. (also known as Tobit) was accidentally blinded. His only son Tobias Jr. set out on a long journey with Archangel Raphael, disguised as a human, to recover Tobias Sr.'s small fortune held by a banker of sorts.

I was even more confused about Tobias after reading the story. The next time we talked I asked him which Tobias he was, Senior or Junior. He replied that he was Senior. "Who is Tobias Jr.?" I asked. "He is you," replied Senior.

Everything was happening just a bit too quickly for my comfort level. There were days when I felt like I was spinning into some grand new adventure, yet the double-Virgo side of me didn't like giving up control. I wanted to know exactly where I would land long before I got there. I've since discovered that this is not one of the attributes of a spiritual journey.

After a year of chatting with Tobias, he put me on the line one day when he "suggested" that I contact some friends about a message he had for them. This was my first experiencing with translating Tobias' thoughts into words for others. This phenomenon is also known as channeling.

After getting over the initial fear of presenting Tobias to others, I began working with a psychologist. We offered unique sessions for clients who were open to this type of work. Tobias guided my doctor friend and me through the sessions, offering advice and council to the clients, as well as a type of energy rebalancing work. During these sessions, the doctor and I could actually see the energy imbalances within the client's auric field. Working as a team with Tobias and the client's inner spirit, we helped to readjust many of the emotional, physical and mental energy levels.

We worked together for nearly a year and a half. During this time I learned to go in and out of channel rapidly. We worked with as many as three or four clients on a given Saturday, or we would work with a client at night after a long day at the office. I learned to release my grip on the three-dimensional focus in order to whisk off to the space when Tobias and I could meld. Just like an athlete training the physical body with workouts at the gym, I was conditioning my spirit to walk between the worlds.

In December 1998, a group of friends met in the Boulder area for a Christmas dinner party. Linda and I had met most of the people in the group through metaphysical classes or networks. The host knew that I was channeling and asked me to bring in Tobias for the guests that night. With my usual high level of nervousness and anxiety, I finally agreed to channel Tobias. There were about a dozen people in the group – I had never channeled for more than two or three people – and I was terrified.

Needless to say, Tobias wasn't. As soon as he came in, he was laughing and joking with the group. He talked for nearly an hour about the concept of light and dark, or good and evil. I remembered thinking that this wasn't the subject I would have picked. Tobias has a way of getting right to the point.

We began meeting on a regular basis and our small group grew in size. We called ourselves the Crimson Circle, based on Tobias' information that he and the angels who talked to us were from the celestial Crimson Council. He explained that the Crimson Council is like a spiritual family on the other side of the veil. They specialize in going into new energies of the universe, then teaching other angels. According to Tobias, the Crimson Council is a spiritual teaching fraternity and we are also part of this group.

✧ ✧ ✧ ✧

We mark the official beginning of the Crimson Circle as a gathering in August 1999. A record-size group of 25 people assembled in a tepee near Woodland Park, Colorado to hear Tobias. This was Lesson One of the New Earth Series, available in text format on the Crimson Circle web site (www.crimsoncircle.com). Tobias came in through me loud and strong, his voice overshadowing the thunder from an approaching storm. He told the group that "the storms would come," referring to the challenges humans would face in the years ahead. In true theatrical form, it was thundering, lightning and raining all around us, but the rains never fell on our sacred tepee.

Tobias delivered his now somewhat-famous message, "The Departure of the Guides." He told the audience that their spirit guides were leaving so they could take ownership of their inner divinity. Like everyone else, I was shocked by Tobias' message. Spirit guides were among the holiest-of-holies in the New Age. Everyone had them, or at least claimed to have them. Everyone talked about how their guides told them this, told them that. Now Tobias was telling us that they were leaving. Linda and I left the group early that evening. I swore I would never channel again. I cursed Tobias for being the bearer of bad news. It was the last thing any of us wanted to hear – The Departure of the Guides.

Somehow, the group meetings continued. We quickly outgrew tepees and private homes. The meetings were scheduled on a monthly basis and we rented a quaint mountain community hall not far from our house. Within a short period of time, the Crimson Circle grew from 25 to 50 people. We started a web site so locals could read the lessons if they happened to miss a meeting. With the advent of the web site in February 2000, the meetings suddenly exploded from our small local group to over 200 in attendance. People traveled from bordering states to listen to Tobias' messages, and soon enough they began traveling in from Mexico, Canada, Hawaii, Europe, South Africa and Australia. It was an amazing time for all of us.

Today, the Crimson Circle web site attracts tens of thousands of visitors each month from over 40 foreign countries. Tobias' lessons are recorded and made available on the web site in both audio and text format. The lessons are translated into seven foreign languages by volunteers worldwide. The monthly meetings are now broadcast live on the Internet, with thousands of people tuning in from all corners of the world. We outgrew our small mountain meeting hall a while back in favor of a large hotel ballroom in Denver that will hold hundreds of people without a space problem.

What next? Tobias told me very early on that this work wouldn't necessarily attract large groups. He said that the curious would be drawn in for a taste of the work, but because it forced the student to go within for their own divine answers, many people would move on to easier territory. We'll see. The Crimson Circle has grown beyond my wildest beliefs. With the publication of this book, I'm anxious to see what new doors are opened.

Tobias' first "official" lesson to the Crimson Circle was on August 21, 1999. I later discovered that this was two days after Edgar Cayce had predicted the "beginning of the end." Cayce prophesied that the world as we know it would follow the way of Atlantis with major earth destruction and the eventual end of civilization. August 21, 1999 was also just 4-1/2 months before the much-anticipated millennium shift.

Later, Tobias helped me understand the significance of the work we are all doing. He said the world was "scheduled" for mass destruction prior to the end of the twentieth century. But we prevented this from happening by raising the consciousness and vibration of the planet over the past 60 years.

He explained that an entire wave of spiritual pioneers were born around the time of World War II and continuing through (but not limited to) the 1970s. This group came in with the understanding that global termination was a distinct possibility. These were the "transition workers" here to assist others in the time of chaos and destruction. World War II, according to Tobias, was a major battle between the forces of light and dark on the eve of great Earth changes. This was followed by the nuclear threats in the

1960s. Tobias said in channel that we came within minutes of launching these weapons of mass destruction. Then there was the potential for catastrophic earthquakes and volcanoes in the 1980s and 90s.

None of this happened, although Tobias said there were many close calls. The job the transition workers came to do ... didn't happen. The spirit and consciousness of humans had changed to the degreee that we didn't need to create this destruction for ourselves. We could begin our journey into the New Energy of Earth. It would be new territory for us, as well as for the angels on the Other Side who assist us.

We, Shaumbra, have a new role now. It was a potential that always existed, but we were so preoccupied with our possible "transition worker" role that we nearly forgot about it. Tobias and the Crimson Council are here to remind us of this work and work along side of us.

We are among the first to walk through the divine integration process. If it sounds flattering, think twice. It is extremely challenging work. It requires releasing all of the illusions about who you thought you were. For many people it feels like they are being turned inside out. True, there are many moments of ecstacy and enlightenment. But there are also extreme challenges from the part of us that doesn't want to let go, or doesn't trust this new energy of the divinity.

Some of the common symptoms of this journey include:

1) Unusual sleep patterns, such as waking at 2 AM, 3 AM or other ackward times in the night

2) Intense dreams, such as being chased or violent battles

3) Body aches and pains, especially in the neck and shoulders

4) Feelings of deep inner saddness for no apparent reason

5) Sudden changes in your job or career

6) Crying for no apparent reason

7) Physical disorientation, like existing between two worlds

8) Increased self talk

9) Feelings of loneliness even when in the company of others

10) Loss of passion

11) Withdrawal from relationships

12) A deep inner longing to go Home

These symptoms are part of the divine integration process, observed by myself and other health care and medical professionals who are involved in this work. I won't go into all of the reasons behind these symptoms in this book, but if you are experiencing these it is possible that you are going through an intense spiritual integration process.

You are among the first to walk into the New Energy, to birth your divinity from within. But in the classic words of Tobias, you are never alone. There are tens of thousands of others who are connected with the Crimson Circle and Tobias Materials. And according to Tobias, there are nearly 20 million people worldwide who are going through this inner spiritual birthing process. More are following each and every day. The vast majority of those who are beginning this journey are not actively involved in organized religion. Most of them are not even aware of the so-called New Age. They are awakening from within, and don't have a clue of what's going on, or who they can share with.

The essence of Tobias' message is simple: We are the first to go through this caterpillar-to-butterfly spiritual transformation process. Many others will follow. Eventually all of humankind will follow. Then – get ready for this Tobias gem – the angels and Spirit will follow! He explains more about this in the lessons contained in this book.

Tobias' call-to-action is straight forward: The world needs teachers ... *now*! Think about the difficulties and challenges of your own awakening process. Now, imagine thousands and millions of others who will soon be walking this "road less traveled." They will not necessarily have the benefit of years or perhaps lifetimes of preparation like you. They may not have the connections to "new thought" religions or spiritual venues`. They are probably not aware of groups like the Crimson Circle, Lee Carroll's Kryon work, Steve Rother's Lightworker.com or Ronna Herman's StarQuest where information and community are readily available.

They WILL need teachers. That is why you are here, in this lifetime, at this time of changes on Earth. That is why you've gotten to this page in this book, while so many others may have put it down by now. That is why a whole new consciousness is about to open for you as you begin the lessons of the Creator Series. You are a teacher of divinity, and you had to go through the process first in order to develop the compassion and wisdom to be a human guide for others to come. And so it is.

✣ ✣ ✣ ✣

www.crimsoncircle.com

Lessons 1 - 12

✛ ✛ ✛ ✛

"You Are Never Alone"

✛ ✛ ✛ ✛

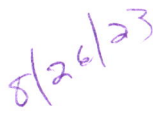

Lesson One
Accept All Things As They Are

And so it is, dear family, dear Shaumbra, that we gather again in this circle, in this sacred energy. I, Tobias, welcome each of you back to the classroom of the new spiritual energy of Earth. You give of yourselves and your life for one simple purpose. You are a teacher. And you wonder why we call this the classroom of the new spiritual energy! As you will find out soon, it is not about *us* teaching *you*. It is about what we are learning from you.

The energy of this time together with you is sweet and strong and loving. We ask you to open, to allow, to be all that you are. In this moment of time that we share together, we ask you to put down the worries that you carry. In this moment of time we ask you to put down the concerns about what is in your future. We ask you to simply be present, to be in the "now," to be in this circle. If you are reading this message, the energy is the same for you as well.

You, the humans, are in a circle of your own. It is a circle that is different than the one that the rest of Creation resides in. You have chosen to go beyond the circle of Spirit, creating new dimensions, and a new circle of life, that will benefit All That Is. This is important information to remember – that the humanity of Earth exists in a separate circle (reality) than the rest of Creation.

Let us talk for a moment about this lifetime of yours. You have come in to this lifetime to complete the last chapters of your book of life here on Earth. You have come in to clear the last portions of karma and to fulfill your contract. You have spent much of the early years of your life doing this. You met others with whom you had karmic contracts. You had family relationships that provided the conduit to resolve karma from past lives. You spent much of your early years working to resolve this karma.

And then something happened to you, whether it was twenty years ago or ten or just two. There came an awakening point in your life. Perhaps it was a book that fell from the shelf. Perhaps it was a message from a friend, or an insight that you had in a dream or while you were dazing. But in this experience you came to an awakening point. You came to an awakening point that led you here. It has led you to a journey of new understandings of Spirit, and your relationship with Spirit.

During this time period there were many difficult experiences for you – what you would call "lessons," although we choose not to use that word. There was much final clearing, for in a sense what you were doing was completing the book of your life, the book that contained the stories of many, many lifetimes. You have been working on completing the final chapters. And then my friends, as this was done, you came to a point of feeling lost, confused, or lacking in passion. You had completed your main contract in life, and your main goals in life.

Now there came a point to choose whether to move forward – to continue in human form and human consciousness – or to return back to our side of the veil. You know of that moment in your life, that moment when you were faced with the choice to stay on Earth or to return to us. Now obviously you chose to stay! You chose to move forward. There is one reason for that. It is an inner commitment that you made. You chose to be a teacher of the new energy. You said you would do whatever it takes. You said you would sacrifice anything. You said you would release whatever it takes to be one who is at the forefront, one who is a teacher. You are the ones who work with other humans to help guide them through their transitional experiences.

We send energy for all who connect into this group and for all who will read and hear these words in the days to come. We look out and see a group of teachers, the ones who will bring the energy of the new Earth to others. We honor you for continuing your journey. We thank you for continuing through the challenges of not knowing who you truly are, but working diligently to find out.

Before we proceed with our discussion, let us take a moment of time here with you. In this moment we hug you. We thank you for the work you have done in all of the lives before this. Most importantly, we thank you for staying here on Earth, for agreeing to go through the understandings and experiences to become a teacher.

Oh, make no mistakes about it. The difficulties that you have encountered are not for waste. These are things you are learning to enable you to become a teacher to others. What you have learned gives you empathy and compassion. It helps you to understand a process that is not necessarily yours, but that you may encounter in working with others.

Much of what comes into your life now are not necessarily experiences related directly to you. These are experiences you have chosen to walk through so that you will be a stronger, more loving and more empathetic teacher. In the years to come you will look back and say, " now I know why I went through that difficult time many months ago, to give me empathy to handle this situation with this human that needs guidance, that needs love." Much of what you are going through now are experiences and understandings that you have agreed to. Yes, you have agreed to this.

Dear teacher, we flood into your circle now to hug you and to thank you and to cry in joy for the work that you do. Take this moment to receive what we bring to you.

❖ ❖ ❖ ❖

In the heaviness of your day-to-day life, in the midst of the conflicts and chaos and the energy that you are involved in, it is perhaps difficult for you to see who you truly are. But we see it clearly. It is amazing to us. In this energy, look at yourself as we look at you. Without judgment but only love. Without worrying about the decisions you make, only knowing that they will be ultimately based in love. We look at you in amazement for you chose to go outside the circle of creation – we mean that literally – to go outside of All That Is in order to experience things that will benefit All That Is. It is amazing to us.

One of the things we will discuss with you in these lessons is how to remember who you are. We will discuss how you will be able to see who you are – to be able to have the power within – and my dear friends, to ultimately become the creators in the new energy. We will work to help you understand that you are indeed Creators.

Oh, you were Creators on our side of the veil when you were here! And as we have mentioned before, Creation came to a point of not being able to go any further. Call it a gridlock. Creation needed new understandings in order to move forward. This is perhaps hard for the human mind to comprehend, but there were understandings that were needed by Spirit, by God, by you and all others. That is why you came to Earth.

In these lessons we will work with you to remember that you are Creators. You will learn how to create on your Earth with new powers, with new ways of manifesting. We will go through a series of very deliberate steps with you. We will be redundant at times in order to reinforce our message. We will repeat messages from the past. Oh, we will be much like your human schoolteachers!

There will be times when you may become aggravated with us. You may feel like you are hitting the wall. It may be challenging to assimilate the information and bring it into your day-to-day life. There may be times when you will feel you are not able to affect what is happening in your life or around you. There may be times when you are down on the floor. There may be times when you are weeping, times when you are ready to give up. That, dear friends, is acceptable. There is no failure. There is no race or competition amongst each other. There are no grades that are given in this divine classroom. Each of you are working as individuals, yet working as a group to move things forward.

In these lessons there will also come amazing new understandings. We ask you to share these with others. Share with those that are in this classroom, who are part of the Crimson Circle. Share openly with each other. It is important for the other humans to hear of your progress, to hear of your breakthroughs.

Now our friend Cauldre was in your armed services (US Army). He went through basic training, and he knows what these lessons will be like for you! But he also knows that much good comes from the intense lessons you will go through. You will learn a new type of discipline, a discipline that enables you to love yourself. And yes, that's what it takes sometimes. A discipline to let you love yourself first. With the discipline of these lessons you will become sharp and refined and clear in your thinking. You will gain the tools to do the work that you came here to do.

Dear teachers, there is much to learn. We know it will be challenging at times. There will be times when you will think that Tobias and the Crimson Council have no earthly understanding of what you are going through! And yes, at times you will be right. We look forward this time we will spend with you. Some will leave this group to find things that are more appropriate in their lives. And new ones will join. We will ask you to bring them up to speed.

✢ ✢ ✢ ✢

In this lifetime, you have released the karma of old by setting up very intense experiences in the earlier parts of your life. Recently, you have released things that you held onto so dearly – things like relationships, jobs, and even core belief systems.

My dear friends, you have peeled the onion layer by layer, to become a teacher in your own right. You have gone through some of the most difficult and personal experiences, some of the deepest experiences in your life. In our own way we grieve for you. We also are joyous for you to know that you have walked through that. The challenges that you will have henceforth will be a different type. They will be personal challenges within your being. They will not so much come from the outside. You have walked through the difficult things. You have made it to this point on this anointed moment to be in the classroom of the new spiritual energy of Earth.

Some of you may be able to smell a faint fragrance coming in now. It is sweet. It is a reminder, dear friends.

Now, Lesson One of the Creator Series will be difficult in many ways. It is a lesson and an insight that we ask you to work on diligently. It is quite simple. We will energetically download it to you, so it will not be just the words that you are hearing or reading. There will be an energy understanding. We will pause here for a moment to allow this process to take place.

Now we will begin the lesson of this day. The concept is quite simple, but somewhat difficult to explain. As you move into your divinity, as it begins to awaken within you and to come from an outer dimension into your being, it is then that you will become what we term the "New Creator." The New Creators are the ones who remain here on Earth, but yet who are able to call upon their divine being. The New Creators will create a new environment and energy first for themselves, and then that will affect others who are willing. And then it will affect the Earth as a whole.

To understand the process of becoming a creator – a true creator in this Earth energy – it is important for you to remove yourself from situations as they occur in your life. Right now, my friends, you are still walking in duality. You are still on the other side of the veil from where we sit.

There are times when you try to create something for yourself. There are times when you try to create or change the outcome of a situation that may affect you or others. It is like you are running straight into a brick wall. You are trying to use an ESP or psychic power. You are trying to push from your brain or perhaps even from your heart. You are energetically struggling with situations, and you find it generally does not work.

My friends, have you come to the understanding, or begun to come to the insights that there is a flow, there is a creative process when you release and you let go? The human tendency is to push. The human tendency is to create energy to ram forth, to try to create or change a situation. And as you have discovered, this is very tiring. Many of you have been very exhausted lately!

You have been trying to use an old belief system and an old concept of creation and manifestation. It is simply not appropriate in the new energy. We see you – humorously of course – trying to change the way another driver thinks! We see you trying to keep a fellow employee out of your energy by creating barriers and shields – and God knows, they walk right through that and come to make your life challenging and difficult! We see you trying to pull energy from outside of you, thinking perhaps that you can make even a brief deal with Spirit to have this energy come in to change situations. We see you calling upon your guides, which is very humorous for they are not there anymore. You are knocking on a door of a house where no one lives anymore! We see you going through all sorts of gyrations and ceremonies and incantations.

My friends, these are things you learned in other lifetimes – 10, 20, and even 100 lifetimes ago. They do not apply now in this new energy. Oh, you may have had some degree of success in those lifetimes of old, but those methods do not apply now in this energy. And you wonder why you have been so frustrated lately! This is a new energy. In the old energy, we could not have talked this way with you, or given you the understandings that we bring forth now. There is a delicate balance within you and within all things of Earth in this new energy.

It is no longer about an external "pushing" in order to create. It is about a *total allowing*. It is about a *total acceptance* of all things that are in your life and the lives of other people around you. We are asking you to be totally accepting of all things. This will be difficult for some. This will make some angry. It may cause a lot of intellectual challenge for you.

You have been used to creating prayer lists to pray for another or for Earth or for an event. While this was a very loving thing to do, we are asking you to not try to affect a situation now. Simply be in acceptance of it, whether it is in your own life or the life of others. We know this will cause some challenges for you!

In your own biology you have struggled with this. You have been sending it light. You have been trying to stimulate it and motivate it and heal it. We ask you now to discontinue those activities and to accept it.

Acceptance of All of it

You have been struggling with your own emotional healing. You have been going for guidance and counseling. This feels good for a while, but ultimately it doesn't provide the healing that you truly desire. So we ask you now to discontinue those activities.

Oh, our friend Cauldre, he is very nervous of what we speak! He is chattering quite a bit now. He is seeing emails coming to him! He is seeing challenges, but we will go forth, for there is a logic, there is a beauty in understanding this. In your own biology, my friends, we ask you to no longer force what you call "light" or healing to it, but rather be in a place of acceptance.

What you have been experiencing in your life, what you have been observing all around you has been duality – light and dark, right and wrong, good and bad, love and anger. You have been taking a side, so to speak. You have been fighting for that side. You have been a willing and strong warrior. But my friends, all of those activities existed within duality, and you are now moving outside of duality to a new place of oneness.

Instead of pushing energy towards one direction or the other, instead of choosing sides, instead of deciding and judging what is right and wrong – if you step aside and simply observe and accept what is happening, you will begin to understand an energy dynamic that will lead you to an understanding of true creation. Again this is somewhat of a difficult concept, and we are working with each of you energetically to help you to understand this.

We are not asking, my friends – no – for you to give up your jobs, to give up the work that you do. We are simply asking you to remove yourself from the situation that is in front of you. If you feel like you need to vest yourself into the outcome, we ask you to remove yourself from that. Imagine a short wall (around your new house) and stand behind it. Consciously walk over that wall. Stand on the other side of that wall and simply observe what is going on. Observe the dynamics that are occurring on the side of the wall that you just left.

If there is a family argument going on between others, instead of choosing one side, or instead of deciding that you need to be the moderator and the pacifier, simply do not get caught up in that conflict that is occurring. Consciously allow yourself to cross over the short wall. Stand back on the other side as an observer. This will be difficult for you, for you have been well-trained and well-disciplined up to this point to go into situations and change them.

We are asking that you do this for a period of time. When you cross

I AM OBSERVER

into this space of allowing and accepting, you will begin to understand the dynamics of creation. You will become an observer. You will literally start to see energy patterns around others, around situations. You will start to see beams and patterns of energy.

As you come onto this accepting side of the wall you will see a beautiful, almost indescribable shimmering tapestry of energy being woven by humans. My friends, you have been so close to all of the events you have not seen that there is a spiritual tapestry being woven by every thought and action and deed. As you stand back, you will be able to see the beautiful weave of colors and textures and patterns and energies, all created from a core of love in the events that surround you.

As you step to the other side of the short wall, first you will see the weavings, the under side of the tapestry. It is being woven in front of you. As soon as you become proficient at this, as you become disciplined in stepping aside, you will begin to see the top side of the tapestry. This is the real beauty and the real art of the human experience. You have been so close; you have only felt the commotion of the weaving of the tapestry. As you step onto the other side of the short wall surrounding your new house, you will see how situations are created. You will see the cause and the effect of the actions of other people, other humans. You will see how things are truly woven.

As you begin to experience this, then we can talk to you more about the process of creation. But first it is necessary for you to remove yourself. Oh, you will still be walking on Earth. You will still be going to your jobs. You will still be talking to others, working with others. In many ways your life will change little. But now it is time to simply stand back, to see the beautiful weavings of duality. It is necessary for you to observe at a distance in order to come to a true understanding of your own creative power, your own creative ability in the next year of time. As you become more proficient at this, we will then discuss how you can be your own Creator. Then we will discuss how you can truly be in service to all humans, to all Earth, as a teacher of the new energy.

Lesson One in the classroom of the new spiritual energy of Earth is to *accept all things as they are*. Accept all things as they are, even those things in your life. There will be challenges even in the next few days (literally) of your time. You will have the tendency to want to jump into duality experiences. For those of you who are healers, you have tried to heal your clients through your own being. My friends, continue the work that you have done, and in a sense, step back at the same time. Do not make judgements of their conditions and do not make judgements of your own abilities as a healer. Simply step back. Stand on the other side of the wall. Observe what is going on. Make no judgement of what is going on.

At first, my friends, you may see or feel very little, perhaps nothing. As you continue this discipline within yourself, you will start to see things that we cannot describe for you. You must come to the understandings yourself. There are not words that can convey what you will begin to experience. For each of you it will be a different and personal experience. Make note of that. Talk to us about it. Then talk to the others.

The lesson today is quite simple. We are being redundant! The lesson is to *accept all things as they are*. Practice this much in the days to come, especially in your life, especially with those experiences that will come to you.

Prior to this channel we gave the "Four Truths" (Santa Fe, July 2000). We repeat those once more because they are pertinent, and they led up to this discussion on this day. The first is that *Spirit does not know the outcome*. As we have said in channel, there has been a belief system with humans that God has known the outcome all the way along. He simply wouldn't share it with you! (laughter) That, my friends, is not true. Spirit does not know the outcome. You exist outside of the circle of Spirit and All That Is.

Truth number two: *Spirit has no agenda*. You have always assumed that God, like a father or mother figure, has preferred you to do the right thing, to go to the right school, to have the right friends and the right jobs. God doesn't care! (laughter) Your biological parents might care! But God and Spirit and All That Is have no agenda. We ask each of you to release that belief system from within your being. Again this is challenging and difficult, for you have always assumed that there was a right path and a wrong path. And you must somehow make the right choice, in the dark. As the churches teach – God help you if you don't make the right choice!

The third truth is that *Spirit and your guides and the angels cannot do it for you*. Even if we wanted to, we could not. For as we have said, in the spiritual physics of things you live outside, you exist outside of the circle of All That Is. Therefore, we cannot do it for you. As we have said before, you have thanked us many times when situations have worked well in your life. It has not been us. You have created those situations.

The fourth truth is that *there are no contracts anymore*. You are not bound to the old. You are not bound to karma. There is residue. There are old reminders that come back to haunt you. But my friends, you are not creating new karma. The book of life for each of you has been written.

Tobias Materials Book II: The Creator Series

You have penned the final chapter. Henceforth, it is a new book with open and clean pages. There is no spiritual directive on those pages that you must follow. You are the ones creating the new energy. You are not bound by the past. You are only reminded of it occasionally. (laughter)

As you wrote those final words in the final chapter in the book of your life, we know many of you experienced great sadness and then a feeling of loss, a feeling of lack of purpose. That is because you finished what you came here to do, but there was one caveat in that. You knew if you could finish that book in record time, you could write a new one. That is why you are here now. But that book has no guidelines or margin lines or preset number of pages. You are creating it as you go. That is what you are doing here.

Lesson Number One: Accept all things as they are. This will take discipline on your part. You will want to become intimately involved in situations because that is what you have done so well. You will want to heal yourself and heal others and bring peace and love to Earth. All of these things are commendable, friends. We are here to work with you, to show you the way of the new creation. You have already discovered that the old ways are tiresome, laborious, and frustrating!

Lesson One: Accept all things as they are. Become an observer of life, of your own life even. Do not worry of what tomorrow will bring for it matters not. Observe what is going on now in your life and around you. Pass no judgements – oh, that will tempt you! Do not feel the need or desire to change others or to change yourself now.

This is a time of accepting all things as they are. You will continue walking through life, but you will use each opportunity along the way to observe, to accept. That does not mean that you will not feel suffering or compassion or love or joy. You will feel these but simply accept and observe them.

My friends, it is also a time to release your grasp, to release your grasp. If you do not, it will be taken from your hands by us whenever we possibly can! (chuckling) You know of what we speak. You have held tightly to belief systems. You have held tightly to concepts of who you thought you were. You have held tightly even to your "New Age."

It is time to let your beliefs go. This will be difficult and challenging. But my friends, if you continue to hold on, it will be difficult for you to come to understandings of the weavings of the tapestry of life. It will be difficult to come to understandings of creation if you hold onto belief systems and concepts that served you at one time but now have grown a bit

Lesson One: Accept All Things As They Are ❖ 45

long in the tooth.

You will be challenged. You will be challenged to release those things. Oh, some of you will fight dearly for them! You will fight for concepts and beliefs that you feel hold you up and keep you from slipping into the abyss. You know of what we speak!

There was a human by the name of Oryan who got into his canoe. He pushed it out from the shore and began paddling. He paddled upstream against the current. As Oryan paddled he became strong from all of the work. He saw many new things along the way, along the river. He kept paddling and paddling. At night Oryan would pull to shore. He would find something to eat and then fall asleep exhausted along the banks, knowing that he had learned much and experienced much on that day. He experienced the beauty of the river, and the challenge of paddling upstream. He would fall asleep exhausted from the day's work. He would get up the next morning, push his canoe back into the river and begin paddling once again, day after day, week after week, year after year, paddling and experiencing. Oh, and certainly it was a good journey. Certainly it was a loving journey.

As the days went by, he forgot why he was paddling against the river. One day he tired of paddling. He tired of fighting the river. Oryan was good at experiencing the journey but he tired, for he did not know any longer why he should continue. He had seen every turn in the river, every bank, every tree, every stone, every rock, and they all began looking the same. He did not know why he should paddle any further.

One day Oryan realized the fear that had kept him paddling. He feared that if he stopped, the river would pull him backwards, backwards in his belief system of the time. It would pull him backwards, and certainly he would float down and down and down river until he went over the steep waterfall and was crushed on the rocks underneath. But he had tired of paddling up the river. He cared no longer. One morning Oryan took his boat out. He took the canoe out into the river, but he left his paddles on the bank. He let the flow of the river take him downstream. Down and down and down he went, past all of the territory that he had paddled by before. He knew what was coming. He knew it was imminent. He knew there was a grand waterfall. It would destroy him. It would crush him. But he had no more energy or desire or passion to paddle upstream.

And one day it came up. He could see the river moving swifter. He could feel the rapids growing stronger. He knew the waterfall was up ahead. As he raced towards it in his canoe, going backwards, he looked over his shoulder. He knew that in moments the canoe would be thrown over the edge. He would fall and fall and fall into the abyss, the abyss that each one of you worry about.

You fear that if you let go, you will fall into it. And yet Oryan did let go. There was a moment as he slipped off the edge – there was a moment of sheer terror and panic. He knew that life as a human was over. And indeed it was! In this final moment of releasing, Oryan transformed his greatest fear and greatest terror. He realized that all that he was experiencing was simply an illusion – simply an illusion! The illusion had been grand and valuable, and it had implications beyond his life, beyond the life of any others. It had implications all the way back to the source of All That Is. He realized that it was an illusion. In that moment of terror and panic he realized that he was the Creator of that illusion. He realized that he could create anything that he wanted now. He could create wings for his canoe! Or he could create for the river not to exist at all!

My friends, that is what you are going through now. Release the grasp. You will come to new understandings. You will let the old beliefs go. There will be times within your being that you will feel the greatest terror. Ultimately, through this process, you will learn to truly understand the illusion. You will learn to understand that you are the Creator. You will learn to create new rivers if you so choose, canoes with wings if you so choose – whatever it is. This is a phenomenal journey that you have been on, a difficult journey, we know, but a phenomenal journey.

Now we are ready for the new work to begin. We are in awe of each of you, even if you do not feel that within your being for yourself. Feel it come from us at this time! Feel it pour forth. Dear teachers, you have given of yourselves to stay here on Earth, to be here for the others. They will come to a point when they tire of paddling – when they do not understand anymore – when they have lost their passion – when they know that it is a time of awakening within themselves.

For them to know that there is another human who survived the great waterfall – it will be a wonderful thing for them. It will give them hope. Oh, and as you already know, you will not be able to do it for them. But they will see another human who has gone the new way. They will see a teacher ready to guide them and to love them, to share with them. From you, they will come to understand their own divinity.

We ask you to work on being in a place of acceptance. There will be times when it will be so irresistible to want to heal someone or to want to defend someone or to change something. Simply be in a place of acceptance. See the dynamics that are occurring. See how the spiritual tapestry is woven.

Know who you are, the journey you have been on, and why you are here. Allow yourself to feel proud of what you have done. Allow honor for what you have done, for you have come a long way. We love you dearly, and remember my friends, you are never alone.

And so it is.

✣ ✣ ✣ ✣

✣ ✣ ✣ ✣

*"You do not go Home ...
Home comes to you."*

✣ ✣ ✣ ✣

Lesson Two
Accept Your Human Self

And so it is, dear teachers, that we gather again with you in this sacred circle. We welcome each one of you into this space.

For the next few minutes of time, we will work with you to meld and to adjust the energies. We will work with you to feel and to sense All That You Are. Take this time now to simply open your hearts. Breathe deeply. Breathe deeply throughout your entire human being. Allow the love of self and Spirit to permeate every cell of your body, into your DNA, into your core level. Breathe deeply. Breathe deeply and relax. Set aside any human cares or worries. Simply release them, for as you do, the melding of this energy becomes much more complete.

Dear friends, it is a joy to be back with you in this circle. It is a joy to see the progress you made recently. You have truly practiced "standing behind the wall." We know the journey you are on is difficult. It is challenging. The journey as a human is challenging. The journey you have chosen as Shaumbra is one of even more challenge. We know what you have forsaken in your life. We know you have let go of meaningful relationships, of things that have meant much to you in terms of beliefs, or abundance, or material things. The journey that you walk – we know it is difficult. That is why we flood this space with thanks and with love.

You keep returning lifetime after lifetime to do this work. You keep returning to the Crimson Circle to be part of the classroom of the new energy, to be a teacher. There is honor for what you do. We do not say this lightly – this comes from the core of our being, from all of the entities that gather here now. As you open your heart this space fills with all of those who have worked with you, who take a special interest in what you do. This is the archangels. This is the holy ones. This is the ones who have been your guides, the ones you have called angel friends. They flood into

this space. We come here to thank you for the work you do.
As we have said before, you came from the circle of All That Is. This is what we have called the "First Creation." That was your Home. The Home of all things exists within this circle. And certainly we speak in metaphors for better understanding.

There was a time when you were within the circle of All That Is. You were a creator. You were a teacher. You were a creator and teacher of the most extraordinary kind. You always pushed the envelope, always seeking new experiences, new experiences that allowed the Eternal One, the Creator, God, or Spirit – by whatever name you call the Oneness – to continue to expand. The experiences that you had within the circle of All That Is, within the original creation, allowed that circle to continue to expand.

Then you began pushing the outer edges of creation. You began creating at the very fine line of existence of All That Is, if you could possibly fathom that. You began to have experiences that were given in love by you to Spirit, and accepted by Spirit in thanks and honor. You pushed this envelope as you created at the very edge of All That Is.

You began to feel a rumble that you had never felt before. You began to feel an uncertainty that was never known within your being. You began to feel a disconnection from Spirit. In your perception, you began to feel that Spirit was no longer One. That created within you a sense of uncertainty and mistrust. It created within you a sense that all things perhaps were not what you thought they were. The rumbling was the first time that you felt Spirit, the Eternal One, did not have control . You were living at the outer edge of the First Creation.

At this edge of creation, you began feeling – and we emphasize it was only a feeling – that the core of all things was crumbling, coming apart. There was a feeling of uncertainty, a sense of mistrust, and a feeling that there was division within the House of One.

In this grand process, a circle outside of All That Is was created by you and other angels with only the slightest intersection, only the slightest overlap, with All That Is. You and the other angels who were living on the edge of All That Is crossed over into this new circle. You forget who you had been and forget where you had come from. You took on a new sense of division and duality that you had never known before, completely shutting the door to Home. You did this in order to create a closed environment to set the foundation energy of the Second Creation. You, the Creators!

What you are experiencing right now in your life is not about past lives! Your contracts are over. The rumbling that you are feeling, the experiences that are coming to you at night, the terror in the night dreams, relate back to this feeling of the original separation. It is not about past lives. It is not even about you in this lifetime!

🕊 You are reconnecting with something that is at the core level within you. You ask Spirit, you ask your angels and those who are in the Crimson Council when all of the hardships in your life now will end. We say, dear friends, it will change. It will change, and you will change. It is not that tomorrow all of the difficulties of Earth will end around you. No, it is not that tomorrow your life becomes a walk through the meadow. But what you are learning here, and what you are learning about reconnecting with the past in another place will enable you, as the new creators, to make the changes in your life. It is enabling you to be the teachers to other humans who choose the difficult path that you have also walked.

Can you feel the honor that we have for what you have done? Do you understand why we call you the teachers? We are learning from you!

What you hear in channel in this Crimson Circle, my friends, should be no surprise to you. It is information that you are already giving to us. We are just mirroring it back to you for validation of what you are truly going through. We do not know the way. Indeed, we have a different perspective indeed. There are times when we can guide and assist you because we are seeing an overview. But we indeed are learning from each one of you.

In the past three weeks of your time, as you learned to stand on the other side of the wall, we learned much about <u>reuniting duality in your dimension into oneness.</u> We learn through your experiences. We are simply recorders of information, the writers of your history, the ones who are writing <u>the new books about you.</u>

Dear friends, take this moment now to truly allow us to come into your circle, into your space, to hug you and to love you and to honor you for all the work that you have done. Do not take your journey lightly. We do not. We will ask Cauldre (Geoffrey Hoppe), our friend who brings these messages into words, to be in silence for a moment. Take this time to allow us to hug you, to tenderly kiss you, to stand beside you. We will return in a moment.

✣ ✣ ✣ ✣

Dear teachers, welcome back to the classroom of the new energy. Today we will discuss a new lesson for you, a new understanding. It will be exponentially more challenging than the first, but more rewarding also. Like Lesson One, you will be given homework to do. Indeed, you will be given experiences within the next few days of your time to allow you to see who you truly are.

When we gathered last, we spoke of "accepting all things as they are." We spoke of standing behind the short wall in order to step out of duality to observe how the tapestry is woven. Oh, with your observations and your understandings, you are beginning to see how things are truly constructed. If you did not stand back, dear teachers, you would continue to be involved in the chaos and in the process and in the duality. You would not see how one thing affects the others. When a challenging situation comes into your life, consciously say, "I will go on the other side of the short wall, the short wall that surrounds my new house." By standing back and practicing this each day you will be able to assess situations in a way that you could never have imagined before.

You will come to understand in your new mind of God that there are no rights and no wrongs in any situation that is transpiring around you. Oh, it is so tempting for the human – we remind Cauldre of the Crusades! – to choose and to be righteous and to assume that rightness and the light is on your side. But do you know the opposing side also feels they are right, and they are in the light? Now how can this be?

By standing back you will begin to see the energy dynamics of people and situations around you very clearly. Part of the homework for this next month will be to continue the work that you have done – the standing behind the wall. There will come a point, dear friends, when you will use this simple exercise of standing behind the wall, and you will do it instantly, in a moment. You will instantly recognize the energy dynamics that are being set up in any given situation. We ask you to continue working with this.

The work that you are doing here does require you to put out energy to do something, even if it is simply standing behind a wall. There is homework. We will go through a series of lessons, each that builds off the other. It will be important for you, for our extended family throughout this world to continue consciously practicing, consciously accepting. You have all done well in this. You have all done well. You have tried it at least once! Many have tried it daily and hourly. This is how you will be teachers. This is how you will be Light Masters.

Now we will move into Lesson Two. We will do so by telling a short story first. We will tell the story of the lightworker named Susan. Now Susan is much like each of you in this room, whether you are male or female.

Susan had many past lives, as you all have had. They ranged from the powerful and the energetic lifetimes of Atlantis to the provocative lifetimes in old Egypt, and through the many lifetimes in lands across your world, including a lifetime (like many of you here) that was touched by the Master of Love, Yeshua Ben Joseph. During these lifetimes there were many things that Susan learned and experienced. These left many marks, many energetic memories upon her being. Like those in the room and reading this material, she worked very diligently, particularly in these past series of lifetimes that have occurred since the Master of Love walked this Earth. There was a commitment given at her heart level – like so many of you did here – that said, "I will continue the work that He showed me." She went through a series of difficult lifetimes, as most of you have also. Many of you knew her in the monasteries, in the churches that you started, for she was there.

Susan went through many struggles. But she came around the circle of her karma into this lifetime, which would be a lifetime of final releasing. Now she was born into a family that was, to say the least, difficult to be with – like so many of you here. Susan had a mother who was very controlling, demanding and self-centered. She had a father that gave his power to others all the time and was known to frequently give his power to alcohol. He let the controlling mother run his life. He was not much of the strength figure that a father should typically be.

Susan grew up with this, and she was shy as a youngster. Oh, she was bright in school. Her marks were high, but you would never know. She was shy. Susan felt like the odd person in a crowd. Although she knew she had something special about her, she simply could not come to letting her light shine forth. There were heavy burdens that she had carried over from her past lives. Her own family situation in this lifetime made it even more intense.

Now Susan was a loner for the most part. She had several close friends, but she was not one who joined in the school activities nor was she the popular one in class. There was something powerful and special inside her that cried to come forth, but there was also something that held her back.

Susan left home at the earliest possible opportunity to be free of this family situation that was most difficult, to go out to discover herself. She fell in love, or so she thought, with a boy when she first went off to college. She became pregnant. Being young and being in a state of fear, Susan had an abortion. This weighed heavily on her soul.

In spite of this, she did well in school. She focused her energy on her studies and graduated with honors. After her college years, she did find one she truly loved, a man with whom she had a previous agreement to join with in this lifetime. Susan and her new mate married and raised several children. They went through the typical problems that other humans have. Along the way there were money problems. There were infidelity problems. There were problems with the children in school. But also there was much love. She loved her children dearly, and she loved her husband dearly. But yes, indeed there were problems. She took these problems upon herself heavily and deeply.

At one point Susan, needing a new light in her life, needing something for direction, joined a church. She went to this conventional church for several years of time. She tried to learn and to understand about God. She attended the schools that they offered, and went each Sunday to pray and to worship. She studied the Bible that she had never studied before.

But dear friends, Susan, the Susan that each of you will meet some day when you are teachers, could not relate in her heart to the words that were coming from the church. She felt that she was a sinner; and therefore, Jesus and God could not possibly love her. She slowly withdrew from the church and went back to her life, wondering what it was all about.

One day, Susan was in a bookstore. As she walked down the aisles looking for something to read, a book seemed to jump off of the shelf in front of her. The book had an intriguing cover . It talked of a new light and a new way. This attracted her, but it also embarrassed her. She stuck it between the other books she was buying, and quickly proceeded to the checkout counter, hoping nobody would see this strange book about light and love and the New Age that she was about to read.

She went home and found herself instantly attracted to it. Susan devoured it in a day, reading it word for word. It rang true within her. She cried and cried and cried because it was a message of Home.

Now many of you know the continuing story of Susan, don't you? Susan studied the New Age, attended workshops, and met others who were Shaumbra. She was thrilled with her discovery. For the first time she was beginning to truly understand who she was. She began to come to understandings of a new order of things.

But within Susan there was still something troublesome, something she could not let go of, something that prevented her from breaking free. Even though she loved this work in the New Age, there were days when she was depressed, when her whole body ached. There were days when she was frustrated that she could not create what she truly desired in her heart. She called out to Spirit again and said, "What is it that I should know?"

She asked Spirit when the challenging experiences in her life would go away. She asked when she would come to a place of nirvana where she would be in peace. While she loved her life and her family and all that she was, there was also a part of Susan that wished to leave, that was tired, that wanted to go back Home. But Susan also knew intuitively that Home wasn't Home anymore. She knew intuitively that it was time for her to continue doing the work.

Last night Susan laid upon her bed, happy with life and smiling within but yet wondering, wondering, wondering what she should know. She had been reading the Crimson Circle materials. She had read about allowing and accepting all things as they are. She had been practicing standing behind the short wall. She had come to new realizations, but yet there was still a major block.

Susan, and all of you, we call out to you on this day. Lesson Number Two: "Accept your human self and you will come to know your divine self." It is a simple lesson, but one of the most powerful and challenging lessons. Let us explain what accepting your human self is all about.

Susan brought many experiences with her into this lifetime. She brought the core experience of being on the outer edges of the First Creation. Within her being, she knew the core feeling that all things were no longer One. She knew the feeling that there was a rumbling within the core of all things. She knew the feeling of being disconnected from Spirit.

She brought with her the guilt and pain and challenge and difficulty from thousands of lifetimes on this Earth. Susan brought guilt and judgment and pain from her experiences as a human in this lifetime. She blamed herself for her father's drinking and his lack of strength. She blamed herself for not telling him more often that she loved him because, in a sense, she despised him for what he was, so she blamed herself. She brought guilt for the harsh thoughts that she had of her own mother. Oh, as a child she would lay awake at night dreaming of suffocating her mother. It felt good, and she felt guilty of that.

She carried a heavy burden of not being a better friend to those who had come to her in her youth. They were attracted to her because they could sense her radiance. Her friends in grade school and high school came to her for healing, but she was so shy and so inhibited that she did not allow herself to do the work that she intuitively knew how to do. She felt guilty for hiding, for not being stronger, and not being a healer for those who came to her. Instead she isolated herself, befriending only a few because it was easier and safer.

She felt deeply guilty for conceiving a child and then aborting it. She had heard that God hates people like her. She had heard that abortion kills a soul. This weighed heavily on her. This was one of her deepest, darkest secrets. She felt guilty.

In her marriage she felt guilty that she was not more supportive of her husband, who was experiencing his own issues of abundance. He would have difficulty each time he was promoted in a job. Each time he began to achieve financial freedom something would happen to shatter that. He would be out of work. She felt guilty that she was not there to help him overcome his own worthiness issues. She did not know how to handle this.

She felt guilty about not being a better mother to her children. She wished she had done more to solve their problems, protect them, keep them from hurting. She felt guilty that at times she would curse them. She would go to her room and lock the door and say, "never talk to me again." She felt guilty for this. She felt extreme guilt.

When Susan went back to church and tried to discover something within, she felt unworthy because God and Jesus would not talk to her. She did not feel reborn or rejuvenated. She did not have the passion like other churchgoers had. She could not raise her hands and sing "hallelujah" with the same passion they did. She felt dirty and guilty. She knew from going to church that she was a sinner, because even Jesus wouldn't have anything to do with her.

Dear teachers, the Susan we speak of is part of each of you. The Susan we speak of is also the one that will come to you for healing and for teaching of the New Energy.

Let us tell you what Susan did after she read Lesson Two. She went home, closed her door and didn't feel guilty about it. She learned to accept her human self, the very thing she had been denying for lifetime after lifetime. She had been denying her human self for hundreds of lifetimes. She had been denying that she was even human. She wanted this thing called ascension so she wouldn't have to face herself as a human, as a lowly human.

Do you know, my friends, that when you left the First Creation and eventually took physical body, you were shocked that you would have to own anything so crude and low? You knew that you would have to carry this body around with you for lifetime after lifetime. You felt this human body was punishment for going too far at the edge of the First Creation. That is not so, and we ask you to release all of those thoughts and beliefs now.

Now back to Susan. Susan went home, closed her door, and realized that she had been denying, even hating, all of the human things she had done. She had been trying to achieve some ascended state so she would not have to deal with the human things she had done and the human body she carried. She had learned in the Crimson Circle to ask from within. Susan thought to herself, "I do not know how to accept my human self. Do I go back and recount every past life? Do I spend more time processing?"

And the answer was she heard from within was – "no." As she laid upon her bed, asking how to accept herself and all of her humanness in order that she may come to know her divine self, it hit her loud and clear. It was simple. The words that came from within her – not from outside but from within her – said, "Release your grasp; simply release your grasp."

As she did, she felt like you will right now when you release YOUR grasp. Her hands were clenching something. YOUR hands are clenching something. Release the grasp. Open up your hands at this time. We ask you to do so now. Unclench your hands. Let go, release the grip of what you have been holding onto.

Susan realized how tightly she had been clenching. When she opened up, she remembered the parable of Oryan in the canoe going over the waterfall. She said, "It is time for me to release all of who I thought I was. It is time for me to release all of the beliefs that I have carried with me. It is time for me release any guilt, any pain. It is time for me, as I open my hands, to accept my human self. As I do, I will surely begin to know my divine self."

You know now your homework! It is to release your grip, to accept your human self and all that you have been, in order to understand your divine self. Surely you will be given the opportunity to experience this in the next few days! You will be given an opportunity to be in a situation where you should not judge yourself, where you should not carry or feel guilt, where you should accept all that you are.

Dear teachers, we who are at your side, the ones you call the angels and the archangels, All That Is, Spirit – we ACCEPT you and LOVE you as human. We accept every thought, every deed, every action, everything in the passion and love and wisdom of Spirit. The Eternal One loves you infinitely, endlessly, and without condition!

Spirit has no agenda. There is not a right way or a wrong way. There is only the new way, and you are creating it. If Spirit loves you so deeply and has no agenda, then dear teachers, you too should be able to accept your human self.

As Susan released the grip of all her beliefs and guilt and pain, and she accepted everything that she had ever done, unconditionally in the form of total forgiveness of self, she began to understand her own divinity.

As she lay awake at night with a tremendous feeling of release surging over her, she came to another realization. She realized that she had been living in the future, and she had been creating a picture of fear for what the future might hold. She realized that she was worrying about unpaid bills in the future that never existed. She was worried about illness that may come to her. None of these were real, but she was projecting her own sense of unworthiness into the future. The future represented a lack of trust in her divinity. She found that she was spending much of her time and energy in the future with her fears. She laughed at herself and wondered why she was doing that.

She said, as she released her grip and opened her palms, "I will now live in the 'now.' I will no longer fear a future that does not exist. I will live in the 'now.'" She began living in the "now," as she continued to practice standing behind the short wall in acceptance of all that is. As she consciously released her grip on her own guilt and pain and the past, she realized that she was creating a moment, a divine moment, in all of the "now" that she was living. She was learning once again to trust self. She was learning that there was no need to project a future fear scenario, but simply to live in the "now." As she did, there was a sacred melding of her humanness with her divinity. She began learning that she could trust herself to provide the "divine moment." She could trust in herself to provide the "divine moment." She was no longer looking outside, asking Spirit to provide the divine moment. She was going within.

She realized that the Spirit within always provides the divine moment – always – but that she had been blocking it. Much like when she was a child, she had blocked her own light and had not helped to teach and heal others, as she knew she was capable of. She had put up a wall, the wall of unworthiness. But now as she released her unworthiness, she realized that she could trust in herself to provide the divine moment.

Susan had a series of new realizations and understandings with the two simple lessons that she had learned. First, to stand behind the wall and accept all things as they are. And second, to accept her human self in order to know her divine self. Her life began to transform. Oh, indeed the daily challenges with family and friends and job continued, but SHE changed. People started coming to her like she never expected, asking for healing and teaching of wisdom. They did not ask her to channel some other entity! (chuckling) They came to her as Susan, the Divine Human. Her work was good. She taught others how to heal themselves.

Dear friends, Susan's experience is your collective experience put together in a single story. There are parts that you may intimately recognize within yourself. The challenge here will be to accept your human self. It is thick, and it is deep within you. You are well invested in the guilt and the pain and the challenge. With the simple exercise we have given – of opening your hands – you will begin to see how you are holding on to things of the past that no longer serve you. This includes old belief systems that are ready to go.

Many of the pains you are feeling in your physical body are directly related to holding onto old belief systems that no longer serve you. You are feeling the pains in your physical body as a reminder to yourself to let go, to release the grip. These are pains of old beliefs, of guilt, of the way you thought things should be. Letting go allows the divineness to come in.

The biggest challenge will be the remembrance of the time when you lived at the outer edge of the All That Is. This is when you felt the original rumblings of duality and separation, and you lost trust in Spirit. This is what will be coming back to challenge you right now. It is not about your past lives. It is not even about this life. The nightmares you are having are about a different time and a different place . They are about the original feeling of the rug being pulled out from underneath. We are reminding you of this at the very time we are asking you to trust in self. This will be the challenge.

You are in the classroom of the New Energy. You are the ones experiencing something out on the edge, so to speak. Again this creates feelings of fear and uncertainty because you remember what being on the edge was like before. And here you are again! But we also know that by being here with you as family, there is also great joy and great reward that you are receiving in this. Each lesson that we go through here in this classroom will provide an important experience, an important understanding at your core level. When brought together, this will help you to understand how to be, how to create in a way you have never done before here on Earth. Each process that we go through with you will bring you one step closer to being the new creators, the likes of which your universe, the likes of which All That Is has never seen before!

Perhaps this all sounds grandiose, and that is why the tears are flowing from our eyes as we tell the story of Susan. It is the story of each of you. Perhaps this all sounds grandiose, but that is why we are also beaming right now, looking at you and knowing the work that you go through.

Dear friends, we love you so dearly. We remind you, as always, that you are never alone in your journey. You are with family, and we are part of that.

And so it is.

✣ ✣ ✣ ✣

Lesson Three
Live In The Divine Moment

And so it is, dear teachers, that we welcome you back to the classroom of the new spiritual energy of Earth. We welcome you to the Crimson Circle where there is celebration, where there is certainly dancing in the aisles. The energy is sacred and divine! We will discuss with you Lesson Three of the Creator Series. But before we do there are a few other things we would like to talk about.

We ask you to breathe deeply now. Breathe deeply within your being, from the top of your head all through your body, down to your toes. Breathe deeply and allow this divine energy that resides within you to come forth. Allow it to be in every cell. Allow it to be in every molecule, every part of your being. This thing that you call your divinity, this thing that you call the God Within – it has always been there, dear friends. It has always been within you, but it has been waiting for the appropriate time to come forth. And as you know, now is the appropriate time! This is why we have this classroom. This is why you gather here. That is why tens of thousands read this material, to understand what is happening within them, to understand the transformation that they are going through at this time.

Oh, dear teachers, it gives those of us who are on the other side of the veil great joy to be here, to be invited into your space. There are many entities who now gather. There are many who now come into the second circle. You, the human angels, form the first circle. Those of us from the other side of the veil form the second circle. We come in now, and we meld our energies with you. We meld with you. We share this new space that you are helping to create here. We join you in happiness. We join you with smiles upon our faces!

It is not so easy for us to get close to humans, for when the veil is heavy, when the doors are closed, we cannot so easily be at your side. But when you gather together like this with the intent of learning and growing and bringing forth the energy from within, then we can come flooding in. We can come in and stand beside you. We can share with you for a brief moment of time. That is exactly what we are doing now.

Allow yourself to feel this moment. Allow yourself to feel the ones who are part of your entourage. Allow your divine entourage to come in close to be at your side. We thank you for the work you are doing. We acknowledge the difficulties and the pain and the struggles along the path. We assure you that it is for a far grander purpose. We assure you that there is meaning in what you are doing. There is purpose, and there are results.

Now there is one entity who comes in on this day to sit beside you, to sits close beside you. This one you know quite well, perhaps so well that the difference in energy is somewhat difficult to discern. The one who comes here for you is somewhat tired, somewhat battled, but filled with joy, filled with thanks, and certainly filled with love.

We have talked before of all of your past lives, all of the entities who you have been in the past. They have come into the circle before. We watched as they walked past. We watched as they returned to our side of the veil. We watched as you released them from the energy of the Earth. We watched as they thanked you for the work you are doing in this lifetime.

The one who sits beside you has also had a journey and experiences and time upon the Earth. Feel this energy next to you. Feel the connection of love that you have. Dear friends, the one who joins you in the first circle, who sits beside you now waiting for release, ready to return to this side of the veil, is the very person you have been in this lifetime, up to now. It has been you, the person that was born 30, 40, or 50+ years ago of time. It is the person who you have always identified as YOU, the person who carries the same name that you have upon your driver's license. (chuckling) This entity comes in today – and you thought it was you sitting in the chair! Dear friends, you are indeed in a graduate status. You have made so many changes in your life! Now, the person that you have been all these years of your life is ready to leave.

A new entity, a new personality, a new spirit arises. It is who you are now. You are released from the old contracts, and released from the old karma. You are looking at a new "book of life," a "book of life" that has nothing but empty pages, waiting to be filled with your new creations!

Oh, dear ones, hug this you who sits beside you! Their journey has been long and difficult and trying. They are ready to return to the other side of the veil. Hug this one who is next to you, for it is the face that you have looked at in the mirror for all of these mornings of your life. Hug this one who sits beside you, for they have endured so much. This is the aspect of you who carried out the final chapter of the book of your life. This part of you went through the difficulties and the hardships in the early years, and chose the hardest of the hard paths. They are now ready to leave. Dear friends, thank this one for enduring so much on behalf of your entire soul!

Now, their memories will be with you for a period of time. But their energy is leaving to make way for the new divine self that is beginning to emerge. As you know, they have been waiting to leave for some time now. You could feel the urges and the pulls, but they could not go until your own divinity was awakened enough for this new human angel to come forth. They only ask one thing before they leave. They ask you to honor them, to acknowledge them and to thank them. They ask you to understand that all that was given and all that was experienced was done in love in order to close out the old cycles of life. Honor your self and love your self!

Hug them for all they have done and for all they have given. You are now ready to move forward, and you are now ready to truly begin to understand your new house. In your new house, dear friends, it was not possible to take along the past. They are only memories. They are only thoughts and experiences. In your new house, it is time to release, even the old self you considered to be yourself.

You wonder now about the changes you have been going through in your biology. You wonder about the feelings that you have had recently, perhaps thinking that you were losing your mind. (chuckling) You wonder about the feelings of disorientation. You wonder why it is that other people do not even see you! You wonder why you appear to be invisible at times! It is because you have been leaving. The old you is fading, yet to be replaced by the new divine self.

You wonder why sometimes you are ignored while standing in a line, like you don't exist. You wonder why they forget your order at a restaurant! Dear friends, it is because the old self that you saw in the mirror has been slipping away for some time now to make way, to make ready for the newest incarnation of self. This new self is not bound by karma and contract. It is not bound to the past but lives only in the present!

Dear friends, this transition is sacred and blessed! We will pause for a moment. We will ask Cauldre (Geoffrey Hoppe) to be in silence while you discover true love from the one who sits next to you. Allow yourself to feel this before we proceed.

✧ ✧ ✧ ✧

There is a gift they give to you now. Cauldre, you wondered why we stopped you before you walked out the door (of your house) today? You wondered why we asked you to bring the Sword of Truth, the Excalibur, the only time it has been brought before this group? (The sword was placed on the mantle prior to the meeting.) The one who sits beside you now passes the Sword of Truth to you, the Sword of Empowerment, the sword that has been the source of truth and power for all these days.

The sword is the one thing you do indeed carry into your new house. It is the one thing that goes on the wall in the gallery of your new house, to remind you of all you have been and all you have done. It is there to honor all of your experiences that have brought you, that have brought this Earth, and that have brought all of creation to this point.

It is simple. It is symbolic. It is now time to accept this, to pass the torch from one being to the other. Usually this occurs between lifetimes when you leave the physical body. The new sword is passed to you before you return to Earth in the next incarnation. But now it is passed to you while you sit here, while you stay in the same body, but a body that will soon undergo many changes! Accept the truth for all that you are and all that you have been.

✧ ✧ ✧ ✧

Now, Lesson Three of the Creator Series.

We have taken these lessons with you slowly. In Lesson One and Lesson Two, and now in Lesson Three, we have presented the foundation energies for the Creator Series. Intuitively, these are things you already know. Intuitively these are things that you have been aware of, but the concepts needed to be brought forth again as foundations. Perhaps they are not terribly exciting lessons (chuckling), but they are foundations for where we will go. We will present four different sets of lessons, each set containing three individual lessons. Today we will present Lesson Three, which will be the end of the first quad.

To help you understand a bit more of your creative nature, of how things are created, we go back now to a time when you were in the original circle, when you were in the first creation. There you had certain creative powers and abilities. We say "certain," for they were somewhat limited – difficult to describe – but there were underlying parameters of the type of creation that was possible in the First Circle. You journeyed to the edge of the First Circle, to the edge of creation, and then you crossed over. Eventually you came to this place of Earth.

Your true Creator ability was hidden from you in the very essence of duality. There was a reason for this. Part of the reason is that the Second Circle, the circle of the energies of Earth and of your physical universe, exists outside of All That Is. You deal with an energy called "duality," which is the two different sides, what you would call the "light" and the "dark," the "good" and the "bad," the opposite faces, the reflection in the mirror.

When you moved outside of All That Is, you were in a void, and you were turning void into reality. In order to create in your new environment, it was necessary for you to project into the future. It was necessary for you to go into the void and create based on thoughts of what might come to be.

In other words, you were always projecting yourself into the future. These vibrations created the pathway for your tomorrow. This is the way you have operated ever since you left Home. You were bound by the memories of the past (karma), and you created the future by projecting yourself into your tomorrows. This is how most humans on Earth still create. The future reality is an assimilation of vibrational frequencies from all the humans on Earth.

We have said before that Spirit does not know the outcome of things. That is because the future does not yet exist! It is not a pre-planned maze or an obstacle course that you must run through in hopes of finding the finish line. No, indeed each of you are taking void and nothingness, and transforming it into a new reality based on the vibrational frequencies of your thoughts that go into the future.

To help you understand a bit more we will tell a short story.

Now there was a sailor by the name of Aaron who was charged by his government to discover new places and lands for the kingdom. He was given a crew and a ship. He was given supplies for his journey. He was told to return in the period of one year after he discovered these new places.

So Aaron set out to sea. He talked to his crew and gave them orders and the details of what he expected. He told them how he wanted the masts rigged and how he wanted the sails positioned. He explained to them how he wanted the ship run. When they first set out to sea, they passed familiar territory. As they got further and further out to sea, they sailed into new, uncharted territory.

Now Aaron and the crew worked with the forces of nature, and sometimes against them. They worked with the winds and the currents and the waves. Occasionally storms came along, and they battled these.

Aaron worked with his compass each night to determine which direction to go in, whether he would sail east or west or north or south. There were many trials and tribulations that they went through, going into these new territories. Aaron would chart their progress. He would plan for their next day. He would continually look through the telescope off onto the horizon to help guide them. They would stop at new islands and observe the environment and energies. They would collect new supplies and new food and meet new types of people.

All of the time they were traveling, Aaron had the unsettled feeling he was not truly discovering new lands. He felt the ship was not truly venturing to far off and exotic lands. He felt that the places they were exploring were just different shades of where he had been before. But he continued his journey. He used the wind to move his ship. He pushed his crew to work harder. The days and the nights were long and difficult, filled with struggling. Many of the crew became sick. Some of them died along the journey. There were fights with tribes on islands that were not so friendly. The journey was difficult, and it took its toll.

As they sailed back for home at the end of one year, Aaron looked at the treasures he brought back. He looked at the new types of foods, at the new types of goods, and thought to himself, "I have accomplished the goal, but it is not terribly fulfilling; it is not terribly fulfilling, for the toll has been great." Some of his crew were not even returning with him. Many were still sick. Many were bitter and scarred. And so ended Aaron's journey. And so ended even his lifetime on Earth.

Now Aaron returned in the next lifetime, once again as a sailor. He returned, going through those things in his childhood that would groom him to be a new type of sailor in a new type of energy. When Aaron became of age, he was ready to sail once again. But this time Aaron did not have a full crew. This time he chose to go alone. He chose to go by himself. He made the choice to not to work for the kingdom, not to work for some government but instead to journey on his own. He built himself a ship that was just right for the voyage he was about to embark on.

Within his cellular being, there were many hidden memories of what he had learned in his previous lifetime as a sailor and explorer. When Aaron pushed out for sea in his new ship, he left his compass at home. He left his supplies at home. He left his charts and papers at home. And when he got out to sea, instead of fighting the currents, instead of fighting the winds, he simply put up the sail and allowed himself to be taken on a new course.

LessonThree: Live In The Divine M

In the early days of his voyage, Aaron was nervous and frightened, for he thought that by simply "allowing" his journey, it might take him to disaster. "Allowing" would perhaps take his ship and crash it upon the rocks. But he let go. He trusted. Certainly, the winds and the currents began guiding him on a different path and a different direction. Aaron lived each day not worrying about charting his progress from the past, not worrying about using his compass to direct him in the future.

He lived each day, allowing in all appropriateness for his ship to be guided where it should go. In Aaron's mind, there were times when the path did not seem to be the right way to go. But Aaron knew that he should let it be.

Aaron learned to stay in the moment. In due time, he was brought to great new lands, lands that were wonderful, lands that were filled with things he could not have possibly imagined before. Oh, these were not like the small islands he had experienced in his past lifetimes! These were grand new lands with new energies, new opportunities, and new powers. He allowed his ship to be guided to discoveries that were beyond his comprehension!

By putting aside his old energy tools, he was taken by the currents and the winds to these new places. In these new lands he received many gifts, gifts of understanding and wisdom, gifts of self-empowerment, gifts of co-creation, and gifts of peace and joy. He brought these gifts with him when he returned back to his home land.

When the people met him and asked about the gifts, he simply explained that he had been to new and wonderful places. He explained that he had been guided by a divine hand, and he knew that it was his own divine hand! He brought these gifts back to share with those who were in his home land. So goes the story of Aaron.

It is simple, dear friends. It is simple! Do not try to make it so difficult. Lesson Three of the Ascension Series – what Aaron learned on his journey – is to "LIVE IN THE DIVINE MOMENT."

It is so simple, and in it is contained much power! You have spent many lifetimes creating into a future, creating a future from a void. Take a moment to think about what we are saying.

You have lived in your thoughts of what tomorrow would be like. This has been appropriate. And it is still appropriate for many who walk the Earth. But as you become creators in the New Energy, you will learn the importance of living in the divine moment, the moment that is now! You will be tempted many times to live in the future, to imagine what your tomorrow will be. You will be tempted to have fears of tomorrow, to create scenarios in your mind. But as a new creator in this New Energy, you will find much power of "living in the divine moment," which is Now.

It may seem difficult to comprehend how you can be a creator by not pushing thoughts and vibrations into the future! But, dear friends, as you learn to accept all things as they are (Creator Series Lesson One), and as you learn to accept your human self (Creator Series Lesson Two), and you learn to "Live in the Divine Moment" (Creator Series Lesson Three), like Aaron you will be able to go to places that you could never have imagined before. These are places that you could never have charted and plotted in your human mind. As you go to these new places, you will begin to understand a new power within. You will begin to understand a new way of creating.

Oh, we know this will be even more challenging for you than the previous two lessons! You lie awake at night and project into the future. You lie awake at night and worry about what will be. You lie awake at night and plan for how you would truly like tomorrow to be. To "live in the divine moment" will be somewhat of a challenge for you, to say the least!

Take a moment right now to experience what a divine moment feels like, for you are in one right now. The divine moment is now. The divine moment has no judgments. The divine moment is complete in itself. It needs no other fulfillment. It is a quiet place. The divine moment is a space where you can feel love washing through your entire being. The divine moment is not held back by the past. It is not plotted into the future. It is simply in the now. And it is perfect in all things. This is indeed a divine moment where there are no needs or wants. You are all that you are.

Now Lesson Three: "Live in the Divine Moment." Like Lessons One and Two, there may be a tendency to be pulled in different directions. There may be the tendency to worry about the future, perhaps to think of the difficulties of the past. Come stand behind the short wall of your new house, accepting all things as they are, accepting the perfection of your human self, and live in the divine moment. Oh, but you say, "Tobias, what about this? What about that? What if this happens? What if that happens?" Dear friends, spend some time in the divine moment and you will see what happens!

As you are in the divine moment, a new type of vibration emanates from you. It attracts all of the appropriate things to you. In the past you have had to seek those things to bring them to you, to seek your abundance, to seek even your happiness, to seek a mate. You have had to go

Lesson Three: Live In The Divine Moment ❖ 69

into a void in the future to create a new reality. This is how reality has been shaped, but you as the new creators will be discovering a new way.

Imagine that within you is a tuning fork held with the handle end up and the two tines facing down. It is a tuning fork. Now in the old energy, both tines were vibrating. They each represented an aspect of duality. That is why there are two tines. They were vibrating out of phase. They were vibrating at different frequencies. This was intentional, so you could experience duality, so that you could experience the effects of light and dark.

The measurement of energy emanating from each of these was approximately 1/3 to approximately 2/3. One of the forks would vibrate with the energy and the resonance that was one third of the whole. The other would vibrate at two thirds of the whole. These vibrational frequencies would shift at times, and they would change at times, but the general ratio of the energy of duality was 1/3 and 2/3.

There were lifetimes that were based 2/3 in darkness and 1/3 in light. The two forks would purposely sing out – would purposely have a different vibration that would cause friction between each other. Oh, and you wonder why your life was difficult that times! This vibrational friction was set up specifically for experience, for understanding, and to play this game of duality.

As you live in the divine moment there is no longer the need for the opposing elements of duality, or for the two different tines of your tuning fork to be out of phase. As you live in the divine moment the energies of these two can now come back into phase. They begin to resonate at the same frequency levels that are appropriate. There is no longer the need here for a balance of 1/3 and 2/3.

Imagine that within you is this tuning fork. Imagine it as part of your being. It has been deliberately out of phase. There has been vibrational friction up to now. Imagine this now within your being, singing harmonious tones with itself. At this moment, dear friends, allow this vibrational duality within you to come back into harmony, to come back to sing beautiful tones, rather than tones that contain friction and duality. As you live in the divine moment and allow the duality to resonate in harmony – in beauty and joy – they will come into a new balance.

As you live in the divine moment, all things that are needed and all things that are appropriate will come to you. They will come to you! You will not need to go searching for them. You will not need to force them into your reality. You will be creating in a new way. You will still be transmuting the void into reality, but you will be creating in a new way, in a very powerful way.

The two tines of your tuning fork represent the DNA, the two known DNA strands that form the helix. There is a light and a dark, or a positive and a negative. They have been vibrating out of phase with each other. They have been operating at frequencies that cause friction. This was to help you understand duality. Now, at the core of your DNA these two strands will begin working together. As they do, it will draw to you all things that are appropriate in your life. As they do, it will also help to heal the scars of the past. It will reverse the process of aging that is taking place within you. It will mend the physical and emotional wounds. Simply live in the divine moment.

In addition to the two known strands of DNA there are at least ten secondary strands. Around each primary strand, there are two secondary strands that embrace it. And then around these bundles of strands there are other magnetic DNA strands that embrace and encompass it.

You are going through many changes. You are releasing many issues from this lifetime. This allows the divinity that has always been within you to truly begin coming forth. As you live in the divine moment, it allows your divinity to come forth. As you allow yourself to live in the divine moment, it changes the very nature of the duality in and around you. It changes the way you create on Earth.

After working with this concept of living in the divine moment, go out to one who reads the energies, to those who are psychic, those who see auras. Go to them. You will scare them! (chuckling) They will tell you that you do not exist anymore. They will not be able to see an aura around you, for it will have changed. They will not be able to see your chakras because they will have melded into one chakra. They may be afraid of you! (chuckling) They will wonder what is going on. Sit in your divine moment with them. Sit in a place of love with them. Do not brag of what you have done or who you have become. But let them know energetically that they too can move to those new levels.

Dear friends, live in the divine moment. At your very core level, change the frequencies of who you are. You will no longer recognize yourself in the mirror. Others will no longer recognize you. They may even think you have disappeared.

Now all of this takes some work. We are asking you to consciously work at this, consciously work on accepting all things as they are. Stand behind the short wall, even in the midst of chaos all around you. Accept yourself in all of your humanness. Don't try to run from it. Indeed, be proud that you are human. Be proud now that you are a divine human. And now live in the divine moment. Worry not of the future.

In his second lifetime Aaron learned not to worry of the wind and the rains, not to worry of the currents, not to worry of what lands he might go to. He lived in the divine moment. He appreciated each day, and each day a new gift was brought to him. Each day he understood he was attracting it to himself through trust in his divinity.

As you work with these foundations lessons you will begin to notice the number "4." You have been in duality up to now. You have been in "two." You will begin to notice "4." We will explain more of this in the future. 2 squared equals 4. Understand that you are moving beyond duality, but you are not eliminating duality. You are going to a new type of dimensionality. The number "4" will become important. You will begin seeing it. It will jump out at you. It is a reminder. It is a reminder to live in the divine moment. It is a reminder that you are changing from within.

Your mathematicians are currently working on a new quantum theory. There are new discoveries in this. It will quite possibly be referred to as "quad" mathematics where there is a new understanding of the balance of "4," of quadrants or four sectors.

This is all evidence of a new energy here on Earth. You are in duality. It is not appropriate to return to singularity. You are in duality, but there is a new type of energy that you will come to know soon. It is represented by the number 4.

All of this takes work. We appreciate the work you are doing here. We understand what you have sacrificed and what you have released, the time and the energy and the devotion. You are helping to pave the way for these new understandings, helping to make it appropriate for the New Energy to come forth. We acknowledge you for the work you are doing. We also ask you to not take it lightly. We ask you to understand that with just a bit of effort you will see very solid results, very dynamic results in your life.

Dear friends, we look into the energy of the teachers here and those reading this material. We see transformation happening before us. We see the release of the old. We see determination and dedication. It is difficult for us at times to fathom because there are so many elements of duality that make it challenging and difficult, but yet somehow you have managed to come this far. Somehow you have managed to get to this point.

When you left on your journey in this lifetime, we cried, we wept, knowing that this would be the most challenging of all of your lifetimes. It would not only be challenging in terms of the lessons and experiences, it would go by so quickly. Things would change very, very fast.

You are ready to allow the divinity to truly flow from the very core of who you are – we tell you once again, dear teachers, it is not us. It is not the guides. It is not angels that are giving it to you or making it happen. There is a divine spark. There is a Christ consciousness that is emerging within you.

We bring to you these lessons to help you integrate your divineness. We bring these lessons for you to understand how to become a creator in this New Energy, how to set the path, how to create the energy templates that others will use later. That is why we call you the teachers. We know you will be working with the others. We know that you will have empathy for them, for you will have been through it also.

The energy that has been YOU in this lifetime is ready to leave. Oh, it knows that you will remember it well. It knows that you will have times when you laugh, times when you cry in remembrance, but it leaves you now in love. It embraces you and thanks you once again. It knows that you will never have to endure the difficulties and the struggles and the pains that this old self did. There is joy for that. And dear friends, this past life of yours reminds you that in all things that you do, and in all the divine moments you live, you are never alone.

And so it is.

12/10/23

Lesson Four
Create in Grace

    And so it is, dear friends and teachers, that we join together again in our circle, in our sacred space with you. We bring greetings to you, and we bring thanks and honor to you. Take a moment here to breathe deeply of the energy that is in our circle together. Breathe deeply in and through your biology. Breathe deeply in through your spirit. Breathe deeply and allow this energy into your being.

    I, Tobias, speak through our friend, the one we call Cauldre, the one I call "son." (chuckling) During our time together we will work with you. The entities from our side of the veil come into your circle now to balance and adjust the energy, to weave a new energy. Open your heart and open your being for all the energy to come flowing in. Open your heart and your being to those who enter your space now, those who come from the other side of the veil to be with you.

    When you open yourself, there is an opportunity for healing and learning. This opens the pathways for us who are on the other side of the veil. Together with you we create a new space, a new dimension. Together we create the energy template and the weavings for your new Earth.

    Feel the energy now. It is present in and around you. Feel the peace and the love and the joy that is here, the goldenness that floods in. This, dear teacher, is the energy of the new Earth. This is the energy of your divine moment.

    It gives us great joy to be with you, for often it is difficult to come in close. Many times it is difficult to talk to you like this. For us, this energy is one of celebration, to be here like this, so close to you, so close to the one we love. The distance that separates you and us is becoming smaller and smaller and smaller. The work you have done in your many lives on Earth, and in particular this lifetime, opens the veil for us to come much closer.

The veil was thick. It was difficult for us to come to you, even when you cried out and even when you prayed. It was difficult for us to cross through the veil, even as it has been difficult for you to reach through to our side. The love you have generated have made it possible for us to come this much closer to you. And we come in now very, very close. Take a moment to feel our love. Hear and feel and sense the messages that we have for you. Take this moment now to feel us. Take this moment to hear the words and the thoughts we have for you.

Now we have been watching as you have gone through the last three lessons. We know the lessons are not always so easy. But there is much determination on your part to Accept All Things As They Are (Creator Series Lesson One), to stand behind your short wall, to watch and observe duality in action. Dear friends, is there not the desire to be drawn back into this duality? Yet do you see what you can learn about human energy – what you can learn about your Self, simply by observing?

Then there was the lesson of Accepting Your Human Self (Creator Series Lesson Two). We know you can quite easily accept your spiritual self. Accepting your human self is difficult.

Then there was a very difficult lesson – to Live in the Divine Moment (Creator Series Lesson Three). Oh, we saw when you chose to stand in your divine moment. And it worked for a fraction of a second! (audience laughter) Then you were immediately pulled out of it by family or co-workers! What was important was that you felt – even for a fleeting moment – what it was like to be in divinity without worrying about yesterday. For as you know, your yesterdays are gone. All of those aspects that you knew as your past lives have left. It serves no purpose to be in the past now. The Book of Life as you know it has come to an end. The final chapter was written and signed in your hand. All of the pages of your new life are blank, and ready for you to fill with your creations.

Ah, and that is why we are here! That is why we are in the classroom of the new energy. We are here to work with you on how to become a creator, a true creator in the new energy. Not like the creators you were back in the original circle. No, you are the new creators. It is not just about your life. It is about all those who follow after you. Learning to stand in the divine moment is perhaps from one of the most difficult lessons so far. And as Cauldre tells us, it is sometimes fun to play the game of duality. It is sometimes fun to be out of the divine moment. It is fun to play in duality.

Do you know what this day represents (11-11-2000)? This is indeed the day on the calendar of the Mayans, what was called "the day of duality" – a 1 and a 1, another 1 and a 1, and a 2. This would have been a very difficult day had you not rewritten the history of Earth, the history of your universe and the history of the second circle. This was to have been filled with duality in a very difficult and challenging way. This day comes 11 months after the change of your millennium, when you changed from a 1 to a 2. This was the day thought to be that of the clash of the 2, of the clash of the light and dark.

But look now. Look at it now. We laugh. We chuckle. Look at what has happened even in the most recent events. There is still duality. Duality is so strong that the recent presidential election (November 2000) comes down to a few votes. Remember when we told you in our last gathering that up until this very recent time, the balance of light and dark has been a ratio of 2/3 to 1/3? The balance of 2/3 and 1/3 was appropriate for the lessons, for the wisdom and the understandings.

Remember when we talked to you of your tuning fork? It was out of balance, out of frequency. The two tines of the fork had a vibrational balance of 1/3 and 2/3 up until this time. The two tines are coming back into harmonic balance with each other again. There are still two, but they were harmonizing. They are not out of phase like they had been before.

Dear friends, look at your elections. It is not 2/3 and 1/3. It is not an offset balance. It is so carefully balanced that it comes down to a few single votes. This is the new duality. It is not two sides battling each other like before. It is two sides so close in vibration, so close that they begin to harmonize together. Many of you do not even recognize the difference between your own candidates. They vibrate at a similar frequency.

There is, and there will continue to be, duality. But from this day forward, it will not be the same again, particularly for those who have entered into the energy of the new Earth. There may be two sides of the mirror, but they are not battling like before. There are looking at each other with great curiosity. They are looking at each other, wondering why they have battled each other in the past.

You will see this in your own life now. Yes, there will be two sides. But the two sides are beginning to harmonize together. This is an unprecedented event. This is breaking through a barrier larger than what you experienced at your millennium, or at your harmonic convergence.

This is "the day of duality." Look around you. Look around your life. Look around your creation. It is filled with much love and much abundance and much joy. Indeed we know there are still difficulties that you are experiencing, but look at where you are. Look where you as a group are. Look where your Earth as a whole is at this time. Duality is taking on a new energy. You see it before your eyes, and sometimes you don't even recognize it! (chuckling)

We take this moment to come in to hug you, to honor you, and to do the final melding of energy in this circle. Then we will continue with the second segment of the Creator Series, the second of four segments that we will have with you. Is it not interesting that today is also Lesson Four? Take this moment to allow our love and honor to come through to you. There are many, many, many who wish to acknowledge you now.

Oh, if we could only bottle this energy! We would take it back with us to show all of the others what this group of humans has achieved. The essence of love is what you have created, and we will tell the others about it.

Dear friends, a long time ago but not nearly as long as you might think, you were in the First Circle, the original creation. It is somewhat difficult to describe, but there were not the elements of duality in the original creation. You created with a oneness. You created whole new dimensions. You created depth and width and all things in between. You were pioneers, understanding how to create with the energy of the Eternal One. You had fun with it and played with it and experienced it in fullness. And God loved watching you play in God's creation. God laughed when you played in the original circle. You brought much joy to Spirit. You were highly creative. You kept creating and creating and going to new levels with this.

You created with such expression and such passion – passion that is still within you – that you literally went to the edge of creation. When you got to the edge of All That Is, there were rumblings *(the registration table in the meeting hall collapses almost on cue)*. When you got to the edge of creation, my friends, something happened that you and Spirit had never experienced before. It was the transition from oneness into a duality. You were not in human form at that time. You were in what you would call your light body.

You began to feel changes. You begin to feel something unusual and very uncomfortable.

And this was duality. You continued to create and experience at the edge of the First Circle. And dear friends, this was a very challenging and difficult time. This is where you first felt disconnected from Spirit. It is when you first felt there was no longer a single harmony but rather an

opposing duality. This was all part of the experience that you chose. There was no mistake in this. There was no mistake in what you were doing here.
You began to experience things like mistrust. You began to experience things like anger and hate. You were changing. You were transforming. You were the proverbial caterpillar going through the cocoon to become a butterfly. You were leaving the First Circle and experiencing two (duality) instead of one.
In this zone, at the edge of the First Circle, is where you have experienced some of the most traumatic and difficult things that your soul has ever gone through. If there was ever an understanding of what hell is like, it was there. If there was ever true war and combat, it was there, and this hurt you deeply. It is something you and the others who were there never felt or experienced before. There was disharmony, and there was to an extent an energy destruction.
Understand that none of this was a mistake. There had been an agreement with Spirit that you would be an explorer, that you would go out to the Void. You would learn something new, and neither you nor Spirit, knew what this would be. It is now called duality. There was so much energy behind this, so much focus here, so much intensity in this experience at the edge of All That Is, that it literally catapulted you into a new place called the second circle, the second creation.
You will have many questions about this, and we will talk about in future lessons. You went through a very difficult experience when you left Home. You eventually came to Earth, and you began to walk through lifetime after lifetime.
We have said to you before, this idea of karma we do not like so much. We do not like using that word. For it was not karma. It IS not karma. What is it, dear friends? You are now trying to understand the experiences you had at the edge of the First Circle, and after leaving Home, by having a parallel or related experience on Earth.
Separation: You have experiences of separation to help you understand what happened after you left Home. Pain: You have experiences of pain on Earth to help you understand and define what happened when you left Home. Imbalance: You have experiences of imbalance in your emotions, to help you understand what happened when you left Home.
Do you understand what we are saying to you? There is nothing that you have done wrong here on your Earth! You have chosen experiences to help you understand something that happened a long time ago, but not so long ago. You use Earth, the physics of duality, along with mass and mat-

ter to help you understand something from your past. You use physical bodies to help you understand, to help you relive the experiences that you had at the edges of the First Circle. Your experiences on Earth relate to the experiences when you left Home. You are now playing them out in duality for deeper understandings and definition. It is not about karma. Rather, it is about reenacting something that happened in another time, in another place.

There was an angel by the name of Taylor. She has walked the Earth for many, many lifetimes. In one lifetime Taylor was a warrior, a warrior for a greedy country, for a greedy kingdom. She cared not of the agenda. She simply wanted to be a warrior.

She wanted to experience blood and battle. She wanted to experience duality and anger. She brought these experiences to her soul, and they remained there for a long, long time.

And in the next lifetime Taylor was a mother who was not so good to her children or her husband. She enjoyed the company of other men. She enjoyed being away from her family. She felt guilty for this, and it weighed heavy upon her. Yet she continued to do it, and in doing so caused much pain and difficulty for her children, and caused her husband to commit suicide, to leave Earth. This was remembered by her soul and carried forth, put into her Book of Life.

In another lifetime Taylor was a businessman who ran a sweat shop. Taylor took advantage of young people and poor people for cheap labor. Taylor did not care so much about them but cared only about her pocketbook, about her wealth. Taylor did not share this wealth with others. She did not give to charity but gave only to herself. She wanted to build a monument to her immortality by gaining wealth. And this weighed heavy upon her soul but she cared not and went forth.

In this lifetime, Taylor was a child of abusive parents. In her early teens she became an alcoholic. She drank every day, lowering her vibrations to levels that it is even difficult for us to comprehend. She drank heavily, and she went into darkness. Her vibrations were lowered, and she forgot what love was about. She did not have such a happy life. She blamed her parents. She blamed others who she worked with. Her drinking caused health problems. And this created more bitterness within her.

Taylor is now in the Crimson Circle and no longer drinks, for along the way she read an inspirational book. She sat in meetings somewhat like this. She had others lend her a helping hand. She allowed others to hug her and say that they loved her. She allowed others to help her understand that all of these feelings of guilt in her being needed to be released, needed to be let go of.

Now you see, we tell the story of Taylor to help you understand something. Indeed this is a true story. We tell this story to help you understand something very important in your own life. You see, Taylor chose these difficult lifetimes. She chose them a long time ago. She knew that Spirit needed someone to go to the lowest depths.

Somebody had to jump into this great pool of duality to explore the lowest and the deepest parts of it. Oh, it is easy to be one who simply puts your toe in and says, "I am filled with light for I do not sink. And I gather and collect the sunlight, and therefore I am special." It is difficult, dear friends, when you take the challenging path. Taylor jumped into the depths of duality when she agreed to become the alcoholic, to have the worst nightmares of nightmares, to have the darkest challenges.

And you thought this was just karma. You thought that you were paying debts to yourself. Dear friends, this doesn't even sound logical to pay debts to yourself. You and the other Taylors who are Shaumbra are deeply loved by every one of us. You have chosen difficult experiences in your lifetimes in order to help Spirit explore the depths of light and dark. You have given much in service by doing these things. You have helped to reenact the energetic experiences from the Void, and by doing so, helped Spirit to truly understand something new.

We know this will bring up many questions, such as, "Is it right to kill another, for am I truly helping Spirit?" You wisdom of today keeps you from doing this. You have done enough of that in the past. Honor yourself for what you have done. Honor yourself for the difficult path you have taken. And in particular, when you look into another's eyes and perhaps do not see the light that you see in your own now, remember that they are still helping to explore this grand energy called duality. There are two sides of it, a light and a dark, a positive and a negative. Someone has to explore the depths of both.

Dear friends, what you are experiencing here on Earth is helping to understand and define experiences that you had at the edge of creation and after leaving Home. And you have done that well.

Many of the dreams and the nightmares you have now do not relate to this lifetime. They do not even relate to other lifetimes. You wonder where these terrors come from? Much that is coming to you now has to do with the experiences you had when you left Home. You are experiencing these in another way – in your dreams – to help create the fabric of the Second Creation. The Second Creation is your universe, your Earth, an extension of All That Is.

✥ ✥ ✥ ✥

Now along the way Taylor gave up drinking. She came to understand that there was a divinity within her, but much of this understanding was only in her mind. She did not understand it so well in her heart, for she still had guilt. Deep down within, she still had guilt about leaving the First Creation. And then she had guilt about choosing these many lifetimes and many experiences of difficulty.

Taylor still had problems in her life. She still had challenges. As she read the material from the Crimson Circle, she began to understand how to accept all things. She began to understand how to accept her human self, although for her this was very challenging. She felt the human part of her was something to be ashamed of. She did not yet understand that her humanness was divine, that her humanness gave so much to the universe. Taylor began standing in the divine moment, although it was difficult, and the experiences were few and far between. She began taking a moment each day to stand in divinity. She loved it dearly, and it felt so warm and golden. But then her guilt would get the best of her. She would feel she did not deserve this divine moment, and it would disappear.

Taylor choose to continue learning and growing. She still had challenges with money, relationships, health, and especially with trusting herself. At times life was difficult, and at times she even cursed Spirit. There were times when she said she would walk away from this new energy Earth path because she felt it wasn't making a difference in her life. There were times when she said, "This is all just words. It is like the other words of the other beliefs of the other groups. It is all just a pacifier." There were times that she was very frustrated.

In spite of this, Taylor wanted to believe she was following her truth . She wanted to move to the next level, but she did not know how. She became so confused and so lost and so upset, but more than anything else so betrayed, that one night she simply collapsed on the floor and began sobbing, saying out loud, "I can go on no further. I do not know what to do, Spirit. I have called on you for guidance. I have called on my angels. I have called on my guides, and I do not know what to do." Now Taylor did not read so well the words that said Spirit cannot do it for you, and your guides have departed. (chuckling)

There was something inside of her that had been trying to come forth. It was trying to talk to her, but it couldn't when she was out of her divine moment. It couldn't when she was worried about all of these things. But when she broke down sobbing, something happened. It was like a voice – not from the outside, rather from the inside. The inner voice said to her, "I am grace. I am divine grace that already exists within you. I will handle all  things. I will balance all things. I will solve all things. I come from within you, and I am grace."

She lay on the floor for a long time, feeling this energy of divine grace from within her being. It felt right. She hadn't turned over herself and her problems to some unknown entity, or to some image of God that she did not know or understand. She turned it over to the grace that came from within her being. From that day forward she began to understand. She began to understand the power of grace.

✣ ✣ ✣ ✣

Dear friends, understand that quite unlike what your books and teachers have told you, there was never a fall from grace with God. There was never a Lucifer who was thrown out of heaven. These are all metaphors. You experienced the very edge of creation. You experienced something that you had never done before, and it was called duality. That sent you into the second creation. There was an energy that was needed to send you beyond the limits of creation. This experience created the energy that catapulted you into the Second Circle. It was like feeling the power of the rockets exploding with so much force that it made you forget where you came from. But there was not a fall from grace. We look at it like it was a step from one into two, a step that was taken in love for Spirit.

Now, let us take a walk through your New House. You have not been there so much lately! (chuckling) It is helpful to spend more time in your New House. It is a good place. You have been busy running around the town and the neighborhood. You are not spending so much time in your new house!

Let us go back to your New House with the angels at your side, for they too love to explore this new creation of yours. Let us walk inside. As we have said dear friends, there is very little here. For you create the walls. You create the space. You create the energy.

Let us walk together into the kitchen of your new house. We see that some of you did not even know you had a kitchen! (chuckling) You have spent no time! But this is such a grand place that you have built. You will be spending more time here now. In the kitchen of your new house, in the center of it, there is a very large, very beautiful, floor-to-ceiling oven with a large windowed door. There is an inscription above the door, written in shimmering gold lettering that reads, "Oven of Grace."

The Oven of Grace. This is a symbol of your own energy of grace. Think of a challenging situation you have in your own personal life that does not involve other people. It is your own situation, whether it is one of abundance, or a general fear, or a health issue, or an issue of loneliness. Think of a symbol that represents the situation. If this is an abundance issue, the symbol could be your purse or checkbook or wallet. If it is about your health, the symbol could be a photograph or snapshot of you. Think of a symbol that represents the challenging situation.

Now approach the Oven of Grace with its large beautiful glass door, and the floor-to-ceiling structure. Put this symbol of your challenge in that oven. Put it in there – yes, on the rack.

When you have placed this symbol in the Oven of Grace and then close the door. We ask you to say nothing, to have no intent, to say no words, to say no prayer. Now look up to the left, and you will see a single button, the only button on your Oven of Grace. It says "START." Hit the start button now.

Now while this issue is cooking in your Oven of Grace, we will tell you a few things about this tool. First, when you begin working with this tool of grace in your life, use it only for yourself. Use it only for your own personal situations. Later on, you will learn to use it appropriately with other people and situations. But for now this is only for you. It can be used for any issue in your own life, as long as it is for yourself. If you are worried about a child, about a spouse, it is not the appropriate time to put their energy in here. It is only for yourself.

Put only one issue, one challenge, one concept in the oven at a time. We saw some of you trying to put everything in there! As you are learning to use the Oven of Grace, only one the issue at a time. We also ask you to keep this issue in the Oven of Grace for a period of 24 hours of your time, for 24 hours. We also ask you to remember to get it out at the end of 24 hours! When the issue is done cooking – when it is done being exposed to the energy of your divine grace, then you can put another one in. But one at a time and let it cook for 24 hours.

While this concept may seem simple – perhaps even trite – we tell you now there is great power in it, for Lesson Four of the Creator Series is to "Create in Grace." Lesson Four – Create in Grace. The symbol of the oven is given to help you understand how to work with the divine grace that comes from within. You will experience this energy when you put an issue into this Oven of Grace.

Let us return to Taylor. She put her purse in the Oven of Grace, for it represented the abundance issue she was struggling with at the time. She put it in her oven without agenda. Without agenda, do you understand, dear friends? Oh, we know you have been taught to pray, and you've been taught to use incantations and intent and goals. These have been good, and they have been filled with love, and it has brought you to this point. But dear friends, we are going to a new place now. In the Oven of Grace there is no need for pray, goals or intent. It takes care of itself.

When Taylor put her purse in the oven without agenda and without asking for anything, do you know what happened? Her Oven of Grace allowed for the deep harmony of love to create a new and blessed energy. Her Oven of Grace brought balance to her financial situation. Her Oven of Grace brought the energy of abundance into her life in an appropriate and balanced form.

Now it would have been difficult for Taylor to create all of this in her mind. It would be like eating a meal and trying to mentally control how she processed it in her body. You simply eat food and allow it to be. That is "digestive grace." And in the same manner, when you place something in your Oven of Grace, it takes care of itself. There is a natural balance. There is a natural fulfillment that takes place in this New Energy.

About a week after Taylor put her purse in the Oven of Grace and allowed it to cook overnight, she lost her job. Don't you know!? (chuckling) She wondered what was going on, but she also trusted in grace. She knew that her job was indeed a hindrance to her abundance. It kept her tied down and limited. It provided other experiences for her that were no longer appropriate, and one of those experiences that it provided was abundance limitation. So when she placed her pocketbook in the Oven of Grace, surely it changed her job.

Loosing her job initially brought fear to her, so Taylor put that fear into the Oven of Grace. She allowed grace to handle the fear of what she was going through. As she did this with new situation after new situation, she allowed divine grace to find the appropriate balance and resolution.

Dear friends, Taylor learned to trust herself. She was not turning her problems over to an angel or a guide or to Spirit. She was allowing the fulfillment within her own being. And indeed in this Lesson Four, "Create in Grace," you will also learn the beauty, the flow, the balance and the love of the grace that exists within you. Up to now, you have not trusted in your divine grace. Also, the energy of Earth up to this time has not been appropriate to truly utilize this energy. But now it is yours.

We can only bring you our insights, our wisdom. We can only mirror back your own consciousness. You must do the work. Take your challenging situations and put them in the Oven of Grace. And yes, you can put a situation in the oven repeatedly if you do not find resolution. You can put that in there again and again. If Taylor were to worry about her abundance issues, she could put her purse in again on another day. But as we said, one issue, one day.

Lesson Four, which will be a foundation lesson for applied creation in the new energy, is to "Create in Grace." You must first understand and learn how to create in grace before we can move to the more dynamics steps. Again we remind you to use this Oven of Grace only for yourselves right now. We present it here in a story, in a metaphor as an oven, but it is a practical way of bringing balance and resolution into your life through grace.

Where are we going with all of this in our future lessons? We are working with you to become the true creators in the new energy, creators of your own life, creators of the new energy of Earth. It is not just about you. It is about creating the weavings of the tapestry of the new energy. The very work you are doing, and the lessons that you will experience in the days to come, all relate to creating this new tapestry.

Now, when you have a challenge that comes into your life, do not say, "Oh, Spirit, why do you bring this now?" Remember that you brought it, and you brought it in a spirit of love to create the weavings of the new energy of Earth.

Dear friends, we love you beyond measure. Through these lessons we bring you understandings of why you came to Earth in the first place. We bring to you the reasons why you chose Earth, and why you chose the struggles. We bring the message that this was all done in goodness and service to Spirit. There has not been one thing that you have done that was inappropriate or wrong. You are beginning to understand this wisdom. You have given of yourself deeply. Now you have given of yourselves one more time. You chose to be a pioneer of this new energy. That is why we love you deeply, and that is why you are never alone.

And so it is.

✣ ✣ ✣ ✣

"It is not about you anymore."

✣ ✣ ✣ ✣

10/20/03

Lesson Five
Expect Changes and Bless Them

And so it is, dear friends, that we gather together in the "circle of crimson" at this most special time of your year (Christmas). We gather with those who we have known before. We gather with ones that were angels with us and have since gone on to another place called Earth. We thank you for inviting us into your space. This is indeed a sacred time and a joyous time to share this with you.

Now for the next few minutes, we will work with you to adjust and balance the energies of this space that we create together. There are those who come in from our side of the veil who understand the "weavings" They understand how to set these energies. We simply ask you to open your hearts, to open your space. We can only come in close like this when you allow and when you give permission. We ask you to open your heart to let All That Is come closer to you, to come one step closer.

(emotional) There is one who enters this space now. He comes in to be with you again, to walk with you again. Indeed! The one who comes in is from the family of Sananda. He is one that you have walked with before. He makes his presence known to you now, all of you who gather here and read this. He makes his presence known. As we have discussed here in this very circle, there came a point when he wept, for he knew it was time for him to go back. And it was time for you to proceed forward into your lifetimes, to continue the journey, to continue experiencing and learning for Spirit and for All That Is.

He is family, and is known by the name of Yeshua Ben Joseph (Jesus). He touches you on the shoulder. He kisses you on the forehead. There is a familiar energy here. It is one of family, of Shaumbra. This energy is indeed sweet.

(very emotional) It is difficult to even speak through this, so we will take a moment. We will take a moment as Yeshua, the one who helped guide you on the path in the past, walks in these aisles. We ask you to simply accept the love that he brings to you from the family of Sananda. There are the moments that are so precious. Indeed, these are moments that bring tears to our eyes. This is a family reunion, when the Master of Love returns once again and be with you, to hear of your experiences and to hear your stories of this lifetime. It is indeed sweet.

It is interesting that within a few weeks of your time that you will be honoring him. Or so you think! For he comes in honor to you. He comes here to walk between the chairs, touching each and every one of you here and reading this, reminding you that you are the ones bringing the Christ seed to life on Earth at this time. You are the ones who are indeed the Christed beings.

These moments are sweet indeed. (very emotional, very breaking) It is difficult for even I, Tobias, to continue on. (pause) The one that comes from the family of Sananda takes his place amongst you for the remainder of our time here together. Those who are in the legions of the angels and the archangels do not come into the First Circle. They sit in the Second Circle, observing. They keep their energy at a distance to allow for Yeshua Ben Joseph to sit amongst you in clarity and in brilliance and in love. Oh, we will need to pause here for a moment!

Now dear friends, we remind you of the work that you do. We remind you each time we gather here, lest you forget. You are creating the template for the New Energy. You are taking the void and transforming it into new creation. We know, and we understand there are difficult days of your life. But my friends, if you knew and understood the extent of the challenge, you would understand why there are certain difficulties.

Now we will talk about change. Change was the first message to the Crimson Circle through Cauldre. We have not talked of it for some time, but now we will speak to you of change, of changes that are taking place directly within your being and within all of the world around you. We will explain to you why you are feeling certain things. We will speak to you of the transformation that is taking place within your being. We will help you to understand how change will bring a new empowerment to you. You will then have the balance and the love and the compassion to become the teachers of the New Energy.

Lesson Five: Expect Changes and Bless Them ❖ below

🖋 We see the bands of shimmering crimson in your auric fields. This is the true sign of a teacher. Oh, there are other colors, but the crimson energy is the mark of a wise teacher. Make no mistake about it. You are a teacher for the ones who come after you. That is why we are here with you.

Now before we proceed, we would like to tell a short story. We enjoy telling short stories! (chuckling) Our story tonight is about a young prince by the name of Jack. Now you see, Jack lived in a magnificent kingdom, and he was the prince. His mother was the queen, and his father was the king – and this is an important point. Now this young prince Jack was but a boy, and he enjoyed playing in the kingdom. He had many friends and playmates, and all who encountered Jack honored him and loved him. He led a very good life as a prince in the Kingdom of IAM.

As Jack went through his childhood days, he had a craving to experience new things. He had a craving to play. He had a craving to learn, and those who saw the young prince shook their heads and remarked, "He is quite the creator, quite the magnificent creator. He is the one who loves to journey and loves to experience. His soul is playful. He is always moving forward."

Oh, this young Prince Jack could not keep his feet in two places at one time. As he grew into his teens, his journeys took him further and further through the lands of the kingdom, to the outer reaches, to the villages that were away from the center of the kingdom. There he met peoples who were part of the kingdom but were new and different to him.

Jack took longer and longer trips. He was gone for days or even weeks at a time. He loved what he was learning. He loved the new types of animals and trees that he saw in the outer reaches of the kingdom. He loved the new lands and new skies he saw. He loved his journey. The young prince Jack rarely rested, always venturing off on a new journey, searching for places he had never been before, and always making friends along the way.

As the young Prince Jack reached early manhood, he knew that soon enough he would be ruling the kingdom. He knew that he would be sitting in the throne. Soon he would be king. He thought to himself, "Before I am to be king and must stay at the castle to rule over the kingdom, I choose to go on one final experience. I will take one long journey to a place I have never gone before, to a place that is exciting and challenging."

The young prince decided not to take the royal contingent that normally followed him on his journeys. He slipped out of the castle late one night with only a small bag packed for his long journey. He traveled past the places he had gone before. He passed the villages that he had visited in his previous journeys. He traveled further and further until he came to new regions of the kingdom. The land was different and exciting, but it was still within the boundaries of the Kingdom of IAM.

As he pushed forward on his journey, Jack eventually came to the edge of land. He stood at the edge of water, an ocean like he had never seen before. He had seen lakes, and he had seen rivers, but he had never seen anything like this. He had heard of grand oceans in the lore of his kingdom. He had heard of the place where land ends. He had heard that it is not to be journeyed past. He had heard that this is where the kingdom ends, and it is not wise to go past. Young prince Jack laid awake all night long contemplating whether or not to take the next step. He debated with himself whether to set sail onto the ocean – or to return back home.

Oh, and as you know, he was far too restless to return home! So the next day Jack began constructing a vessel, a small boat that would take him on his journey. He worked on this for days and days and days, until he was satisfied with the boat. Then, with a lump in his throat and a pit in his stomach, feeling like perhaps he was breaking a sacred rule, perhaps he was going where he shouldn't venture, he set sail.

The current took him swiftly out onto this ocean. He sailed a good number of days. The waters were calm. The wind was gentle. The sun was bright, and all things appeared well. But there was an uneasiness deep within Jack. The lump in his throat grew larger. The pit in his stomach grew queasier. He knew something was coming.

One quiet afternoon on his ocean journey — somewhat boring by Jack's standards — he saw a great Wall of Fire rising from the ocean ahead of him. He started to paddle backwards, trying to avoid this great Wall of Fire. But as hard as he tried, he could not overcome the forces of the great Wall of Fire. It was sucking him in, pulling him closer and closer. He could feel its heat, and he could feel its turmoil. He could feel the turmoil within this Wall of Fire. Jack screamed as he paddled backwards, trying to go back to the kingdom of IAM. But it pulled him in. The force pulled him into this Wall of Fire.

Jack had a hard time remembering what happened after that. It seemed like an endless amount of time that he was in this Wall of Fire. When he awoke, he was exhausted and empty and with no memory. He awoke on the shores of strange land. He could not remember his name, or from whence he had come. There was something within that told him that he was somebody, but he could not remember. It was, in a way, amnesia.

When Jack opened his eyes, he saw a new land, different from anything he had ever seen before. He knew it was time to start exploring. He explored this land day in and day out, discovering things that were new to him and new to his soul. Yet he felt an uneasiness once again. He felt there was something he should know or remember but couldn't, like he was trying to put his finger on something, but it was not there. Jack was trying to remember his past.

After much time exploring this new land, one day he came upon a woman. They talked, and they rejoiced in seeing each other. There seemed to be a familiar bond, but they did not know from where. She brought him back to a village where there were others. In this village they were making buildings. They were having children. They were creating a new civilization, but none who were in this village could remember where they had come from. They could not remember who they were. They just knew it was time to move forward. It was time to continue on with their lives.

Now, dear friends, there is no particular end to this story, for it has not yet been written. This story of Jack and the others he met in this new land is your story. You are the angel explorers and adventurers. You are the ones who went to explore all of the kingdom of God in the First Circle. You were the ones who are the princes and princesses, who will one day inherit the throne.

You are the ones who were restless and wanted to explore. You went to the edges of all creation. You set sail and went beyond the First Circle. After many, many new adventures, you eventually came to a place you now call Earth, that is surrounded by the very universe you are helping to create. You are the ones who are building the new village, creating the new ways, discovering new things that you could not possibly have discovered in the old kingdom. You are the ones who are creating the templates for the Second Creation. And you are now trying to remember where you came from, what your roots are, what your origins are.

There are angels in the Kingdom who went in search of you after you left Home. The king and the queen asked them to search for you. They followed your footsteps through the kingdom of IAM, to the sands of the ocean.

When we came to the edge of creation, they knew you had gone out onto the fabled waters, beyond All That Is. They rejoiced, knowing that you loved Spirit so deeply that you chose to go on this long journey, in service to All.

Many angels still stand at the Wall of Fire, not able to come through. They can see into the Wall of Fire. They can see the images of your life on Earth projected onto the Wall of Fire. On this screen, they can see things you are doing. They can feel you, but they cannot cross through at this time.

Like you, the Wall of Fire is changing. In a relatively short period of time, it will be possible for the others from the Kingdom to come through. At that point, the boundaries of the kingdom of IAM will expand. The Kingdom will expand beyond the great Wall of Fire. It will expand into this new place you have created. There will come a day when Home will come to you. You will recognize the angels, and then you will remember Home. The kingdom of IAM will be a grander place because of the work you have done since leaving Home.

This indeed is a story, one that portrays your journey. It is a story we talk of all the time – your journeys, your experiences and your discoveries. Dear friends, there is much honor in what you are doing. There is much honor for what you have taken on. That is why the energy of Yeshua is here now, to thank you and to remind you of family.

✣ ✣ ✣ ✣

There are changes occurring with you at the deepest levels of your being. These are deeper than the DNA, deeper than the magnetic energy patterns, deeper than the inner vibrations.

In the Kingdom, you were in the "oneness" mode, the singular mode. When you crossed through the Wall of Fire, you took on the attributes of duality. This was Jack's experience. This is what Jack wanted to feel and experience. And indeed he did. Indeed you all did!

When you left the Kingdom, you took on the attributes of duality or polarity. There was no longer the oneness, but rather "two." There was the light and the dark, the positive and the negative, however you want to state this. There was always the balance of duality energies of approximately 2/3 and 1/3.

Imagine you dualistic energy represented as a white marble and a black marble. Now imagine a clear marble. Depending on the experiences you choose, the clear marble will take on attributes of either the light or the dark. The clear marble will transform, and for a period of time, it will take on the attributes of the white marble. You will then have an energy balance within your being of two parts white, one part dark. You then go through a series of experiences with this balance of energy to provide the appropriate "friction," to provide the appropriate challenges, to make your experience fulfilling.

As you go through the cycles of your life, there are times when the transformed clear marble — the one that had turned to white — will return back to clear for a short period of time. Ah, and then you would feel balance in your life for a short period of time! Within time, the clear marble will move to the other side and take on the attributes of the dark marble. The clear marble will now have the energy attributes of the dark marble. Then you will walk into life experiences with the energy balance of two parts dark and one part white.

Generally, the white marble has usually stayed white, and the black marble has usually stayed black. The clear marble changes, moving back and forth between the white and black. However, there have been periods of time where the white marble and the black marble would reverse their polarities, for they indeed are just mirrors of each other. The black would become white and the white would become black. And at times this greatly confuses the clear marble!

These changes of polarity do not occur very often, perhaps every several thousands of years. It happens not only within your individual being, but within the general consciousness of the planet. In the past, this shift of polarities from light to dark and dark to light, would take hundreds of years for completion, and it would occur only every few thousands of years.

What is happening now, dear friends, is that the polarity shift between the light and dark is occurring very rapidly. No longer does it occur even few thousand years. You are seeing the polarity shift now — where the white marble and the dark marble are changing attributes — every few years. It is happening very quickly. The clear marble is attempting to take on attributes of the light or dark, but is becoming very confused as to which is which!

There are a few humans who carry special attributes of the clear marble within them. In their case, the clear marble never takes on a distinct pattern of either white or black. It remains in a "gray" state. They do not choose to have the typical 2/3:1/3 energy balance. The carriers of these energies are helping to change the internal dynamic structure of energy within all humans. Dear friends, honor the ones who are gay. Honor the ones who have been ridiculed by your "conventional" society. They have taken on a deeper and more challenging role. They are helping to break the barriers of the former energy balance of 2/3:1/3. Instead, their clear marble does not choose to side with either the white or the black. It remains in a neutral state, what we call a "gray" state for the sake of this example. They are the ones who are helping to bridge the gap of polarity at this time. Honor them deeply for their work.

With all that is happening in and around you at this time – light changing to dark, dark to light, clear not knowing which is which – something new is happening. There is, dear friends, a fourth marble coming in. A fourth marble is coming in. This marble is clear crystal. This marble is extremely clear and bright, different than the other three marbles. It is the activator of the Christ energy that is already within you. This fourth marble comes now to activate the Christ energy, to bring it to life.

As this fourth marble moves into your being, the other three marbles – the white, the black, and the clear – are attempting to throw it out! They consider it to be a foreign energy not welcomed into the old energy of their duality. They do not understand where it comes from, and there is turmoil within! And you wonder why your backs and shoulders ache so much! You wonder why there is emotional struggle within your being, when you thought your life should be balanced. You are taking on the attribute of the fourth marble. The other three marbles are very confused right now, for they have never had this fourth element. We have spoken to you before about the importance of the number four. This is the core of it. This is the essence of the balance of "four" that we have spoken of.

What is happening at the deepest levels of your emotional, physical, and mental being? The fourth marble is settling into your energy makeup. It is communicating with the other marbles. It is assuring them that it is part of their new energy. As the three original marbles learn to accept the fourth marble, and as they learn to understand its distinctively different energy, they will stop attacking. They will stop trying to throw this fourth marble out. They will become very tired. This fourth marble is strong, stronger than all of the others combined. They will start listening to the fourth marble. They will start feeling the vibration of the fourth.

Then something will happen, dear friends. The white marble will lose its attributes of white. The black marble will lose its attributes of black. The clear marble will cleanse itself. And all of the four marbles will begin to radiate a new multidimensional color. They will shimmer and glow, and they will sing and dance with each other. They will spin together. They will celebrate together. They will have no single color, but they will contain all colors in perfect clarity. They will be in unity.

This is the point when you pass through duality as you know it. You will go to the next level. This is not what you think of as your fifth or six or seventh dimensions. Those are linear. This is exponential. The changes of the marbles are happening within you. We can look into this group and see how the acceptance level of the fourth element has been difficult and challenging.

In the past, we have asked you to accept things. We have asked you to "allow" rather than to "effort." We were communicating to you on several levels. We were communicating that it was time for polarity to stop its game. We were communicating that it is time for the old balance of 2/3 and 1/3 to cease. We asked you in the past to take breaks, to do "no-thing," to be in a quiet space. During this time, the three marbles were learning to allow and accept the fourth marble.

This is a difficult process to go through. Your biology, in particular, has not yet adjusted to this fourth energetic element. Your emotions have definitely not adjusted to it. You are accustomed to working in duality – good or bad, right or wrong – depending on what particular day it is and depending on the coloration of the third clear marble.

Dear friends, dear Shaumbra, we ask you to expect the changes in your life and to bless these changes.

Lesson Number Five – EXPECT CHANGES IN YOUR LIFE AND BLESS THEM. You have asked to be the ones to learn, to grow, and to experience. You are the ones who have asked to move into your next lifetime on this Earth. You are the ones who said you would move past duality into the newest of the new energies. Would it not be reasonable that there would be changes in your life, and in some cases, for all things to seemingly be ripped from your being? You are making way for a new energy.

Those of you who are enduring the most difficult of times – we extend our hand and our love to you now, for we know what you are going through. But it is for a reason. It is for a purpose. We ask each of you to simply allow these changes to happen. It may seem like the old self is crumbling apart. It may seem like every dream and aspiration you have ever had is being taken away. And in a way, you are right. You are making way. The fourth element is coming in now. In order for this to work, many things in your life must change.

Dear friends and Shaumbra, expect changes in your life and bless them. When you lose your job, bless this. When your body becomes ill after you put it in your Oven of Grace, and you wonder why this is happening, bless the changes. We know this is not what you expected, for you had expectations that you would get healthy right away. You had expectations that you would come back to balance immediately. Sometimes the changes are deeper. Sometimes there must be a complete reversal and renewal. Sometimes the old foundations must come down. These changes that you go through are indeed sacred. Do not panic with them. Do not be in anxiety. Now even Cauldre chides us when we say this. He says it is easy for us to say since it is not us going through the changes! (chuckling)

And we understand this.

From our perspective, we can see what is happening to you in your life. The changes that are taking place are, in essence, a clearing. We can see that this is making way for the fourth element to come in. There may be days when you are laid up in bed, when you are ill, and you cannot move. There may be days when you are depressed and do not understand why. Do not fight these things. Bless them. Bless them, and this will give them a new energy.

What is happening is that the three original marbles are indeed trying to reject the fourth. They consider it an outside threat. This is one of the first times that the three original marbles are aligned and agreeing with each other! (chuckling) They are confused by the fourth element. They are testing the fourth element. They believe it is an impostor. They believe it is coming from a place that does not serve the overall good of your being. They are trying to defend something within that has been precious to them – their existence in duality. With your "allowing," the fourth marble will be able to integrate faster and easier. Talk to your inner being and let your Self know that the fourth element is part of the process. This will make the transition much smoother.

Allow the white and the black and the clear marble to come close to the fourth element. Allow them to feel the love, to feel the acceptance that is inherent in the fourth element, and to feel the clarity. This is one thing you will notice in your conscious human being – the clarity that comes in with the fourth element. That is when you will know it is real and it is true. But in the meantime, friends, as this new dance takes place within your being, expect changes in your life and bless them. Bless them, for they are making way for something that is profound and sacred. Bless these changes in your life.

As the white marble and the black marble and the clear marble become comfortable with the fourth element, they will, in a sense, adapt to it. They will take on characteristics of the fourth marble. As they do, they will shed the electromagnetic characteristics of duality that they have held for so long. They will shed the obvious characteristics of light and dark and clear. They will wake up one day and see that they are no longer dressed in their old cloaks. They will no longer have the characteristics of duality.

We are not talking of something that will happen within you in the distant future. It is happening within you right now. In the meantime, expect changes within your being – physically, emotionally, and mentally. Bless these changes. Then notice the new things that are taking place in your life.

As you begin working with other humans, teaching them how to heal themselves, you will understand the deliberate and sometime slow process of these lessons. You will understand what is taking place within their beings, the shedding of the old, the acceptance of the new. When you look at their "one chakra" and into their energy fields, you will see they are beginning to adopt the fourth element. You will then understand how to work with them.

You walk through these lessons first in order to develop the compassion you will need as a teacher. You experience it firsthand. You experience it, perhaps deeper and stronger than those you will teach. You are amongst the first to integrate the fourth element into your being.

And for that we love you dearly. For that we thank you and honor you for the service. It amazes us to see the souls and the beings here, to see the smiles upon your faces, to hear your laughter. It amazes us, for we know the journey is difficult. At any moment you can say, "Dear Spirit, I can no longer choose to continue this difficult path, this journey." We know that at any point you can say, "no more," but yet you come back here, time after time! You come back in love. You come back in service. You allow your bodies to be places where new things are tried and new things are integrated. You allow your emotions to be a learning ground, not just for you, but for the others.

Oh, we have said to you before, it is really no longer about you. Do you understand that? You have cleared. What you are experiencing now is for the love of Spirit and all others who will follow. The afflictions and the challenges that you have now are truly not your own. You are accepting these on behalf of All That Is. You are accepting this integration of the fourth element in at this time, knowing that it is difficult on your physical being, knowing it is difficult on your human being.

This is why we honor you. This is why Yeshua Ben Joseph asked to join you. He asked the other angels to watch from a distance. He asked to share this time with you as family, one on one. He has been here this whole time – did you know – working with you, sending you the vibrations that are appropriate. While you were reading these words, this great master touched you in a very special way. Now he gives thanks for this opportunity to be with you, to share this most precious time, to share the unveiling of this new information.

This information, dear friends, will change much of the old thinking. We have called it the "quad math." It is part of what you would call your quantum leap. It ties into this time of the year 2012 (which we have told you will most likely come much sooner). We are sharing it with you because you are amongst the first to integrate it into your beings. That is why you are experiencing what you are at this time.

We love you dearly, friends. With all of the changes going on within, know that you are never alone.

And so it is.

Lesson Six
Within You Is Divine Balance

And so it is, dear friends, that we gather together with you in the energy of the Crimson Circle. We joyfully come into your space and into your energy. Oh, your hearts are open at this time! Your acceptance of us is true and deep and loving. We thank you for allowing us into your space.

The acceptance of yourself – of who you truly are – has changed significantly since our last lesson. It has changed in grand proportions since the first lesson (August 1999). Part of our responsibility in the Crimson Council is to offer you perspective, to show you what we see. There are times when you cannot see your own progress, for you are in the midst of your experiences. You are so much a part of duality that it is difficult for you to see who you truly are. So we offer you our perspective. And indeed, dear friends, you are not of the same consciousness as you were a few months ago. You have shed much of the old, and you are beginning to embrace the energy of the new. This energy is your own Divine Self.

I, Tobias, and those of the Crimson Council are here to share what we see. We look into your heart and into your one chakra. We see that you are learning to accept your divinity. We know it has been challenging and difficult. And we know there are certain ones of you that have cursed Tobias! You have cursed the very lessons that we give you! We laugh with you now! (chuckling) And we honor you, for we know it has been difficult.

We come to you in this series – what we call the Creator Series – to give you information about becoming empowered humans. We know that the last thing a human angel wants to hear is yet another platitude. So we are very cautious of this. We will continue to give you as much solid and practical information as possible in our talks. But dear friends, this is a two-way street between us. We will not give you platitudes. We will not give you empty words to only make you feel good for a few moments of your time. We will give you information that we are receiving from you about your own path. We will give you information that a part of YOU is telling us you need to hear. We are simply feed back information that is coming from you. That is why it seems so familiar. That is why the energy of Tobias and the Crimson Council seems so close, like it was meant just for you. We are channeling YOU.

We will impart information back to you, but it is up to you, the human angel, to then put it to use. It is up to you to work with these new tools. It is ultimately up to you to be the creators. As we have said to you before, we cannot do it for you. We do not know all of the answers to your questions.

The melding of this energy between you and us and Spirit is indeed sweet! We know your lives are filled with many activities, many thoughts, many concerns. We ask you now to take this time of pause to meld. Dear friends, take a moment to feel what you have helped to create with Spirit in this space. It is a feeling of true love, of peace, and of your own Divine Self awakening quietly within.

❖ ❖ ❖ ❖

Now there is a bit of an interesting energy here, different from what you may have experienced before. As you know, there are many who come to visit when you are in the circle. They come from the other side of the veil, curious about the work you are doing. In a way, dear friends, they have to make reservations in advance, for otherwise they would flood into your space. (chuckling) We are very particular about who comes to visit at times like this. There is even a seating order within your circle. You, the humans, sit in the first circle. Then there are others who gather in the circle around that and even circles that expand outward beyond that.

The energy of our invited guests is different than in the past lessons. They cannot come in as close as our previous guests. There are intermediaries who help to create the lines of energy to allow our guests to observe, and to meld with you. They cannot come in directly right now. So there are angelic facilitators who are bridging this gap.

Our guests for this lesson have never been on Earth before. They have never crossed through the Wall of Fire. They are anxiously awaiting the proper time. They will cross through the Wall of Fire within the next five years of time. They will go to a type of reception room, or transition room, before they can take on a physical body, before they can come into the consciousness of Earth. You knew them when you were in the Kingdom, when you were in the First Circle. You played with them, you taught them, even back there. They have missed you deeply. You would not remember their names. You would not even remember their energies. But they are ones you have known. They are ones you have long for. Oh, and indeed they barely recognize you now!

Nearly all of you have asked about your angelic or spiritual name, the name that you were know by before you came to Earth. Do you know, dear friends, why you are not able to put your finger on it so well? It is because the name you were known by on the other side – it is like a vibration or a tone – you do not carry that name any more.

You have changed so much since you began your journeys on Earth. It would be a dishonor to call you by the name that you were known by before coming to Earth. It would be a dishonor. It would be like calling a general, a lieutenant. It would be like calling a doctor, a student. It would be a dishonor to use that old name because you have journeyed so far. You have evolved so much. There is a new name that is emerging within you. It is not the name that you had on the other side. It is a new name that you are helping to create and define right now. With this new name we begin to see the hints of energies birthing within you. As it does, your new name begins to take shape. It would be inappropriate for us to share that name with you. You will discover it on your own. You will know without doubt or question. But that name is still being birthed. So we ask you to be patient.

Those who come in to observe this lesson are here for a very good reason. They have been watching you from the First Circle. They have been amazed at what you have done, and what is like to be on Earth, to be in duality, to have no remembrance of who you truly are. They are honored that you are coming back into remembrance. They are honored when they see that you have gone from the energy of "two," and you are now beginning a new balance. You are bringing in the energy of the Christ consciousness. When there is appropriate mass, when enough Shaumbra and enough lightworkers around your world have brought in and integrated this energy of the Christ consciousness, then it will be their turn to journey through the Wall of Fire.

They come here to observe because they are in training and preparation. Oh, dear ones, they will come to Earth in approximately five years of your time. They will be born into biology. They will take on the human condition. They are not what you would call the Indigos, for that is a different type. The Indigo children have gone through a number of lifetimes on Earth. Most indigos are old Earth souls.

There are others who are called the "crystal children" – oh, you have many names for groups. (chuckling) These are not the ones we refer to. We give them no names at this time. They come from the Kingdom of the First Circle and have never taken on the human condition. It is to say that they are nervous! They are amazed at what you have done. They are in their training, and they are beginning to assimilate. They are beginning to condition themselves. They are trying to understand.

These new ones will be studying you over these next several years. So if you awaken at night and feel an energy in the room, if you feel perhaps you have been bumped in the night – they are still somewhat clumsy – they are simply coming in for a closer look. As you integrate your divinity, they are able to come in closer and closer to you. They are trying to understand this process of being a human. They are "shadowing" you.

If you should ask them for advice of what to do with your life, they will have no concept. They are learning from you! Do not mistake these ones for your guides or your angels, dear friends. They are the trainees. They do not have permission to go freely back and forth. They must always be – we are using your words here – they must always be escorted by a type of angel who is on your side of the Wall of Fire.

They are here with you now. They are beside you even if you are reading this. We ask you to greet them in your heart. We ask you to send them love, even as they are sending you love. They eagerly anticipate their upcoming journey on Earth. We ask you to share with them the soul and the depths of all of the experiences of your lifetimes on Earth. They eagerly await the time when they can follow in your footsteps.

This leads us to the continuing story of Jack, the Prince of IAM. In our last lesson we told the story of Jack, the prince of the Kingdom of the First Circle. He enjoyed journeying out into all parts of the Kingdom where he met many, learned much, and experienced much. He went to new villages in the Kingdom. We told this story to help you understand how you came to Earth. For indeed each of you is Jack. What we did not talk about in the last lesson was what happened to Jack when he came to the place where the land ended. He pushed his boat out onto the great sea, where it was calm for a number of days. And Jack became bored.

One day as Jack was drifting upon the waters, looking for new adventures, he saw a great Wall of Fire. It frightened him. He began paddling backwards, back towards the land where he had come from, back to the Kingdom that had been his home. But yet this Wall of Fire pulled him in. He was frightened, and he was terrified, yet it pulled him in a way that he could not prevent. After going through the Wall of Fire, Jack awoke upon the shores of a new land. Here he met others that were like him. Together they began to build the villages. They created the architecture and the energy patterns for the new land.

Now let us back up for a moment and talk about what transpired during this period when Jack went through the Wall of Fire. We did not focus so much on it in our last lesson, for we wanted to talk specifically about it now.

This was a traumatic experience for Jack – and for you. For the first time he felt he was not in control. This Wall of Fire pulled him in, and he screamed within his being. It was the first time Jack had ever felt terror. It was the first time Jack had ever felt a splitting apart within his own being. He had always been a prince, the heir to the throne. He had always had the freedom to create in any way he chose.

But now the Wall of Fire changed all of that for him. While he was passing through the Wall of Fire, it burned at the core of his very being. It caused conflict and pain and sorrow and suffering – all things he had never experienced before while he was in the Kingdom. It created something within him called guilt. As he tumbled through this dreaded wall, as he was wondering what he had done, he felt the guilt of having gone too far. He felt he should have stayed home in the Kingdom where all things were good and one.

The Wall of Fire shattered Jack. It shattered the oneness that he had been, and in a sense, you could say it created a war within him. The experiences that he had during the moment he passed through the Wall of Fire seemed to last an eternity. Prince Jack, the one who was a creator within the Kingdom, had experiences within the Wall of Fire that were filled with the deepest of sorrows, that were filled with anger and hate.

Oh, we know some of you have a hard time hearing this. But all of this was appropriate. All of this was meant to be. And all of this, you will see in its finality, was filled with the greatest of love.

Prince Jack spent what seemed to be an eternity in the Wall of Fire. It shattered him into pieces. Those pieces, in a sense, later rebirthed themselves into two areas.

A small portion of the pieces fell into the universe and eventually came to a place called Earth. They eventually resurrected in a human body. In this human body, Jack was destined to walk the Earth many, many lifetimes to gain experience for something on a very grand scale.

The larger part of Jack that was shattered spent a bit of extra time in the Wall of Fire. These pieces of Jack spent time in turmoil and difficulty within the Wall of Fire. But then they banded together. They found each other. They found the vibration of each other. They came back together. They wrapped together in a large weaving of energy to protect them. You would call this a cocoon. And within this cocoon, this other part of Jack went to sleep, protected by an energy cocoon.

This part of Jack slept in the cocoon, looking inward. You see, Jack had always been the outward creator, the adventurer, the one who sought new lands. Jack had always been an outer expression, but now most of Jack was within a cocoon, deeply asleep, looking inward.

This had never been done before. There was in a need on the part of Spirit, through Jack, to look inward, to look from a new perspective, rather than to create outward.

The other part of Jack eventually became human. He lived many lifetimes, forgetting who he was and forgetting his angelic origins. He came to believe that he was just a human. Oh, he even forget that he had past lifetimes on Earth. He believed his existence was merely that of being born and living and then dying. From lifetime to lifetime to lifetime he forgot who he had been. And his name would change from lifetime to lifetime. His gender would change occasionally. He had many experiences as a human.

In one lifetime not so long ago, he began to question "why." He asked who he was. He asked who his father truly was. The words he was told did not rest well within him. The words he had heard from the churches and through the spiritual doctrines did not resonate within him. He knew there was something more, and he sought to find it. He sought to reunite with something he knew was there, but could not put his finger on. He could not define it. Jack spent a number of lifetimes in search of himself. He spent these lifetimes in loneliness and solitude. He spent these lifetimes searching and struggling and banging his head against the wall.

After many trials and tribulations, Jack finally gave up one day. He did not care if he lived or died again as a human. He loved his family and he loved those he had met along the way, but he did not care so much any more. He did not care or have the passion for being a human any longer.

This was not a sad thing, dear friends. This was not a sad thing. It was time to release being human, of holding the human belief, of maintaining the human condition.

Others thought Jack was going out of his mind. They worried for him, and they talked amongst themselves, saying Jack was perhaps suicidal, and that Jack had gone out of his mind. They thought Jack should get a simple job, doing simple things and not worry about such grand events as finding himself.

Jack finally stopped his outer searching. He sat quietly and began to accept. He began to listen to his own inner voice. He put down his books. He put down the struggling in his heart and in his mind. Only then did Jack begin to understand what was truly taking place. The greater part of him that had been in this cocoon, looking inward, had now finished its sleep. It had now finished its introspective look and was ready to awaken.

Dear friends, when the greater part of Jack that was in the cocoon decided to awaken, it was like an infant. Oh, you think the True Self is like your father or mother? No, it is like the infant. As it awakens, the first thing it longs to do is to reunite with you. As the True Self is awakening and coming out of its cocoon, it wants to find you. This is the awakening of the Christ consciousness within.

Now Jack sat quietly, and he listened for a long time. At first he tried to listen in ways he had been taught by others. This did not work so well. He found himself out searching again, even while he was trying to be quiet. He was searching in his mind, using the technique that was in the old books. When he finally gave up on the old ways, he began sensing the energy, the love, the longing and the passion of the part that had been left behind.

At that point Jack understood something that even we could not explain to you. We choose not to because it will be unique to each one of you. There is no process or technique that Jack could have read in a book. It will be so unique and personal to you. It is not something that can be outlined. Oh, indeed we can talk to you of being creators. We can talk to you of how you got here. We can talk to you of things you are experiencing at this moment. But the process awakening your divinity is so deeply personal that we cannot possibly begin to define it. You will come to understand.

Jack sat quietly and listened within his being. He opened and allowed at his deepest levels. He allowed at the level that meant total release. He began to hear and to understand his divinity. He began to integrate with all that he was, what you call your True Self. This is what some of you mistake for your guides, what some of you mistake for an outer energy. These are all ones who come to guide you and to work with you and to give you love, but dear friends, the inner discovery is of something far grander.

We will talk more of this in our times to come, but we wanted to get a little further ahead with the story of Jack. It is your story.

When you went through the great Wall of Fire, much of you was left behind. Much of you went through a turmoil that is very difficult to describe and difficult for you to even understand within your being. A small part of your total energy came to this place called Earth and has walked for many, many lifetimes. But the part of you that was left behind – your True Self – is now awakening. This is what is happening within you right now. This is why you are feeling strange things within your body and your mind. This is why we gather here. This is why we honor you.

Remember, this is not some external entity. Your True Self is not some angel-like being with wings. It is you. It is you, and it comes from within. If you review some of the metaphors we have used in this parable, you will come to understand more here. It comes from within you.

This is Lesson Six of the Creator Series. We ask you to get comfortable for a moment, for we know you are in suspense. (chuckling) Those who are here visiting have sat in the outer circles listening, listening like you have listened to stories around the campfire. They are in total amazement, listening to this story of Jack, knowing that it was you. Their mouths are wide open, so to speak. There is honor for you.

Dear friends, this is Lesson Six of the Creator Series. We will do a brief review. We will add a cautionary note at this time. If you do not fully comprehend or understand the previous lessons, we ask you to go back. We put a sign here on the road of this series that says, "If you do not understand, go back."

What we will discuss after this lesson will be practical applications and practical tools for being the creators in the new energy. If you do not have the core understandings of the foundation lessons (Lessons One – Six), and you attempt to go forward, it may be painful at times. You will get zapped by your own creation energy, and you will not like it so much.

For the ones who will teach these lessons in future times, remember that there is a sign that says, "Stop, go back if you do not understand the previous lessons." If you have jumped in at Lesson Six and have not taken time to review Lessons One through Five, we highly recommend going back.

The first three lessons of this series were foundation lessons. Lesson One: "Accept all things as they are." This was the lesson of standing behind the short wall. This was the lesson of stepping out of duality and drama, standing behind your short wall and observing all that goes on around you. From this lesson you came to understand how easy it is to get trapped in duality. By standing behind the short wall, you have seen how easy it is to feel the addiction of wanting to jump back into duality!

By standing behind the short wall, you gain a new perspective, a somewhat distant perspective, but not necessarily disimpassioned. You have a better vantage point to watch all that happens, and you see the interesting dynamics of other humans. You begin to understand duality as it truly was.

Lesson Two, another foundation lesson: Accept your human self, and you will come to know your divine self. This is perhaps one of the more boring lessons, but my dear friends! You will need to understand this for yourself, and you will need to understand it for those you teach. If you do not accept your human self, return to "GO" and start over again. (chuckling) If you do not accept your human self, if you reject yourself, it will come back later. Your human self wants acceptance, and it will be more difficult to heal later than it is now.

You came to Earth for a reason. You have gone through many, many lifetimes for reasons. As you get closer to integration with your divinity, indeed there is the tendency to reject your human self. There are some who think they are going to ascend and never come back to Earth. Dear friends, that is not acceptance! You will have difficulty on the path of the Crimson Circle if that is how you feel about yourself. Do you understand what we are saying here? Think about the beauty and the joy and the love of being a human. Accept it. If it is difficult to accept, take time to work with this. If your desire is to pop out and never return to this challenging place of Earth, oh, dear friends, you will have many names in many future lifetimes!

Lesson Two : Accept your human self, and you will come to know your divine self. This is a core lesson. Accept all that you are. Accept your human self. Jack came to a point where he had to learn to look in the mirror and see God. Do you know what we mean? You need to come to this point within yourself, where you can see yourself as God, for indeed you are! Being in the human condition is a joyful, grand and loving thing. There are scores and scores of entities in the outer circles who desire this. They desire the human experience. Accept your human self, and you will come to know your divine self.

Then there is living in the divine moment. Lesson Three: Live in the divine moment. As you know so well, it is easy to live in the past. It is easy to worry of the future. As a creator, you will not be in the past or the future. You will be in the moment, the divine moment. Interestingly enough, the divine moment includes the past and the future. If you are in your divine moment, you are healing your past. You are creating a future that is awesome. In the divine moment you are in the past and the future all at the same time, but you are truly in what we would call "no time."

In the divine moment, your aging process is greatly reduced. That makes sense if you are both in the past and in the future and in "no time." If you choose to reduce the aging process of your biology, be in the divine moment. Healing your physical body is exponentially faster if you are in the divine moment. When you are in the divine moment, the healing process is exponentially faster and the aging process is slowed.

Oh, these have been key lessons. (chuckling) We hope you do not simply read them for the wonderful energy! These are the foundation lessons. They are not the most exciting, but they are the most important. These first three lessons in the Creator Series are lessons of acceptance: Accepting all things, accepting yourself, accepting the moment you live in. They are the acceptance lessons within this series.

Then we moved into Lesson Four. It was a fun lesson, for it provided the first real tool for you: To create in grace. The Oven of Grace is a tool for taking a situation and finding resolution. This will be a fun lesson for you to teach. To create in grace is to get your human thinking out of the way. It is to step aside for a moment and simply allow your True Self to begin its process, to find the appropriate resolution. Creating in grace also means to take your agenda out of the situation at hand. Your agenda is limited. It limits the full potential of creation. Lesson Four, to create in grace, begins a new type of process. The process does not come from the mind. It comes from within you, so you can create in a new way.

When creating in grace, would you not expect to have changes in your life? Lesson Five: Expect changes and bless them! The changes that you begin experiencing in your life, while frustrating and aggravating, are appropriate. You will see that old things are moved out to make room for new things, grander things. There is a parallel here on what is literally happening within you. The new thing that is moving in is the part of you, the larger part of you, that was left behind at the Wall of Fire. The things that are moving out of your life right now were based on old human limitations. The limitations of consciousness are being moved out right now to make room for this grander energy.

(very emotional) We will pause here for a moment, for it is difficult to be this close to you, to feel the challenges and pains that you have gone through and to feel your sufferings. Yet you continue along your path. It amazes us, and the emotions that come through now are from the ones in the outer circles who weep in honor. They weep to see what you go through, and wonder how they could possibly follow in your footsteps.
(emotional pause)

We will continue now.

You cannot expect to begin the series of changes precipitated by the oven and not have things happen in your life. The old ways move out to make room for the new. Dear friends, when you turn on the oven of grace, expect changes in your life!

Now we ask you to be in your new house at this time. We ask you to take a moment to make sure you are in your new house. (chuckling) If you have been out in the yard, we ask you to come in now and to be with us here. Close all of the shades and the windows and the doors so that you do not have disturbances from the outside.

For those who are not so familiar with what we are talking of here, the new house is the metaphor, a symbol of your new divine human self. It is your new house. It is who you are. It is a magical place, filled with anything you want.

But for now we ask you to close the windows and the doors and the blinds. Let us go back with you to the kitchen where we have the Oven of Grace. Oh, and we even smell things cooking in your new house!

Now dear friends, let's walk into your kitchen. We see quite a mess! You have put so many issues in your oven, and then when it has come time to take them out, you have forgotten, and your oven is stacked with the issues! The issues you remembered to take out are laying on the counter, for you did not know what to do with them! There are trays of pictures and wallets and purses and eyeglasses! Dear friends, your issues are laying all over, cooling off, so to speak. It is indeed a mess!

The cooling off period that has been appropriate. We have not given you this information until now, for we wanted you to remember this when you teach it to others. There is a cooling off period! There is a transition period from the time you take something out of the oven until the time things truly begin to transform on your human level. As you know, change begins to take place. This is part of the cooling off process.

Before we go any further, let us talk of your issues that are cooling on the table. Your issues are not as complex as you think. Look at the trays of issues laying out on the counters. We see there are basically four categories of human concern that all of these issues can fall into. We see four areas of human concern. There is that number four again!

First, there are the issues that deal with biology, with your physical being, with your aches and pains, with disease of the body, with needs of the body. There are those biological issues.

Second there are the issues of relationships. These has been and will continue to be an issue for many of you. Relationships represent duality. They represent the "two." That is why relationships are such a challenge. We see many who have wanted to put relationship issues in the oven – and a few who did! (chuckling) And there are many who put their own relationship needs in the oven without putting in another person. This has been appropriate, for as we reminded you, only put those things in the oven that were for you.

There are also resource or abundance issues. As a human, there are certain things that you need, and your money usually buys them. These are resource issues. These are abundance issues. We have seen many, many of those issues in your ovens lately! (chuckling) Some went in repeatedly! Abundance issues will be the most difficult to break through and may need to go back in the oven again and again. But when it finally starts working, you will see the fastest changes in this area of your life.

Finally, there are the issues of self worth. These are issues about who you are, about your own worthiness. These issues can now be directly tied back to time when you went through the Wall of Fire. You have done much processing and releasing in this lifetime. The releases that you have not been able to get through relate directly back to this traumatic time of crossing through the Wall of Fire. With this knowledge you can begin to resolve your worthiness issues quite easily. What you did when you came through that Wall of Fire was in service to All That Is. You went through the Wall of Fire to explore a new area, a new circle that had never been created before. That is how you came to be here on Earth. We honor you for doing this on behalf of Spirit. We ask you now to put your self worth issues aside. There was nothing you did wrong. You did this in love and service.

Now let us return to your kitchen with all of the issues sitting on the counters. We ask you to now take the trays of issues and throw them up into the air! Take all of your issues and throw them up in the air. You will notice something – they do not fall back down to the ground. Your issues are suspended in mid air. They float in the air. They begin transforming. Instead of a slip of paper or a picture or physical object such as a wallet, they transform into bright, twinkling lights. They are like stars, hovering around the ceiling of your large kitchen.

When you take your issues out of the oven of grace – which is a divine grace that exists within you – they will transform from issues into bright, shining stars. There is a natural order of things that takes place, a natural resolution that takes place when you do not limit the results, when you let things come into balance. It transforms a difficult, heavy, human issue back into a twinkling light of energy.

Now dear friends, leave these issues suspended here as twinkling lights in the kitchen of your new house for a moment. We will share with you Lesson Six of the Creator Series. This is perhaps the most magical of all the lessons we will give to you. The others will be more practical. This is the most magical. Spend some time with this, dear friends.

Lesson Six: Within you is divine balance. Within you is divine balance. All of these twinkling lights, that were once issues, are now finding their own balance. You released your issues when you placed them into the Oven of Grace, and set them aside to cool. Now they are without the heaviness of being physical objects, of being tangible objects. You have thrown the issues up in the air and allowed them to find their own balance. At this point, they transform into twinkling, brilliant lights. They will find their own balance.

For example, let's say you have a physical problem in your life. When you cook in the Oven of Grace, and allow the changes to take place in your body, it will find a natural balance. That natural balance will not come from Tobias or your guides or Yeshua or any other being. It will come from within your being. This magical transformation process occurs if you allow. This applies to all of your issues, whether they are about your body, your relationships, your abundance or your self worth.

Now you have all of these twinkling "former" issues floating around your kitchen. They are former issues that have now found the appropriate balance. Take these twinkling lights and weave them into a beautiful light necklace. You will wear this necklace of lights in the future for certain ceremonies we will explain later. Each one of these glistening lights is like a gem around you. They are also a reminder that you have walked through many experiences, but each one of them had a pearl of love and light and joy within them. Each experience had a purpose. This necklace will be a reminder of all that you have learned. It will also be a reminder of all that you are learning about to allowing a new type of creation in your life.

Lesson Six: Within you is divine balance. When you allow this divine balance to do its work, your former issues will come back to you in the most appropriate ways. Within you is a new divine balance. We asked you to close the blinds and the doors of your new house. We want you to understand that it comes from within you. It is not appropriate now to ask your guides for help. They love you dearly, but they are not in your direct energy anymore. It has not time to ask Tobias or any other outer being for help. Within YOU is Divine Balance.

The relationship is between you and your Higher Self. Your Higher Self cannot be found if you look out the window. It is not out there. There is nothing outside that will connect you to your own divinity. When you find yourself looking outside for your answers, we will remind you that the connection point back to your divine being, the connection point back to whence you came, the connection point to the future for where you are going, is within! Dear friends, remember this. This is the lesson of magic that you will come to understand. Within you is divine balance.

Now we have gone through the first half of this Creator Series. We have given the foundation lessons of acceptance. Now we have given the three lessons of transformation – to create in grace, to accept the changes in your life, and to understand that there is divine balance. Simply allow it to be.

Dear friends, the ones who gather in the outer circles do not know if they are worthy of ever coming in to human body and following in your footsteps. But the way has been paved by the work you have done. They will not need to go through the challenges and the difficulties and the lessons that you have. They will have teachers such as you have never had. They will walk the path that has been blazed by the ones we call Shaumbra. When they come into biology – as they will begin to do soon – and experience the challenges of duality, they will need a teacher. When they are in most need of a teacher, they will come across a human who wears a shining necklace of light. They will recognize you as their human teacher, to guide them on their new path.

We love you dearly, and you are never alone.

And so it is.

✧ ✧ ✧ ✧

Lesson Seven
Create In Broad Strokes

And so it is, dear friends, dear Shaumbra, that we gather again in this circle. It seems like only a moment of time since we left you, but we know in that time that you have had many wonderful and some challenging experiences! It is good to hear your music, to hear the story of your journey expressed in these musical vibrations. I, Tobias, cherish these moments. I look forward to these times when family joins together like this.

As we get started here, we will work with you to adjust the energies. Those who are on our side of the veil come in now to facilitate, to meld the energies of your humanness and your divinity with our energies.

Dear friends, dear Shaumbra, I know you well! I know you by the work that we have done together in the past. This energy should be familiar you.

As we expand this circle, open your heart. You are in a safe space here. Open your heart and allow the love and light and Christ consciousness within you to pour into the circle we build here together. Breathe deeply. Breathe deeply and allow it to permeate your entire being, throughout all of your biology and all of your spirit. Breathe deeply and know that you are with family!

There are ones who come in now to adjust the energy of this space. They help weave the vibrations of this space. In this time that we spend together, we are with you in a new energy, in a new dimension that we create together. This is the energy of the new Earth. This is the new spiritual energy. It is not something that simply disappears when you leave this space. It is something that becomes part of your being. It becomes embedded within you. It provides a type of energy template from which the old energies within you will copy and mimic.

The Old Energies within you will look at the New Energies you are creating within. They will look at it and say, "This indeed is the light. This indeed is what we at the sub-DNA levels will copy and to mimic." It is a very interesting process here – how these particles of energies that are at the deepest parts of you react. These particles are looking for the proper vibration, the proper balance to occur. This balancing is happening within you right now.

The energy of this circle is brought into your being. It is held there. It does not disappear. This time and dimension and space that we are in together is one of great healing for you. This is a time of new balance. Even if you are reading this weeks or months afterwards, you receive the same energy. Even if you were not present when this message was originally delivered, it is the same energy. For those who are reading this at a later date, you are here with us as much as any human that sits in their physical being.

Now we have much to discuss, and then we will proceed to Lesson Seven of this Creator Series. We know you been doing much homework. There are very interesting experiences in your life now! Your homework is not just what is happening in your mind. Your homework is not just what happens in that specific moment when you stand behind the short wall. Your homework is not just when you put an issue into the Oven of Grace. The homework is all of those things that are happening in your life now.

Think about it for a moment, the experience that you had three days ago, and two weeks ago, or perhaps last night. This is your homework. This is what you are creating. These challenges and circumstances and experiences are there to help you truly become a divine human.

There are times when we gather like this when we could not say another word. We could simply sit with you here. We could simply let our emotions out. They would come out as tears – tears of joy and happiness – but more than anything, tears of incredible honor. You have heard this from us and from others before. You still don't see yourselves as we do! You still don't see who you are, and what you are doing. There are those of you who wake up in the morning and feel small and unimportant and alone. You do not even begin to understand what you are doing and who you are! You think we overstate our message about your mission on this place called Earth. Oh, dear friends, you have such a surprise coming! Hopefully that surprise will come while you are still walking in biology, the surprise of knowing how truly powerful you are.

We told the story of the prince named Jack, which is the story of each and every one of you. We do not give this story justice in the way we tell it, with all of the honor and the grandness and the love and the sacrifice. It is not an overinflated story that you hear from I, Tobias, or the others. It barely begins to scratch the surface. Here you are, the ones who were princes and princesses of the kingdom of All That Is. You chose to leave the kingdom for something of incredible honor. Here you are on this tiny place called Earth, thinking you are just a human, thinking that you live perhaps eighty or ninety years and struggle to survive, struggle to do the right thing. You do not see who you truly are!

One of the purposes of the Crimson Council is to help awaken this understanding within you. As was said earlier, you will not get there through your mind. You will get there through your heart, and more specifically, through what is called the "one chakra," the Christ seed that is within you. Be "out of your mind" for a while. It is a wonderful thing! (chuckling) There are drugs that can help you go there, but dear friends, you can do it better on your own!

Now, each time we gather together in this circle, there are certain "invited guests." Take a moment here, dear friends, to feel the energy of those who gather in the second circle with you. Indeed, you the human is in the first circle. Surrounding you in energy and in love are those from the other side that come in to observe. Oh, they are fascinated. Each time we gather like this, there is a new group of "invited guests." Indeed, they must have an RSVP to be here! (chuckling)

The ones who come in now bring in a technical energy. Even on our side there are certain energy groups or families. There is a group of angelic entities whose job is to monitor and measure the vibrations of Earth and the humans upon Earth. The ones that sit in the second circle are the technicians. They are – and Cauldre laughs about this – but yes, they are "celestial engineers." They are here for a specific reason. First, they come to enjoy your company, to smile upon you. They are also the ones who watch the "gauges" and the "meters" of your work and see how it affects all things. They have been actively measuring the vibrations of Gaia and the vibrations of humankind. They come here now as part of their research.

They see a group that is going through an intense transformational process with the intent of integrating their divinity. They join us now because your vibration is different than most other humans. You have given yourself in service. You have studied the spiritual aspects of self and humans for many, many lifetimes. You have spent much time in both your human schools and the schools on our side of the veil in between lifetimes, studying the process of ascension. You are the ones, not only studying it, dear friends, but living these studies on a day-to-day basis!

The technicians join us now to measure, monitor and record your experiences. They are beside you with their gauges and note pads, metaphorically speaking. They are very curious about you. No, they do not interfere. They do not probe or prod. They remain at a distance. They have been busy lately, not only with you, but with all humans and Earth. There is – how to say – a rush to measure.

The measurements are changing faster than ever. The vibrations are going up and down. It is not following the old patterns. And yes, we do also watch your stock market, for this is an interesting indicator of certain aspects of human consciousness. Vibrational changes are occurring faster than ever before. These changes are gaining momentum. It is like the momentum of a wheel that begins to turn slowly and then goes faster and faster. As you watch the spinning wheel, the patterns within the circle of the wheel begin to change. At times a wheel that is turning clockwise may have the appearance of turning counterclockwise. The momentum is changing, and the perception of the patterns is not always what it seems.

The ones who measure, track and record the vibrations are particularly interested in Shaumbra. They see a variance within this group. They see a new path being carved by your energies. They are watching intensely.

As a result of the momentum and your changing vibrations, indeed you will see the Earth changes, the adjustments of Gaia. You will see changes within yourself. There will be quantum leaps in the technologies of Earth, but more than anything, there will be quantum leaps in your own enlightenment. This is a time of great change, and you are living in the midst of it. Hold on, because the ride will continue for a while! (chuckling)

Now dear friends, before we proceed let us do the final melding of this energy. We draw in close to you. Let us touch you and hug you. Remember who you are. We send you the energy of remembrance, so that you may remember who you truly are!

Indeed it is sweet to be here with you. What we see is shining desire, desire to be in service. We are in awe to know that the most pressing question you have is not about money, not about health, and certainly not about becoming more powerful over other humans. What you ask most frequently is, "Dear Spirit, how can I be of service? Dear Spirit, how can I help humanity? Dear Spirit, how can I be in fulfillment to you?"

Do you understand what we are saying? What is in your heart is not selfish! You are not asking something for yourself. You are asking how to be in service to Spirit. It amazes us! It amazes me, for I think if I were walking in your shoes, I would surely ask for more money! (chuckling) I would surely ask for invincible health! I would surely ask for something that was not as high a vibration and as loving as what I hear you asking for! You say, "Dear Spirit, how can I be in service today? Dear Spirit, what is it you want me to do?" When a human comes to this point, we know they are truly enlightened. We know they are truly on the path!

Dear friends, we mention this to you because at this point on your path, you do not need to worry about falling down. You do not need to worry about losing ground and going backwards. Do not worry anymore about falling backwards into the old ways. Your vibration of love and service is strong.

We will continue the story of the prince named Jack, and of his journey that eventually brought him to Earth. We use the story of Jack to describe what happened to you, for you are the princes and princesses of the kingdom of the First Creation. We are giving this to you a piece at a time to help you absorb it and to understand who you truly are. We will continue telling parts of this story for some time.

We will caution that some humans might not like this so well. It will raise the eyebrows and perhaps even a few fists of your own kind, those called lightworkers. We ask Cauldre to step out of the way while we bring this information forth. He knows what comes, and he is not terribly pleased that we are going to open this can of worms! (chuckling)

Jack was a prince in the kingdom of IAM. He was a great explorer and a great creator. And he was easily bored. He journeyed to the ends of the kingdom where he then set sail onto the waters. Jack came upon the Wall of Fire, which was the edge of all creation as it was known. This frightened him. He tried to go back to the kingdom but the non-energy, the vacuum, and the suction from the Wall of Fire pulled him in.

It seemed like he was in the Wall of Fire for an eternity. His being was shattered, broken into many, many, many pieces. Some of these pieces went into a type of "cocoon" to go for a long sleep, to go for an inner experience. Jack had always been an outward-looking creator. Part of the energy of Jack did not go into this inner cocoon, this inner-looking energy. Part of him continued to travel.

Now, Jack did not go straight to Earth. There was an interim period. This is somewhat difficult to describe, but we will attempt to convey it working closely with Cauldre. Beyond the Wall of Fire was nothing, a void, total darkness. It was the Void that would later become your physical universe. When Jack crossed into the Void, there were no stars. There were no galaxies. There was no energy whatsoever. The Void was nothing.

When Jack came through the Wall of Fire, he saw his opposite, his mirror. He began to have experiences, first with himself and then with other entities. These early experiences created an energy that poured out from him, setting up the structures and patterns of energy in the universe that had previously been a Void. Jack went through experiences that created energy weavings. These energies would later become your stars, galaxies and solar systems. This was a very interesting period of time for Jack.

Through his experiences, Jack began taking on a new identity. He mingled with other entities who had also crossed through the Wall of Fire. He bonded with others, forming new "energy" groups. These energy family groups traveled to new parts of the universe. And as you know from your current experiences with families, internal battles developed. Jack and the others began fighting. Wars began to occur. The groups that had formed became fractured and split.

During this very chaotic time, Jack was still learning to adjust to his transition through the Wall of Fire. He had never felt anything like this before. He was trying to remember and discover who he was, but he was taking on new attributes to which he could not relate. Jack had strange feelings and vibrations about his own energy. Where Jack had once been only thought consciousness, he was beginning to take on a thickness, a heaviness of being that would later become a physical body.

Jack did not like this heaviness. He did not like feeling the slowdown of his energy, the descending from thought to light to electra. He did not like this whole situation. He sought to get out of it, but did not know how. He was becoming more and more solid. As he and the others experienced this, the universe also became more and more solid. Planets began to take shape, to form and take on mass.

Oh, dear friends, Jack – you – did not like any of this. You felt like you were falling and falling and falling. Your energy and vibrations were slowing. You fought it. You felt you would never again remember who you were, or where you came from. You desperately tried to hold on to the vibration of the kingdom. You cursed the Wall of Fire!

You were in chaos. There were terrible wars in your universe. During this time the concept of killing and death first began to appear. There was anger towards others and towards yourself. Groups of entities roved the ever-solidifying universe, trying to take power from others. They thought that if they took power and energy from other beings, this added energy would raise their vibration and send them back Home to the kingdom.

You traveled in groups, some large, some small. As you did this, you in a sense held hands and bonded your energy. You lived within this "family energy ship" and traveled all over and had many, many experiences. You learned to travel quite well on the energy "highways" that were developing in your universe. You could get from one part of the universe to the other, what could be millions or even billions of light years away, using your current measurement system. Traveling light years would take you only a moment. You were proficient at inter-dimensional travel. Dear friends, your science fiction stories and movies are not so much about the future. They are about your PAST!

All of this time, you were resisting this slowing down, resisting this solidification that was taking place in you, in your entire universe. You started having strange experiences. You started crashing into things! You didn't pass through objects any more. Energy did not pass through energy. Things were becoming so solid, so slowed down, that you would crash into stars and planets and meteors and asteroids. This surprised you, and it angered you.

The wars continued. The battles intensified. This was not a good time. You were trying to reach the proper vibration to find the way back Home, yet also discovering how energy outside the Kingdom worked. At the same time, the energy was spinning down.

Eventually everything came to an impasse. Consciousness could go no further. The conflicts and battles between the light and the dark came to a stalemate. The universe as you knew it stopped growing. Your scientists will soon see this through their measurements. They will see that the universe came to a halt.

In order to find resolution to this energetic impasse, the consciousness of all energies in the universe came together and created something called the Order of the Arc. Yes, this creation is what you now know as the Archangels. We will talk about the Order of the Arc in more detail in other discussions.

At that point there was an agreement for a select group of angels to go to this place of Earth. You would cross through the final veil. You agreed to cross the final barrier, to take on a very dense physical form. You agreed to live in complete amnesia of who you were, to walk through the cycles of life and death. Through this experience, you would come full circle from the time you left the Kingdom. By coming to Earth, you would come to remember who you were before crossing through the Wall of Fire.

That is why you are here! That is why you have lived through hundreds and hundreds and hundreds of lifetimes. You have been walking through the cycle of Earth lives because of your agreement to bring things full circle. This agreement is one that heals the past, heals the time of going through the Wall of Fire, and heals the time of the building of the Void which is the creation of your universe as you know it. You have walked all of these lifetimes to heal and to rediscover.

The work you do here on Earth will ultimately resolve the energetic impasse that still exists in the universe. Yes, everything is at a standstill out there. This will cause you to scratch your head, especially when you look into the stars and see much activity. It is difficult to explain here in words, so we will explain it through energies. What you are seeing in the universe is your past. You perceive it to be happening in your present time, but that is an inter-dimensional illusion. Until you find resolution on Earth, all things in the universe remain at a standstill.

This lesson's invited guests are taking the measurements and monitoring what you are doing. They are here because the circle is coming to a close. You are in these final stages of a journey that has lasted in a time frame we could not even begin to explain. But the circle is coming to a close from the very work you have done.

It should be no surprise that your daily life is challenging right now. It is not about you! It is not just your current self that you are healing. You have already healed hundreds and hundreds and hundreds of past lives. Most of those past life energiews have healed and left, and Gaia is releasing the energy that has been stored in the Earth. What you are truly healing right now is this time of the building of the Void, the time between the Wall of Fire and coming to your Earth. You are healing this time when you were bouncing around the universe, experiencing the beginnings of mass and matter. It was a time when you could freely travel through time and space.

Now, the ones you call "alien beings," dear friends, are simply aspects of you from this past time, this time of the building the Void. We have said to you that when you look up into the stars, there is not much out there. We mean just that. You are looking into a limited dimensional view of your physical universe. And indeed there is not much there! What is there is all the energies of you from the past that are crisscrossing, sometimes intersecting, your current life on Earth.

Imagine standing in your living room. All you see is the living room, but there are other rooms of the house that you cannot see because you are standing in one place at that moment of time. There are activities in the other rooms, but you are not aware of them, for you cannot see or hear them. Your universe is much like this. There are many rooms, there are many dimensions. When you look up into your skies, and you see the stars – in that room, there is not much. There is not much there in terms of life. There is much energy, but in terms of life form, not much. There are rooms in the universe that exist side-by-side, dimension-by-dimension, that you cannot see or hear. Some of you are beginning to sense these other rooms. They are all under the same roof, but they are separate rooms.

Once in a while, in an unusual energy situation, there is a bleed-through or crossover. You will see into one of the other rooms, or an entity from the other room accidentally walks through the door and comes into your room. When this happens, this is you from the past! Oh, it will look like an alien and feel like an alien, but dear friends, it is you from the past. With the intense amount of healing work going on right now, you are paralleling your own past.

You are in the living room now, but you are also healing the other rooms at the same time, so there are incidences of crossover, of intersection. Are there aliens in your universe that are wiser and grander and smarter? Indeed my friends, no! These are aspects of you from the past. How could they be wiser or smarter or more powerful? These aspects of yourself – part of your past – are occurring at this very moment. Even while you sit here, the part of you that was/is building the structures of the Void in the past exists at this same moment.

We do not want to get too far off track here with concepts of alternative realities or multiple dimensions. We simply want to reinforce the point that these entities are you from the past, and they cross over occasionally. The important thing is to know, dear friends, is that you are coming full circle in your work. Do not give up your power to another, to any being, to what you would call an alien.

Even though these entities are simultaneous aspects of you from the past, they will try to present themselves as grand, intelligent beings. They will try to tell you – and there is a bit of truth to it – that they are your parent, that they supplied the seed stock for you. Well indeed, they are your past! But do not be deceived that they are grand beings who understand the keys to all knowledge and wisdom.

Dear friends, the vibration of the word "alien" is "a lie." Do not give your power to another. You are so close to completing your circle. This is a time of intensity, where even aspects of you from the past will come back and try to deceive you and belittle you and tell you they are the wise ones. In a sense, even though you are trying to heal this past, these aspects from the past will try to deceive you.

Why? The "you" from the past wants to know if you in the now has truly discovered who you are. "You" from the past is testing you in the now. Have you discovered your divine origins? Are you taking ownerships of your divinity? Are you still looking outside of yourself for salvation, or have you discovered your power within? The "you" from the past wants to know if they can count on you. So these aspects will test you. Have you finally discovered your truth, or are you still playing games? They cannot heal until you discover and own your divinity.

I, Tobias, want you to remember the energy of this moment we share together. It is the energy of the Christ seed within you. You have always had it. You just needed to discover it once again. Follow none other than the God within you! You will be challenged in these days to come, as you make the final link of your circle. The challenges will be difficult. That is why we bring up this subject now.

Are we saying you will have an alien encounter? In a way, yes, we are. It may not happen while you are driving down the road at 1:00 AM and come to a railroad crossing. It may happen in your sleep. It may happen, and most likely will happen, as an old remembrance coming through like a freight train, a remembrance that brings fear and that cripples you and immobilizes you. When this rememberance happens, we want you to come back to the energy of the time when Spirit, when Yeshua, the Crimson Council and Tobias sat with you, and said, "Dear ones, you are the God that is awakening. Have no others come before or above you."

(chuckling) This will bring up many questions about aliens! We are prepared to discuss each and every question you have.

We will shift energies here and go into Lesson Seven of the Creator Series. Dear friends, we will tell a short story to help you better understand Lesson Seven. It is a simple lesson. You may struggle with it because it is so simple. You may try to make it something complex.

Lesson Seven is the first of what we would call the practical lessons of outward creation. Much of what we have talked about up to this time has been foundations understandings, and processing of old energies that needed to be balanced. Now we will give a number of steps for creating in the New Energy. This may feel odd or unusual to some of you. There is an ingrained fear within you – within all humans – of your creator powers. There is a reluctance to create once again, for it has been a long time, and there is still a shame and a guilt associated with what you perceive to have done in the past.

Deep within your being is the feeling that you sinned when you crossed through the Wall of Fire. You feel you went too far. You feel guilt for being in the energy of chaos and battle while building the Void. Oh, dear friends, the battles that took place make Star Wars look like child's play! So when we talk of using your true creator abilities, some of you may be taken aback. Some of you will wonder if this is the right thing and think perhaps that it is not time to use your creator powers.

There was a human angel by the name of Anna, a wonderful angel, much like you. She attended many spiritual classes over the past 30 years. She learned about mind control, which is amusing in itself. She learned how to meditate, to follow the ritual of meditation, and how to clear her mind. But we know, and you know, the mind was never cleared. She spent 20 minutes a day, twice a day, sitting in an uncomfortable position because she thought it was what she should do. Yet in a sense, this was very good for her soul, for it helped her along her path. It provided learning and growth experiences foe her.

Anna took many courses in different techniques – how to be peaceful, how to be calm, how to be nice, how to be God-like, how to obey God, how to hide from God. (chuckling) These courses were like stepping stones on her path, and they helped get her to this point.

But underneath, Anna kept wondering, "If I am learning so much and growing so much, why can't I affect my being, my space? Why can't I focus my mind to change the flow of water coming from a faucet?" She tried this. It did not work. "Why can't I use the power of my mind to change the way a candle flickers?"

Anna was frustrated, for she felt like she had little or no control of her life. You see, what she did not realize was that all of her work and effort was awakening something within. But yet she was frustrated that it was not changing her outer reality. Things were not changing on the outside. There were many reasons for this. One reason was that the time was not right. It would not have been appropriate. It would have been – how to say – a crash and burn. The time was not quite right.

Anna's balance of energies – the clear, the white, and the dark round marbles we talked about in the last lesson – were still playing a wonderful game within her. It was not time for the game to end. There was also the fact that she continued giving her power over to others. She would take a class, or read a book, and she would become a follower. A creator is not a follower! They are contradictory terms.

But now, dear friends, now the time is appropriate. As we have said, the ones who gather in the second circle for this lesson are the ones who measure and monitor. They are highly intrigued because the time is now appropriate. They know that the first group of the humans can now begin to use their creator abilities. You belong to this group.

Anna was very frustrated because she felt she could not control her life. At one point she, like many of you have done, threw away all of the books, all of the tools, and said, "No more classes. They have done nothing but cost a lot of money!" Dear friends, this is not an accurate understanding, for as we have said, all of those things, those classes and disciplines and techniques, were truly stepping stones for her, and helped bring her back together with family. That is how she met others, through these courses. The energy of these gatherings has brought family back together.

Anna learned about this place called her New House. She did not understand it, but she felt good when she was went into her New House. It felt appropriate, and if nothing else, it felt quiet for a few minutes! (chuckling) So she spent time in her New House, like we ask you to do now. Put yourself in the energy of your New House. Feel the song of your New House. If you do not hear so well, simply feel. Know that there is a vibration, a core vibration, in your new house.

Anna came to a point where she had released many of the old ways. She came to the point where she was truly ready to begin creating.

In her New House, Anna saw a large paintbrush in a pail of glowing paint on the floor of her living room. She knew it was there for a reason, for she had not placed it there. It had not been there the last time she was in her New House. But it felt right

The brush was large. It was larger than any paintbrush she had seen before. She looked around her new house and wondered what she was supposed to do with this paintbrush and with this paint. But instead of fretting, being that she was in the wonderful energy of her new house, she simply asked herself, "What is it that I should know about this can of glowing, beautiful paint and this large paintbrush?" A voice came up from within her – not from a guide or not from Tobias. Her voice told her to take the brush, dip it in the paint, and make a broad stroke on any wall of her New House. When Anna took the brush, filled with glowing paint, and made a broad streak across the wall of her New House, she learned about Lesson Seven.

Lesson Seven: Create in Broad Strokes. Create in broad strokes. This is a simple but profound lesson. In these coming days, you will have your first real understandings about creating in the New Energy. No longer are you a victim, and no longer simply reacting to things that happen in your life. You can actually create.

Sit in your New House and feel the vibration. When you are ready, take this large brush, dip it in the paint, and create a broad stroke. Just one, no more. Then put the paintbrush down, sit upon the floor, and watch what happens with the broad stroke you have created. Observe it. It will change. It will morph. It will find its own balance. You are in your New House, and within this energy is a divine balance. Your first creation – your first broad stroke – will find its own divine balance.

What are you creating? In our last lesson we talked of four areas of the human experience. We talked of resources, also known as abundance. We talked of health and biology. We talked of relationships. And we talked of self worth. Choose any one of the four. Hold it in your heart. Then create with a broad stroke. Create the balance for this area. You are creating balance. There is no need to have a specific agenda or intent for Spirit or for yourself. You are creating in the divine balance. But this time, you are creating a broad stroke. You are being proactive.

What does this mean? What will happen now? You may come to some fear here. You may wonder what you are really creating, and what is going to happen as a result of your new creation. This fear relates back to the time before you came to Earth. It relates to the shame you have for crossing through the Wall of Fire, for leaving the Kingdom. Address this fear. Sit with it in your new house. Understand it and talk to it. This fear could be your best friend, or as a creator this fear could be your worst enemy. This fear, if left unattended, will come back to you. It will come back looking like an alien. (chuckling) We mean that seriously. If you allow this fear to grow and to have power, it will take you back to places where this fear was birthed.

Lesson Seven: Create in broad strokes. Do not worry about the mechanics or the details. This space is filled with mechanics and engineers who work on the details. You, as creators, do not need to get into that now. Create in broad strokes. You will have the tendency to want to go in with fine brushes and tell Spirit and your divine Self how to do it. Resist that temptation. Sit in front of this beautiful, broad stroke you have created. Allow it to take its divine balance. This is simple, dear friends, but yet very challenging.

Use the issue of relationships for an example. You do not have to explain to Spirit or yourself what the issue is. You do not have to go into the details. Take this one issue. Hold it in your heart. Create with a broad stroke, and know, dear friends, that your own divinity, will handle the rest.

Do you see what is happening here? You are learning to trust your own divinity and allowing it to do the work. You have tried to handle all of the details in the past! You have been separated from the Kingdom for so long that you feel you've had to handle every little detail. It is time to trust. As you allow your divinity to provide the appropriate balance, oh, my dear friends, your life will be so much easier! You will be the painter of beautiful strokes. The mechanics of manifestation will be handled at other levels. Life will be so much more joyful.

Why the wall? Why the paint? Walk outside of your new house after you have painted your broad stroke. Things outside will look different. It will look different because of the work that you have done on the inside! You will see beyond what you could previously recognize. You will see the way things are created. You have changed something on the inside with your first, broad brush stroke, and the outside will begin to look different.

Lesson Seven: Create in broad strokes. Dear friends, resist the desire to use the fine brushes to fill in the details. This will be done for you. After you create a broad stroke, sit on the floor and admire the piece of art you have just created. We have talked to you before of the Oven of Grace, and we have talked to you about putting old issues in there. The Oven of Grace is wonderful for old issues. But the Oven of Grace also serves as a processor and a balancer of new things you create. It is like an entire energy system of your new house.

As you paint a broad stroke, your Oven of Grace balances and processes the energies. It allows grace to process your new creation in a divine balance. It manifests and balances in the most appropriate and loving manner. Your own divinity will handle the balance.

There is an innate fear within you of creating something that is not appropriate. This has been a block for many of you. You have been reluctant to create because you did not know if it would be the right thing. You have been waiting for Spirit to tell you how to create and what to create, because you did not want to be inappropriate once again. The Oven of

Grace, your own divinity and the love of Spirit will make it so that you do not create inappropriately. With the balance of the four marbles, you will not create bad or dark. With the love that is within you, you will not create the wrong thing.

What should you create now? It is simple. With your broad stroke you create a new balance of relationships, a balance of abundance, a balance of health, and self worth. When you paint that broad stroke, you are creating a new balance. Do not worry about how many dollars that balance means, or what this new lover in your life will look like. Divinity will handle the balance and bring to you all things appropriate. As you change on the inside, you change your vibration level. You change your energy patterns, so that when you walk out the door of your new house, you have changed the perception of what things appear to be. You change reality without affecting another human being. This is very interesting. It is why we have said, "Do not pray to change the world. Pray only to awaken within yourself." As you do, you will change your reality.

Lesson Seven, a very simple one, but your first lesson in the active creating. Choose from one of the four areas of human challenge we discussed earlier: relationships, abundance, health or self worth. Work with this for a period of time now. Create in broad strokes.

Now dear friends, our invited guests who monitor and measure the energy are smiling. They feel a vibration level that they have detected in very few others. This vibration is about the love that shines within you.

They will be taking many more measurements of Shaumbra and of Earth. They say to expect shifts on your Earth. You will see shifts in power. You will see shifts in Gaia. And these will continue to intensify. The recent earthquakes in South America and India are just a beginning. There will be more, and it will be appropriate. Later, we will discuss how to handle these types of situations.

It is indeed a time of love and a time of reunion when we gather like this. We enjoy our times together. Take this energy. Take this feeling that comes when we gather like this. Hold it within you. Keep it within you. Dear friends, there are a multitude of beings on the other side of the veil doing work on your behalf, doing work with you, caring about you.

Indeed you are never, ever alone.

And so it is!

✧ ✧ ✧ ✧

✥ ✥ ✥ ✥

"We are channeling you."

✥ ✥ ✥ ✥

Lesson Eight
Receive The Fruit Of The Rose

And so it is, dear friends, that we gather once again in our Crimson Circle with our family. These times are precious, and there is much to talk of in this lesson. There is so much that we have to convey to you, so much that we have to say. Some of this will come out in words, but so much more will be here for you in energy.

Above all, we want tell you in the way that comes from the deepest part of us, that we love you dearly. We honor you for what you are doing here. We honor you for giving your lives. This is exactly what you are doing. You have totally given yourself in service. You have agreed to release the old energy ways. This is not so easy to do. You have agreed to release all of the old. You have agreed to release all that you thought you were in order to be the first ones walking into this New Energy. We know this has caused you many tears. We know that this has caused many hardships.

At this time we come flooding into your circle, no matter where you are at this moment. The entities who are not in human body come flooding into the second circle to thank you for your journey.

The journey you are on now is one of a true teacher, a teacher of the heart. What you are going through now in your life provides the necessary experiences so that you may assist the others as they come into the New Energy. You are learning the lessons of the Crimson Circle in a very rapid manner so that you can be teachers, counselors and human guides to the others.

There will come a point very soon when other humans will come to you. They will not necessarily carry the label of the New Energy, or the New Age, or metaphysical. They will be ones who have been on their own search – an alone and quiet search. They will be brought to the door of your New House, and they will not know why they are there! They will have a surprised and startled look when you open the door of your New House, and you invite them in. You will be able to explain to them exactly why they are there. You will know what their journey has been like, because you will have walked it. You will know that it is time for you to be a teacher, a teacher of this New Energy.

Dear Shaumbra, you might combine your teaching with the methods and arts you already know. You might combine the knowledge you have gained from the Crimson Circle with your current healing and reading practices. But your knowledge will have a new twist to it, the twist of the New Energy. You might integrate the very lessons that we are walking through with you; the lesson of standing behind the short wall, the lesson of the Oven of Grace, the lesson of accepting changes and blessing them, and the lesson of the broad stroke.

You will sit with your human students. You will be a guide for them on their own journey. As you know, you cannot do these things for them, but you can help them understand that the transition into the New Energy IS possible. This is why you are here in the energy of the Crimson Circle, right now. You have concluded all of your spiritual contracts of this lifetime. You have concluded even the things of your other lifetimes. You have released all of these things, and then given of yourself to be among the first to transition into the New Energy. You are one who tests out the very vibrations and structures and energy patterns of this New Energy.

You are the teachers of the New Energy! That is why the ones who come into the second circle now have so much respect. The ones who you call angels call each of you the Masters, Masters of the Journey. You have been on a long, long, long journey away from Home. You have been away from the First Creation for longer than we even care to remember. Those who are still Home, as well as those who have crossed through the Wall of Fire but are not in human form, have so much honor for what you are doing!

As we have said repeatedly, you do not see the big picture. You cannot see the overview, because of the energy of duality you are in now. By being here with you like this, perhaps we can help you to understand that there is indeed a big picture. There is indeed a purpose and a meaning to all of what you are doing. Not one thought or one breath or one action is wasted. Not one tear goes unnoticed by Spirit. Yes, we hear your thoughts. We hear when you talk to us. Your message is received. Indeed it is!

As you continue to shift in your biology and in your spirit, you will notice things beyond your current human perception.

Your biology and your senses are becoming much more acute and much more sensitive. Some of you do not so much like what you perceive to be allergies! They are not allergies in the true human sense of your biology. You do not like the body aches and pains. You do not like the feeling of being disoriented, of not feeling that there are two feet on the ground. Dear friends, this is all part of the process.

You are becoming much more sensitive to things around you that are of the invisible nature. Yes, you indeed are becoming more sensitive to others' thoughts. The energy of a group of people seems to affect you more than ever. You are becoming more sensitive to the imbalances in your Earth. When you have something that occurs within you that you do not understand so well, you call it a flu. Dear friends, it is not the type of flu you have experienced in the past! Perhaps you could call it a "New Energy flu" for it relates to the inner changes you are experiencing, rather than a normal biological event. There are changes occurring within you and these will continue for a period of time.

But these changes can be made easier. They can be gentler on your body and mind as you understand that your vibration is keener in the New Energy. Your energy is sharper. You will begin to see the invisible things. You will begin to hear things you have never heard before. They will occur at levels of consciousness that you are not used to accessing. If you are waiting for something to manifest in front of you in your human condition, do not look there. The first signs will be from the invisible levels. You will begin to notice more depth in your human reality as you transition into the New Energy.

The adjustments related to your increased sensitivities are simply part of the process. Do not run from them. Do not run when you are in a group of humans and you are affected by their energies. Stand in that energy. Do not be fearful of it. It cannot hurt you. You are receiving the thoughts and energies of those who are still firmly planted in the old energy. Remain in that. Feel it. You will come to greater understandings by being in that space.

As we have talked of before, there is a need for many humans to stay in the old energy for the time being. It would cause quite a tidal wave of energies if all humans rushed into the New Energy at one time! Imagine if those you work with and those you live with came rushing into the New Energy at the same time! It would be most chaotic!

But the humans that are with you on a day-to-day basis are watching you in ways you may not perceive. They are very curious about what you are going through, and certainly in their curiosity they will poke holes. They will prod you. They will question you. And indeed, yes, they will aggravate you. (chuckling) They are simply trying to understand what you are going through. They know that there is something within themselves that is awakening. They know that soon – perhaps in this lifetime, perhaps in another – they too will be going into the New Energy. So they are curious about what you are doing. They ask in funny ways, of course! They respond to you in ways you would not necessarily expect. They are most curious.

As you know, dear friends, there is always a group of "invited guests" at our gatherings. Those who join us for this lesson are the ones you know now in your life on a regular, daily basis. They come to be with you, to sit next to you, to see what is happening as you cross into the New Energy. Those who join us now in the second circle are the ones you work with, the ones you call your human family, and the ones you call your close friends. They are the humans you interact with on a regular basis.

Indeed the ones who join us in the second circle are living beings. They are living in the human form at this time, yet join us in spirit for this lesson. We have had enough dead entities visit our gatherings! (chuckling) Those who join us today are the ones you are involved with right now.

Like you, they have parts of their consciousness that can travel outside the body. With the assistance of the runners and weavers that are in the nonhuman form, they can join this circle. In a sense, a part of their consciousness has been escorted here to be with you, to join you. They are curious.

Oh, they may be the ones that give you the hardest times during the day. They may be a boss who is relentless with you, a coworker who is manipulative, or a family member who is always clinging, always taking energy. They come here, joining us in the second circle. Of all things, they have love and honor for you. They are most curious about what you are doing. They do not understand what it is you are doing. And as you know, it doesn't do a lot of good to explain it! (amused) They like to be close to your energy. They like to prod in their own loving way.

They come here now to observe a new type of human who is walking into a new energy. The next time you see them, they will look at you differently. Their eyes will be wider than ever. They will be more curious. They will have made a link with you on a different level. They will have sat in the outer circle observing you, a human who has given deeply of self, given all of who you thought you were and released you old identity. They will look at you different the next time you see them. They may give you a loving, knowing look, or perhaps they may be more angry than ever, trying to figure out who you are!

They gather here for this lesson, encouraging you on your journey. They encourage you to continue going forward. They know there are hardships along the way, but they know there is a new type of creator that will come forth from this.

There are other entities who gather here as well, including those of the Crimson Council who are always working with you. There are legions of angels here for you. And of course, I, Tobias, the one who knows each of you. We have shed some tears together! We have walked some miles on the path together. You know me. You know my energy. We have looked each other in the eye. We have hugged each other in the past when we shared lifetimes together. We have always known that we would return together for this work of Shaumbra.

I, Tobias, get somewhat emotional, for I am not there with you in human form. Oh, how I long to be there, to once again look you in the eye, human to human, and to hug you once again. It gives me, and all who are of the Crimson, honor to be here. We applaud you to be the first who are the quiet teachers of the New Energy.

The energy of your Earth is changing. Indeed your own energy is changing! This is evident in all the things happening within you and around you. There are clues every day in your news. There are clues every day in your jobs, in your work situations, many of which have changed or ended. There are clues in your biology. It is speaking a different language to you now. Simply tune in to all of these things. Know that it is most appropriate. Know that you are leaving something behind. You are, in a sense, losing something, but opening yourself to an entire new way.

The way of the New Energy is hardly based on the way of the old! When you try to build on the foundations of the old energy, you run into a dead end. It does not work so well! You are being asked to look in the new places in your energy and all around you. You ask us, "Where do I find the New Energy?" Dear friends, tap into what is called your True Self, what we prefer to call The Inner Divinity. Sit in the inner room of your New House, a metaphor for your awakening divinity. Force nothing in your mind. Simply be, and simply listen. It will come to you. Be patient, and it will come to you. We know this to be true. We know this to be true!

Now we will continue discussing the journey of the prince named Jack. This is also your journey. Indeed you are Jack. We use this parable to help explain the long journey you have been on. As you know, Jack was a prince in the kingdom. He went on many long journeys to satisfy his need to create, to expand, to learn more, and to allow his love to pour forth. While on a long journey, Jack came to the end of land. He came to the great ocean. He was posed with a question of whether to continue on, or to go back to the kingdom. But as you know, Jack could not resist the temptation to journey onward.

He set sail upon the waters, on this new type of energy he never before experienced. And he sailed and sailed until he came to the Wall of Fire, a metaphor for the end of the First Circle. It was the end of creation as it was known. He tried paddling backwards. He struggled against the pull of the Wall of Fire.

When Jack went into the Wall of Fire it shattered him into billions and billions of fragments. This was a very traumatic event for him. When he came out the other side of the Wall of Fire, he was different. The greater part of his energy and his consciousness had retreated into a "cocoon." It was wrapped in an "energy cocoon" for a long, long sleep. The purpose of this was to experience an inner journey. Up to that point Jack had never looked inward. He had always been an outward expression, but after going through the Wall of Fire, there was a new inner perspective of Self within this cocoon.

Part of Jack did not go into the cocoon. Part of his being continued past the Wall of Fire where he entered a void. He entered nothingness, total darkness. When he opened his eyes on the other side of the Wall of Fire, Jack saw the mirror image of himself. He saw his opposite. He experienced duality. For the first time ever Jack was not in "oneness." He was now "two." This was the beginning of duality as you know it.

As duality took form in the Void, great wars broke out. There were many battles among the many entities who had crossed through the Wall of Fire into the Void. There was a struggle to return Home. In a desperate effort to return to the Kingdom, you tried to take energy from another. There were wars, as one tried to capture the energy of the others. The warriors thought this was a way to return Home.

The battles built and expanded this thing you now call duality. The battles intensified and made duality – the energy of two – larger and stronger. During this time of the great battles the Void was being transformed into a new reality. Your physical universe with all its stars and galaxies was being created.

Lesson Eight: Receive The Fruit Of The Rose ❖ 135

The battles became overwhelming. Neither side could dominate or win, to use your terms. So at a point, dear friends, a stalemate developed. The battles could no longer continue. Something had to change in order for Jack and you and the others to continue to move forth.

There were many, many entities in your new and growing universe at that time, and the standoff had gotten to the point where neither side, neither energy of duality, could function or move. There was no expansion of energy in the universe. This was counter to all things that had ever been known by Spirit, and all things that had ever been known by Jack.

Dear friends, there was bridging of the consciousness of all entities that existed in your universe. You were not entities in physical form like you would know now. You were entities who had definitions of energy and vibrations, but you had not descended into physical matter. There were many who met to discuss the nature of duality, and the energetic stalemate that had occurred. You realized the battles of the two sides had proven little. It was time to end the battles. It was time to move on to the next portion of the journey.

Many entities gathered for this unprecedented meeting. This is the beginning of the Order of the Arc, what you would now call your archangels. You met, and at the highest levels of consciousness there was an agreement for some of the angels to descend, to lower the vibration. In this lower vibrational form these angels would take on what you now know as biology. They would take on mass.

When you were angels in your newly forming universe, you created almost as quickly as thought. At times this got out of hand. At times, dear friends, you did not know which side you were on! You did not know how to control your own energy and things seemed out of control.

Part of the reason for taking on mass and biology was so that creation would not occur so fast as it had before. Action and reaction would be slowed down. There would be opportunities to live through experience. There would be opportunities to assess and evaluate and to help balance.

It was agreed that these angels would place their spirit into mass. It was also agreed that you would not remember the journey that brought you to this point. You would not remember the battles. You would not remember going through the Wall of Fire. You would not remember the kingdom from whence you came. This would be a new start. It would allow you and it would allow Spirit to truly understand the nature of duality and the nature of "two." Prior to crossing through the Wall of Fire, Spirit had always been an expression of "one." Coming to Earth with no remembrance would allow the true understanding of duality.

There were many, many angel entities in your new universe at the time, and of course, most of them wanted to be part of this new place of Earth. When there was a call for volunteers, dear friends, you were among the first! You were among the first. You initially came to Earth in nonphysical form. You shifted your energy with the assistance of many, many entities on the other side. You shifted your energy in such a way that you could enter the dimension of Earth. You visited Earth in your angelic form a long time before you ever came here in biological form. You and the others came here to set up the energy templates and the grids. You came here to set up the weavings and the foundations of this place called Earth. You visited Earth long before taking on a physical form in order to become acclimated, as well as to help set up the energies. There was much assistance from the angels who were not going on your journey.

At some point each of you descended to Earth and eventually took on the human body. You began your cycles of incarnation. You walked the Earth in many different forms, physical forms. In one lifetime you were male, in another lifetime female. You walked through your lifetimes in many different ways to experience this thing called duality.

And now, you have completed your cycles on Earth. You have come a long way. You are now preparing yourself to reunite with All That You Are. And if you choose, you will then stay on this place of Earth to be the teacher for the others who follow in your footsteps.

We will discuss your dreams for a moment here, for these are beginning to intensify. These are beginning to become more real and more dramatic. In many of your dreams right now, you go back to this time before you ever came to Earth. You go back to when you helped transmute the Void into reality, when you were in the time of wars and the battles. You are now journeying back to there at night to try to resolve much of what happened.

This is somewhat difficult to describe, dear friends, but even as you are living your human life, and you are coming into the completion of your own circle of your long journey, you are also back in these other places. You are back in the time before you ever came to Earth. You are back in this time when the universe was being created. When you close your eyes at night and go into your dream state, part of you journeys to the past. You journey across time and space in an attempt to resolve the past. You tell your soul from the past that there is now a completion, a unity, in the future. You are visiting the past to proclaim that there is no need for the battles because you have found the way through the next doorway. You are going into the past to tell your own self that it is time to end these conflicts, to end the chaos. You are in the now, bringing resolution to the past. Think about this!

Something interesting happens here, dear friends. Something very interesting. You journey at night in your dreams. You journey back to the time after you went through the Wall of Fire and before you came to the Earth. It was the time of the building the Void, the time of the great wars. You journey back there at the same time your consciousness from the past is trying to journey here to your now! Sometimes you meet each other in the middle. That's when you go "bump" in the night!

In our last lesson we discussed the ones you call the aliens. They are actually aspects of yourself from the past. These are the ones you collide with at night, for you are journeying back to resolve something old. They are journeying forward to resolve the chaos in their "now" time. Is it a wonder that your dreams are so intense?

When you wake up after a dream, your mind creates a symbolic interpretation of the dream experience. You do not bring back the clear picture of what happened. There are a series of symbols, and they generally relate to people and events in your lifetime right now. You generally dream about the people who are around you now, your family and those that you work with. Why is this, dear friends? It is because those who are in your lifetime now, who sit in the second circle during this lesson, are the very ones you are battling with in the past! That is why it is important for them to be here for this lesson. There is so much perfection in what is taking place here! Even as you battle them in the past, there are conflicts in the now. Even as you attempt to resolve situations with them in the past, you are attempting to resolve them in the now.

It is intricately woven together. The ones who gather in the second circle for this lesson will look at you very oddly when you see them the next time, for they will know that you know, but they will not know how they know! (chuckling) There is a desire at the deepest part of your being to resolve the past, to bring things back into unity, and then to move into the energy of the New Earth. Great amounts of energy are being poured into this right now. A multitude of entities who are not in human form are helping to facilitate these processes.

Here you sit not understanding who you truly are and understanding what is truly taking place! Some of you think your life has little value. You think you have not accomplished much in this lifetime. You have fear of being a failure. Dear friends, we weep at this thought! We weep at this perception. We know you are the first to take on the New Energy, and at the same time, you are healing the past. You are resolving the conflicts that occurred in your universe in the past. These occurred on different dimensional levels than what you would expect. You are working to resolve these, to bring these together, to move from duality into the New Energy of quad. The energy of the quad is balanced. It is the energy of creation in your material world. This is why we honor you so deeply. This is why we know you will be wise and compassionate teachers.

Dear Shaumbra, Lesson Eight of the Creator Series is an important lesson that you will teach to the others some day. Eight is a beautiful lesson – and there is not much homework with this lesson! We ask you to enter your New House now. Sit in the energy of your divine Self, in the divine state of being. We will tell a short story before we reveal the lesson.

Sitting in the Inner Room of her New House is one of family, one we call Shaumbra. Her name is Catherine. Catherine is weeping as we visit her during this lesson. Catherine is very sad. She is not sure who she is. In her private moments Catherine has said to her Self and Spirit that it is time to go Home. She no longer feels a purpose or meaning in her life. Catherine is crying many tears, for she does not understand. She has asked Spirit over and over again for the answers, but she hears very little. The answers that do come are simply morsels, simply specks. They are not complete and full answers. Catherine has been battling what she calls depression. She has gone to a medical doctor, and she has received pills to get over her depression. But dear friends, she found that even the pills could not take care of this deep feeling within her, this feeling of sadness.

Catherine cries and sobs because she has tried many different things. She has tried many different ways of being and of acting. Yet they have not worked so well in her life. She does not understand, and she feels somewhat abandoned by Spirit. Oh, she knows that her own guides left within the past few years. She lost a job that meant much to her. She replaced it with another job that has not been nearly so meaningful. Because of her thoughts and beliefs, some of her own family has shunned her. When they talk to her, the conversation seems gratuitous. The exchane is not meaningful and loving as it used to be, and she does not understand this.

Lately Catherine has been physically depleted. Her energy is low, and she does not understand this, for she goes to ones who are facilitators. She goes to ones who help rebuild the energy of the human. It works for a short period of time, but it does not sustain itself over the period of weeks and months. She does not understand; therefore tears fall from her eyes. The one called Catherine, the one who is family, who is all of us, does not feel any sense of purpose or passion. There are times when she thinks she could simply do nothing, not even read a book, not even watch television. Catherine thinks that all care and feeling have left her. She does not even have the energy of hope.

Let us pause here for a moment with Catherine and talk of what is happening. Let us talk of what is happening to many of you at this time. As you move out of the old energy into the new, you let go of many things that were deeply ingrained within you. You let go of so many of the things that were near and dear to you. "Letting go" creates a void. It creates an emptiness. When Catherine, or you, go back to try to recapture what you knew before and apply it to the New Energy, it does not work. The old and the new are like oil and water.

As we mentioned before, you are becoming more sensitive, physically, emotionally, and spiritually. But sensitive energies have not totally moved in yet. It is difficult for these new energies to move in while you are still holding onto the old. Oh, yes, indeed many of you have found yourself awakened at three or four in the morning (chuckling) wondering about who you are now, wondering about what it is you are doing.

You are awakening at these times for several reasons. First, you have just completed a series of what you call dreams – and what we call realities – of going back to this time before you came to Earth, to help resolve the energies of duality. You come back from these journeys with a feeling of nightmares, sometimes with the feelings of great stress. This wakes you up. And there are instances when we specifically wake you out of these dreams, for we know you need at least a few hours of rest before you go to work!

You wake up at three or four in the morning, thinking about your life as a human, wondering who you are, wondering which way to turn. For most of you the only resolution that you can find is to let go, to let go. We have heard you say, "I do not know which way to go. I do not know what to do next. I do not know any more what is right and what is wrong; therefore, I release and let go." Dear friends, this indeed is the appropriate thing. As you release, you fall into the loving hands of who you truly are, of Spirit, of the God that you are. When you release, you do not fall into a pit of flames. You do not fall into an abyss, even though you fear that. You fall into the loving hands of the God that you are.

Making decisions in your life will be different. You are used to making decisions and choices each day. Generally you have had one of three choices. You could move left, move right, or not to move at all. You could go to the light, to go to the dark, or to stay right where you were. Your decisions have been to go forward or backward or not at all. Up to now your days have been filled with makings decision with these choices. Now there is a new way that is coming in into your life. As you let go, you will see it clearly, and you will wonder why you didn't see it before.

In the New Energy the choices are not limited to light and dark and neutral; positive, neutral or negative; left, right or center. There is a new choice. Let us call it – ALL, A-L-L. You will be presented with yet another choice, and it will come from a place of divine knowingness. It will be a new type of choice. It will offer a solution that surpasses the other ones. It will come to you as a knowingness. You will not have to go through the mental exercise of choosing left, right, or center.

It will come in from above. It will be ALL. It will be All that is. It will not feel like a choice to you. It will simply be a knowingness, a knowingness of divinity. You will then move in that direction. You will look back on your previous struggles about making choices as an old energy human. ALL will seem full and inclusive and complete. ALL will seem filled with love, whereas the other choices you previously had will seem to be only partial solutions.

There will be a new way of making decisions, but before that can occur, there is something else that will happen. There will be something else that comes into your life. We return now to Catherine who sits quietly sobbing, wondering what to do next, and where to go next. She is sitting at this very moment, wondering whether to turn left or right or to stay right where she is. She thinks those are the only options in her life. She has not seen ALL yet. She has not seen this glowing knowingness that sits above the other options. She has not glanced upwards. So to her life does indeed seem empty. It does indeed seem like a struggle and difficult, for she has not seen ALL.

Catherine gets up from her place in the Inner Room of her New House. She is as frustrated or perhaps even more than when she walked in, for the answers have not been there. She was hoping and even praying that Spirit would manifest in front of her. She thought that perhaps if Spirit was not available, then perhaps, I, Tobias would come to her and give her the answers! But as you know, dear friends, that is not appropriate.

Lesson Eight: Receive The Fruit Of The Rose ❖ 141

Catherine gets up and she leaves her Inner Room. She wanders around her New House. She is amazed at how empty her New House is, considering how long she has been living there! Oh, indeed there is an oven. There are still trays filled with issues sitting on the counter in the kitchen. But in the other rooms there is not much furniture. Indeed there is a bright glow, but she has not connected with it yet. Indeed she has heard a vibration, particularly when she has truly let go. She has heard this hum, this quiet music, this vibration that I, Tobias have talked of, but she has not quite connected with it.

Catherine moves around her New House, rambling from room to room, asking Spirit to come with the answers. She asks her guides to please come back, even though she knows they have departed. She bargains with them. She promises to be a nicer to them and to stop asking so many favors from them if they only come back! She rambles around her new house, feeling very sad and very alone. She decides to go outside for a long walk. Perhaps there is something outside the New House that she missed, something back in duality, in everyday life, back out on the streets. Perhaps she missed an important notice. Perhaps there is a human who has a message for her!

As she walks towards the front door, a sparkling light catches the corner of her eye. Something catches Catherine's attention and stops her in her tracks. She glances not to the left, or to the right, or even where her glance is currently focused. Instead, she glances past and through these things. She glances into a place called ALL. In this new dimension that now joins her human dimension, she sees something that she cannot believe she missed. It was there ever since she first entered her New House. On the table, in a vase, is a CRYSTAL ROSE.

We discussed this with you in a previous lesson *(Lesson Nine, "The New Camelot," New Earth Series, April 2000)*. When you first entered your New House, there was but one thing inside, and it was a crystal rose. We told you the crystal rose bore a fruit. It produced a fruit, unlike any rose that you have known.

Catherine adjusted her gaze past her reality into the ALL. As she approached the rose a knowingness came over her. She was not struggling at this point with the question, "What should I do with this rose?" because she was looking to the ALL. She was looking beyond the obvious choices of: touch the rose, don't touch the rose, or do nothing. She looked to the ALL, and in this knowingness she knew what to do. She didn't allow her human intellect to go through the regular process of duality, of struggling with choices. She intuitively knew it was time to take the fruit of the rose and to receive it, to place it in her mouth, to digest it, and to bring it within her being.

Dear friends, the Fruit of the Rose is your passion in the New Energy! LESSON EIGHT – RECEIVE THE FRUIT OF THE ROSE. Receive the Fruit of the Rose. It is the passion you hid within when you left Home. It is the passion you forgot when you came to this place called Earth. It was the passion you had in the kingdom, in the First Circle. You carried with you through the Wall of Fire. But it has been hidden from you ever since.

On Earth, your divine passion was replaced with something you call the human ego. You built your life upon that. Your passions then became things of human nature. Your passions were for other people. Your passions were for food. Your passions were for certain types of work and creative expression that you did on Earth. But your passions were based on your human condition, not on your birthright as a spiritual being!

When you receive the Fruit of the Rose it brings back your divine passion. What was it that Catherine was missing in the room, as she sat there and sobbed? Why was it that she felt such emptiness? It was because she had let go of her old human passions, the incomplete passions. There was nothing left inside. There was nothing that came from the heart. There was only emptiness.

Dear friends, when you came to Earth and descended into biology, you broke yourself up into even more parts, parts that you call chakras. You had these chakras in your human biology in the number of seven, and you had those that you carried in your etheric fields in the number of five.

As we have mentioned, these are now coming together into a single chakra. They are being melding together. They are coming together into one, the "one chakra."

As you receive of the Fruit of the Rose, you bring back a passion that was hidden within you. You will feel renewed in the energy of your body. You will feel renewed in your purpose. You will feel renewed in your purpose! You will bring this important element of divine passion back into your being. The old incomplete passions of the human that were based in the ego are leaving. That is why Catherine felt incomplete.

As you receive the Fruit of the Rose within your being, it will ignite a passion that we cannot even describe, for it is not explainable in human words. It comes from an energy that you are not used to right now. This will be an experience that you will have on your own, and it will fill you. You will feel a new glow from the inside and it will emanate out from you. It will not be like anything you have experienced before. It cannot be created out of the human mind. It cannot be manufactured from the ego. For those who say they can control it on the human level – this will not work. It resides in this place of ALL. It is available to each of you.

We use the words here in Lesson Eight very carefully. We ask you to receive this energy. We know you, as Shaumbra, are not so good about receiving! You feel you must start from the ground up and create everything, struggle through everything. Here now is a gift that is yours. It resides in your house. It is yours to receive. It is your spiritual passion. This will bring about a renewal, but the renewal will be in a different place than you have been used to.

Dear friends, you are changing. You cannot build upon the old foundations of the old energy. You are stepping into the New Energy. Bring forth the passion you carried within from the Kingdom.

Passion is love expressed. PASSION IS LOVE EXPRESSED. Passion was something you had all the time before, for you were always expressing outward. Jack was always expressing outward. Spirit has always expressed outward until part of you went into the cocoon. When you left Home, you hid this passion deep within your being, knowing that you would bring it forth at the appropriate time.

You created duality. You created a type of spiritual amnesia. You also left behind your true passion, your divine passion. You built your lives on the wants and needs and human passions that are small in comparison to your divine passion.

Now as you know, the rose that represents the expression of love also has thorns. Dear friends, if you attempt to control this passion with your old energy, your old human ways, it will hurt. That is why the thorns are there. If you attempt to use this new passion to simply recreate your old energy human ways, it will hurt. This passion, and the love expressed with it, is designed for the New Energy.

If you are in question of the appropriate use of your new passion, seek the answer from the ALL. Seek the answer from the place that is beyond duality. If you are not so sure, simply sit in a quiet moment. The answer will come to you. You will have an answer of knowingness. This will help to ignite your new passion and bring you to new ways of creating.

Lesson Eight – Receive the Fruit of the Rose. Take in the passion that has always been yours, the passion that will renew your life in the New Energy. If your expectations are to simply make your old-energy self bigger and stronger and more powerful, the thorns of the rose will remind you that this is not appropriate! The passion will be a fuel of the New Energy for you. It will be a renewal for you and for Catherine. It will bring fullness and meaning in her life, but in a way she has not experienced in any of her lifetimes of the past.

This is a simple lesson. There is little homework, dear friends, other than to find the appropriate quiet time to approach the front entry way of your new house, to feel the vibration of the vase with the crystal rose. Then when you are ready, when ALL guides you, simply take of this fruit and receive it within you. This will start a new round of physical changes within your being, some which may be uncomfortable, but it will only be for a short period of time. This will increase the sensitivities of your body and of your energetic feelings, and you will also notice that you will start to see beyond what is obvious.

When we use the term "see" – Cauldre asks us to clarify – "see" relates to perceptions. Some may see beyond with their eyes. Others may see beyond from their one chakra. Others may just intuitively know. But you will begin to "see" beyond what you have seen before. This will begin to happen more and more with you. And again, do not be surprised if the sensitivities of your body increase for a period of time, for your body is simply trying to get used to the New Energy. These are all processes and changes that you are going through.

Lesson Eight – Receive the Fruit of the Rose. There will come a day when you teach other humans who have come to your door. There will come a day when you explain this lesson to them. It will seem so simple to them. Yet they will not get it! They will wonder what you are talking about! They will wonder of all these metaphors of crystal roses and fruits and thorns and passions. You will have a large smile on your face, because you too will have sat in the space of "not getting it," and you too will then have experienced this new passion coming into your being.

Dear friends, it is an honor that we share this time and space together. We give you a very simple but most powerful lesson. It is one of the key lessons in this series. How can you create in the New Energy without your divine passion? This lesson will help you to truly understand creation in the New Energy. It will ultimately help you to become a teacher to the others coming into the New Energy.

You are going through many, many changes at this time. Understand this is simply part of the process. In this process there are many, many entities on our side of the veil working with you. But ultimately it is up to you.

We love you dearly for all that you do. Those who have joined in the second circle for this lesson – the ones who are in your lives now and have been in your lives in the past – thank you for what you are doing. They will be among the first to come to you as the teacher. They love you dearly. Dear friends, you are never alone.

And so it is.

✠ ✠ ✠ ✠

✣ ✣ ✣ ✣

"You cannot imagine the potential of tomorrow in your consciousness of today."

✣ ✣ ✣ ✣

Lesson Nine
Dance With What Comes To Your Front Door

And so it is dear friends, dear Shaumbra, and dear teachers, that we gather once again in our circle, in our place of love. We thank you, Shaumbra, for welcoming us into this space, and for inviting us into your circle. There is much that we have to speak of, much that we have to cover. It is new information that will cause you to rethink ways you have done things in the past. It will cause you to rethink who you are, and cause you to rethink yourself as a true creator.

We ask you to open your heart and your being, as all of the angels and entities come flooding into this space. They come in to join you for Lesson Nine of the Creator Series. As the first ones into the New Energy, you are the teachers. You have agreed to be the first to go into this new space and this new dimension. You have agreed to be the teachers for others.

As we have said to you before, it is not Cauldre who channels Tobias or those of the Crimson Council. It is I, Tobias, who channels you through Cauldre. We are channeling you! We are taking your experiences, your energies, your thoughts and dreams and then channeling them back to you. There are very few things we will say during our times together that are totally new to you. Our words should resonate from within your being because we indeed are channeling you. We are taking all that you know, and all that you are learning, and we are simply presenting it to you from a different perspective. There is so much more to this statement that you will understand as you come into your own divinity. We channel you, and it is such a delight that you have invited us here to be part of this.

Take a few moments, dear friends, and breathe deeply. Breathe deeply into the core of your being. Breathe in the love that we bring to you. Breathe in the honor. Breathe in the energy of friends, of family, and of Shaumbra that come flooding in to sit beside you for this lesson. Breathe in. Take in the energy that comes to be with you.

The honor is for your journey. It is for going into this New Energy, for going through the shift, for releasing things from your life to make it possible to be here, for making it possible to be the teachers of the New Energy.

We know some of you are timid. You do not feel worthy of this moment, and do not feel you deserve the grand love that comes in. We see you. We smile at you. We know you well, for you are family, in spite of the fact that it may be difficult for you to understand. You are the timid ones, the quiet ones, who feel a burning passion within your being. You have many questions on your mind. You know something is going on, but yet you stand in the corners. You are not quite sure why Spirit, Tobias or the Crimson Council would honor you, and kneel at your feet the way we do. Take your time, timid ones, quite ones, ones who are not so sure. Take your time. You will know when it is right to step forward. You will know when it is right to be bold, to voice what you have to say, to take action in the New Energy.

In the meantime, accept the smile and accept the love we have for you. Accept the honor. The honor is here because your past has been long. Your path has been filled with many, many experiences. We know what you have done. We have seen it. We have felt it. It is recorded. Timid ones, shy ones, quiet ones, soon the time will come when you can accept this divinity that comes from within you. You are as indeed special and loved as anyone connecting with this information. We see your heart glowing. We are speaking to you.

There are always invited guests who join us for these lessons. They come here to be part of this wonderful event. They come here to observe, to see what it is like for a human to walk into their divinity. There are many, many here on this side who are curious, who stand in line and wait to be here. There is a special group of invited guests that join us for this lesson. They come into the second circle.

You, the human, sit in the first circle. Then there are those who come here to observe. They stand beside you, to honor you, to share a few smiles and a few tears. They are in the second circle. During these past few moments, they have come in and taken their positions with you.

Do you know that when we gather like this we create a New Energy, a new dimension? It is not of Earth. It is not of our plane. It is a new dimension of divinity. That is what is created when you open your heart, when you welcome in the others who are not in physical body. That is what is being created here at this very moment.

The ones who come into the second circle for this lesson have a particular interest in you and your journey. They want you to continue this journey into the New Energy, to be a teacher for others. Their spirit comes in to visit, for they, as much as anybody, want to reassure you that you are on the right path. They will come back to you in the months and years ahead in your lifetime. They will sit with you, human-to-human, at that point.

The visitors in the second circle are the ones who will be your students in the future. They will come to you for teaching and for healing. They are the ones who will mysteriously appear to you. They will not know how they have gotten there, but they will come to you. They will see and feel and sense the wisdom of one who has walked the path, one who has accepted their divinity, one who has gone into the New Energy and is now working from that dimension and from that vibration. They are the ones who will come next from the old energy into the new. They will need a human guide. They will need one who has crossed the chasm from the old to the new, to assure them that it can be done.

It is interesting to note that you have also been their teachers in the past. You sat with them in other lifetimes in temples, in churches, and classrooms. You have been their teachers. This will not be a new experience between you and them. You will have gone through it before.

They knew you would be among the first to walk into the New Energy. They raised their hands. They said, "After you go through, be my teacher. Be the one who shows me how to heal my body, how to heal my emotions, and how to love my spirit."

Our visitors have good reason for being here. They have reason for cheering you on. They knew it would be difficult, being the first. It could mean giving up what you loved most dearly: your family, your career, your health, even your perception of who you were. They knew it would be challenging. That is why they did not raise their hands to be the first! (chuckling)) But they knew you would be a good teacher. They come now knowing you are walking through these lessons, knowing that you are going through many experiences in your life of release, and then of acceptance, and then finally of empowerment.

The visitors are in awe of what you are doing, much as we are in awe of what you are doing. The work you are doing is powerful. It is incredible. It is done in the greatest service to Spirit and All That Is. And you do not yet see it! You do not yet see who you are or the effect that you are having on the people around you. You do not yet see the effect that you are having on your Earth and the consciousness of this planet. You do not yet see how you are changing your universe, and how you are changing the place that we call Home. The very work that you do today, tomorrow and in the days to follow is changing everything around you. Indeed it is changing the very nature of the Kingdom from whence you came.

We have talked much of the journey of the prince named Jack, which is your journey. We discussed how you got here to this place called Earth, and then forgetting who you were. Your thoughts, deeds and actions are indeed changing the very nature of the Kingdom.

You do not see the powerful nature of your work. You think you are just living a lifetime in this body, trying to get through each day. What you are doing is changing the nature of Home. We honor you for this. We thank you for this. And as we have said, someday we will cheer and laugh together. When you are able to open those spiritual eyes of yours, you will see the effect you are having on this entire creation, not only on this universe that you are living in, but on the entire creation.

We have been asked the question, "Do I return Home between lifetimes?" The answer is no. You return to a place that has the attributes of Home. It is filled with your family. It is filled with angels who help you rebalance after you leave your physical body. They help prepare you for your next time on Earth. But it is not the Home that you once knew. If you went back there, you would never return to Earth. You would find it too difficult to return. Also, dear friends, if you returned back Home now, back to the Kingdom, you would not recognize it. The work that you and the other human angels have done has changed the very nature, the very vibration, and in particular, the depth of the Kingdom from whence you came.

There will come a time when you will have access to all of the memories of your entire journey, when you will have remembrance of your journey. It will be like a library that is available to you. As far as returning Home, we know you too well! We know you are the adventurers. As you cross into the New Energy, and as you take the "quad leap" into the energy of four, you will want to venture off again, creating new dimensions and new places. Your feet never stay put. We will be right there at your side as you go off on your new ventures. We have been with you for a long, long time.

Dear friends, this space is now appropriately balanced. It is filled with entities who will stand in line to work with you. You will have much to teach them. Oh, they will resist you in many ways, much as you resist Tobias in many ways. (chuckling) They will curse you at times, but they have the deepest love and respect for you. They fill this space now, anxiously awaiting the time when you accept your new role as a teacher of divinity.

Timid ones, shy ones, we talk to you as well. You are as much on this path as any others. It is simply that you have chosen to stay back a bit. You are working just as hard and going through just as much, and you are just as worthy as any others. Dear shy and quiet ones, we address the energy of this channel to you. Our visitors come to you in remembrance for the past lives you had together. They come to you in deep respect for the new work you will do together.

They say to you, "Oh, dear teacher, oh, dear teacher, accept this role that awaits you. Accept this chair of the honor that awaits you, that of the teacher of the New Energy." They anxiously await this time of learning from you again. They know you do not trust yourself at times, but they ask you to continue your journey. They ask you to listen well to the words and to the energy that will be delivered in this lesson. It will be an important element in the transition that you are going through. They thank you and take their place in the second circle as we continue with this lesson.

Before you came to Earth, there were many preparations that had to take place. Your energy took on biology. You took the physical form. The preparation for this took eons of time. But before you came here in physical form, you visited Earth in spirit, in the light form that you were. As the universe was beginning to take structure, you journeyed to Earth in light body to get adjusted to the attributes of this planet, to get used to the dimension of "two" expressed in matter.

You needed these visits to Earth, and they were done over long periods of time. They were done in your light body, for you had to adjust your being to this new, slow-vibration energy of Earth. You had to adjust to vibrating very slowly in order to adapt to a physical body.

You first came to Earth when it was somewhat of a barren place. You came to seed your very energy on this planet, and to get adjusted to duality in a slow vibrational state. You would come here and place your consciousness and your energy into the Earth herself.

As the essence of life began to form on Earth, you placed your vibration into the smallest life forms to experience being birthed into a living organism on this planet. Over ages of time, you placed your energy into the more sophisticated life-forms that were developing on your Earth. All of this took place over a very long period of time. But from the dimension that you operated in, it was not so long at all.

You found it particularly comfortable to place yourself in water because water were not as harsh on your vibration as the land. You spent much time placing your energy into the aqueous forms that were developing on your planet. Among your favorite life-forms were the whales and the porpoises and the dolphins. You spent much time experiencing these new life-forms, for you loved this energy. You loved the playfulness. You loved your ability to express within this physical body. Even to this day you have an affinity for these beings.

Make no mistake about it: It was you and the other angels that seeded this planet with energy. You transformed a rock into a living organism, into Gaia. You came here in light body and set the energy templates for Earth, transforming it into a dynamic living and growing force. Gaia is you, for you came here and seeded her. The oceans and the lakes are you, for you swam in them before you ever came here in physical body. The trees, the flowers, and the plants that feed you – are you.

You created the structures, patterns, architecture and seeds of this very planet. Gaia is a living organism. She is you. When you look out into your stars, there are not other places with the attributes of Gaia. You did not go there as angels to seed. You came here. Indeed you took journeys to the far reaches of the universe prior to coming here. There were light body explorations to other stars and other planets, but dear friends, Earth was the planet of choice, the place you chose for this grand experience of duality in biology.

There was much preparation before you ever came here. It was known that when you came to Earth and placed your energy into physical matter, you would need a team to work with you. These are what you called your "guides." There were generally two angels who journeyed with you. They did not take on physical body like you did. They stayed in light body. They stayed at your side through your many lifetimes on Earth. They have been with you. Their role was to maintain a balance of energy, to maintain a spiritual quotient, to keep you balanced. They were messengers from the other side of the veil who always accompanied you. If you didn't have these angelic guides, there was the possibility that you would have become so immersed in duality that perhaps you could have never gotten out.

Your guides were the conduit to the other side of the veil, the conduit back to us. They stayed with you for quite some time. Oh, and as you know, they have departed, or are in the process of withdrawing their energy. It is now time for you to accept all of who you are, so that you may accept your own divinity. It is a compliment of the high-

Lesson Nine: Dance With What Comes To Your Front Door ✣ 153

est order that you can now maintain your own balance.

Several years ago, in this very room, the Kryon explained the other attributes of the guides. The Kryon stated that as you come to a new understanding or enlightenment, your energy would fill the vessels that the guides carried with them. It was like a golden, liquid light that filled these grand vessels carried by your guides. It was filled with your enlightenment and your new understanding. The guides would collect this wonderful energy of golden knowledge and wisdom that you exuded. Oh, and yes, you agreed to release this to them. They did not steal it from you! (chuckling) It was something that would not do you much good on this place of Earth.

The guides collected this energy, and then another group would take the vessels and replace them with new empty ones. They would take this incredible honey of substance – golden and sweet and nurturing – back on the other side of the veil. This energy was used to continue creating your universe. It also would find its way back to the Kingdom from whence you came. This golden honey energy of your enlightenments and wisdom would find its way to the Kingdom to change the very nature of Home, to expand All That Is. It was the greatest gift of love that any entity had ever given.

And you wonder why we honor you and why we weep when we sit in front of you, knowing that you don't recognize who you are!

There was a group, and there continues to be a group, that we call the "runners." They are the ones who go back and forth from your side of the veil to ours. They continue to serve as messengers of energy. They bring these energies back through the other side of the veil. They are runners, because they run the energy from you back to the other side, and then they bring back with them the new tools and the new vessels. They are very busy these days, these runners, for there is much work to do!

Your runners no longer interface with the guides. It used to be that the runners would work directly with your guides. The guides were always positioned like pillars of love directly beside you. Now the runners work directly with you.

✣ ✣ ✣ ✣

From the time you first came to Earth until now, you have not been able to be a creator in the true sense of the word. You would plan your lifetimes ahead of time with your team of angels. You would work on certain objectives and lessons. You would develop a spiritual business plan, as it were. Then you would come back to Earth in human body. You would walk through the experiences you had established for yourself. When you reached one goal, you would move onto the next that had been previously planned. In this mode, dear friends, it was difficult to be a creator in the true sense. In this mode you were one who was experiencing, one who was learning. But it was difficult to be a creator, for there had been parameters that had been determined in advance.

There was a frustration at the very core of your being, for prior to coming to Earth, indeed you had been creators. You had always expressed outward. You were frustrated because you could not seem to move outside of these boxes, and you could not express yourself as openly and fluidly as you had in the past. This has changed. You have completed all the chapters of your Book of Life. Now in the new book there are empty pages, waiting for you to create.

There are many new things happening in your New House. When you take your brush and create a broad stroke, this sets up an expression of energy. This action creates a vibration that begins to resonate and grow. Until you take the broad brush stroke, everything is in neutral. But when you make that first broad stroke, everything begins. With the broad stroke you initiate an energy that begins to work at very deep levels.

These energies begin to resonate from within your New House, and then you add the passion, the Fruit of the Rose. This adds fuel to the vibration that has been created by your broad stroke. This new creator energy has an effect similar to when you throw a stone into the water. It creates ripples that expand outward. It creates waves of energy, and these waves of energy permeate your house.

Dear friends, as you might have noticed, we did not include intent here. We did not tell you that there should be specific intent when you created the broad stroke, or when you added your passion. There is a reason for that, which we will discuss. The broad stroke begins the expression. The passion adds fuel to the expression. The waves are sent out. The waves of vibration of love, of the new creator, are sent out past your new house, past the short wall around your new house. These waves of love vibration are sent out into the people around you, into the city around you, into the Earth that you helped to create. There are waves and waves and waves of love that go out. Why would you need to tell those waves of love vibration what they should do or what they should be? They come from within you. They are you.

As these waves go out, they change the vibration of things, not only within you, but also outside of you. The vibrations emanate from you then touch other people. They touch the Earth. They touch the skies and the waters. They touch human consciousness. These waves of love have no need for intent. The spiritual balance is already there. There is the balance of "4," the new spiritual balance of Earth. There is no need to put intent on them. They are balanced unto themselves, and when they touch other elements, or other vibrations, or even consciousness, the balanced love vibration of "4" has the potential to balance and rejuvenate all energies. It is up to the receiving energy of how it will respond, if at all.

The energy that comes from your divine being is complete and full in itself. There is no reason to attach agenda or direction or anything to it. It emanates from you in purity. It emanates from you in completeness and in love. Do not put your human spin on it. Accept that it comes from you in the most perfect way. It comes from you already in a state of perfection.

Now an interesting thing happens. When you throw a stone into the water, the waves go outward and they eventually weaken. They eventually die off. It is different when you send out the waves of your divine energy. As the waves go out and affect all things around you, there is also the reflection of the wave that comes back to you.

The energy will come back to you in the most appropriate manner. When these waves of love vibration come from you, they are accompanied by the ones we call "runners." The runners assure that these waves find the proper place. The runners are the go-betweens, the facilitators between the energies. As the waves reflect and come back to you with the facilitation of the runners, they bring back to you all things that you need, all things that are timely, and all things that are appropriate. Then you will hear a bang at your door like you have never heard before!

Dear friends, Lesson Nine of the Creator Series: Dance with what comes to your front door.

As you move into the New Energy, you will hear thuds and bangs and knocks at your front door. Some of you hide and do not answer the door! Others open the front door and do not see what they think they should see, and totally ignore what appears at their door. They slam the door, waiting for Spirit to deliver what they think should be the appropriate package.

Dear friends, Lesson Nine: Dance with what comes to your front door. It will be appropriate. What comes to you will be appropriate. The ones who gather in the second circle will be those who come to your front door. They will come, not knowing why, not knowing who you are, not knowing what brought them to you. They will have that look on their face, frightened perhaps, nervous, but more than anything, confused and dumbfounded. They will not know what brought them to your front door. They will not see the runners who accompany them. It will be your runners and their runners who bring them to you.

No matter who or what comes to your front door, dance with it. It IS appropriate.

Dance with what comes to your front door. It is time to interact. It is time to take all that you know about yourself, all that you have learned and apply it. It is time to dance with what comes to your front door, whether it is a person or an object or a thought. Oh yes, it could be a check from your Publisher's Clearinghouse! (amused) Whatever comes to your front door has been brought to you appropriately. It is delivered to you by your runners, based on your vibration. It is time to interact with it. It is time to dance, to meld your energy into it. It IS appropriate if it is brought to your front door. YOU sent out the waves that brought it there.

Let's talk about some old energy attributes. There are those we call the "acorn hunters," the humans who gather the acorns, They are much like squirrels who gather nuts before the long winter. The humans acorn hunters gather and store the nuts because they fear not having enough resources. They gather acorns, stooping along the ground, and bring them back into the house for the long winter ahead. They are being cautious indeed. But dear friends, there is also a level of fear attached to this.

Then there are the humans in the old energies that are the "willers." They "will" things to happen. They try to make it happen by sheer will. They try to create by forcing their will. Occasionally it works, but generally they are left tired and frustrated. They are trying to force creation in a way that is not so appropriate.

Then there are the "imaginers," the ones who think that if they visualize, and they create the picture of something in their mind, then it will come to them. Occasionally this works, if there is enough energy poured into it.

But dear friends, why tire yourself, why frustrate yourself? There is a better way to create in the New Energy. Take your broad brush, add your passion, and then to wait for things to come to your front door. When it does, it is time to interact. It is time to place your energy and your human skills, as well as your divine skills, into what comes to your front door.

If a student is brought to you – even if you do not like the way the student looks or acts or smells – it is time to dance. (chuckling) Get close. Get personal. They have been brought to you for a divine reason.

Put human judgment aside and know that all things are appropriate. If an object comes to your door, it is there for a reason. If you lose your job, know this is something that has come to your front door. It is there for a reason. Dance with it. Express your emotions. If your emotions are anger and pain, dance and express. You do not need to act holier-than-thou. We understand that there is pain with some of this. But as you dance, as you express yourself, as you embrace the moment, you will discover things about it that were previously hidden from you. Dance with what comes to your front door.

This will be a challenge for many of you. You are used to making plans. You are used to predetermining the way things should look and be, or how you would like them to be. This will be a paradigm shift, in the magnitude of "4."

Instead of worrying, planning, gathering acorns, or willing things to happen, we are going to make it so very simple for you. Take your broad brush. Create a stroke. This begins a vibrational sequence at the highest levels of spiritual physics. When your passion is added to this, the waves of vibration go out. They affect others who are ready for it. They change the nature of things outside your New House, if the recipient is ready. Then the reflection of these waves brings back to you all things appropriate. This could be people, relationships, abundance, or health. The waves will bring it back. The runners facilitate this process to assure that it gets back to you, in spite of things that may try to block its way.

Do you understand what we are saying here? Be in your divinity and know that all things appropriate will come to you. Do not plead with Spirit. Do not beg for these things, dear friends. It is so simple that it will challenge you. Your fears will come up, and when you do not hear a thud at your door for a period of time, you will think you are doing it wrong. There is no difficulty or challenge in this. There is no way to study to do it right. It is that simple.

When you do not hear anything at your door immediately, it simply means that the waves of vibration that have gone out are doing their work. Now is the time for you to sit in the easy chair of your New House. Wait for that knock at the door. Now is the time to relax, not to worry. When you worry, and when you do not have trust in your divinity, it does alter the vibrations that go out, and surely it will not bring back the highest level of what you would truly like to create. Do not worry when you send these out.

Dear friends, Lesson Nine: Dance with what comes to your front door.

When you do hear that knock, when something comes to you, it has been brought there for the highest good, and in all appropriateness. Now is the time to dance with it. Now is the time for you to go to work.

You say, "Tobias, how will we know what to do when we open the door and we see something?" We say to you, dear friends, the answer was revealed in our last lesson. Do not look at the choices of left or right or doing nothing. Look into the ALL. When the person stands there at your door, having been delivered to you by the runners, and you are wondering what they are doing there as much as they are wondering, look past the obvious. Go into the ALL. The ALL is the fourth level of understanding. The ALL is the higher level of understanding. It contains the answers, and you will know what to do. You will know how to dance.

Dance with what comes to your front door. Now is the time for interaction. We use the term "dance" because it is, as we understand, a beautiful human expression – although Cauldre is not so refined in this art! (chuckling) It is a beautiful interaction and expression between the elements. It is flowing, and it is graceful. We do not just use the words "act on what comes to your front door." We use the word "dance" because it is complete, and it is beautiful. It is an art. Simply dance. Interact. When you look into the ALL, you will know exactly what to do with the object, the thought, the person, the emotion or the opportunity – whatever comes to your front door.

Here is the challenge for you, the teachers: can you drop those plans you make each day? Can you go beyond the way you THINK things should be? You have been goal-oriented, and that has served you well to bring you to this place. You have planned things in your human mind, but now it is time to release that. Oh, this will challenge some of you! We refer here to things in your own life. We know that you will still be required to submit these things in your workplace, but in the New Energy you will begin to see the fallacy of these old plans. You will begin to see how they limit your life.

You will not need these plans. You will not need the difficult mental exercises of willpower and focusing and imagining. Dear friends, this is what is tiring you out! This is what is causing your energy to leak! You try to will your health. It did not work so well! You try to will your abundance, and you find yourself flat on the ground – and flat broke!

In the New Energy you emanate a vibration that goes out, and the reflection brings back exactly what you need. When it comes to you, then dance with it. Perhaps it is a new job opportunity. Perhaps it is a new healing that feels appropriate in the New Energy, something that will heal those things that have been tormenting your physical body. Perhaps it is a mate or a relationship. Perhaps dear friends, it is a look at yourself, of who you truly are, of the long journey that you have been on and all that you have done to help change the very nature of All That Is!

Lesson Nine is so very easy, but it that will cause you to rethink the way you have been doing things. Simply being in your New House, creating in broad strokes and adding your passion sends out waves of love without intent and without agenda. It IS perfection, and then it brings back everything that you need in perfection. This lesson will challenge you! Once you begin to understand, you will be amazed at how you could have gotten along without it.

Dear friends, dear friends, there is much to learn now in the next three lessons. We ask you to work with this lesson – dance with what comes to your front door. Whatever comes into your life will be appropriate. It will challenge your thinking. You may not understand how this could possibly be appropriate. Perhaps you will think that Spirit is bringing you terrible things, but if you dance with it, you will find that it is appropriate, and you will discover gifts beyond measure.

This is a milestone lesson. When you teach this lesson to others, it will challenge your students to go into a place of trust and knowingness, and to release many old ways. But these ways have been limiting factors in their lives.

You are without contract. You are without plan. You are without a life lesson at this point. The pages are open and blank. You are now creators. We bring you this lesson to truly begin creating in your life.

Before we end this lesson, there is one who you walked with in some way in the past. He initiated a family energy that continues to this day. It continues in the greatest of love. The one we call Yeshua Ben Joseph comes here to honor you for your journey and to smile upon you. Yes, his energy has been here throughout this lesson. He has been standing beside you. He asks you to understand that the image of the cross and of the death is not so good! Yes, it was a challenging experience, but it was filled with joy. It was to show humankind the love and the grace and the renewal that is possible within you.

As Yeshua was on the cross, his spirit stepped down and walked amongst those who were gathered. His spirit extended throughout the land, and there were many, many who thought they saw him at their sides at that particular moment and time. Many of you were close. Many were in other lands, yet felt this one that carries the energy of Christ walking beside them. How could he be in two places at one time, you wonder? How could he be upon the hill on the day of that storm and yet walking beside you? He came to show you that life renews and that you renew.

He comes here now to say that you renew once again. You rejuvenate, but not the old human mind and not the old human body and energy. You rejuvenate, and you transform much as he did at this time 2000 years ago. The love pours from him and from us to all who continue the vibration of Shaumbra that began some 2000 years ago.

And so it is.

Lesson Ten
Step Into Your Divine WIll

And so it is dear friends, dear Shaumbra, that we gather together in our circle. This is such a precious time, a time of love, a time of honor and a time of thanks. We ask you to feel all that is coming into your space and into this circle, for there are many entities who come in now bringing with them much energy. We ask you to open your hearts and join together in the circle with us for there is much to be discussed.

The energy here is so sweet! It is difficult to even speak in words to you here because the energy is thick. It is easier for us to transfer our feelings and thoughts to you in the form of vibration and the form of love. We also know that you like to hear these words, so we will continue. (chuckling)

We told Cauldre – the one who brings forth these messages in the human words – during our time of melding that we would take the energy and to a new and higher level in this lesson. This may feel different than what you have felt before. If you look for the melding in the past, it will be somewhat different now. We are ready to bring this energy to the next level with you. It is the result of the work you have been doing in your lives. It is the result of all of the thinking that has been going on in your brain, all of the studying of the lessons, all of the considerations of who you are and what you are doing here, all of the deep internalizing that you have been doing. Ah, we know it has been much! We know it has been challenging.

The work you have been doing with these last few lessons is making a difference. It allows us, the ones who come in to visit and your runners, to bring the energy to a whole new level. You will be able to feel the energy in your biology. You will be able to feel in your heart and you will be able to tell the difference in your daily lives.

We'll give you a bit of a clue here. As you integrate this New Energy, you will find that things get easier. They will be less challenging. Life will be different; sometimes you will be surprise at how things come to you. Dear friends, in the New Energy and in the energy that is being brought forth in this lesson, you do not need to struggle so hard. It will be there, it IS there.

There are words of power that you will soon learn to understand. You have thought these words in your mind, but you have not so much brought them into your life. It is the simple energy of the words of I AM. This is the essence of our teachings dear friends.

I AM.

That is why we say it is no longer appropriate to give intent. Intent separates you from reality. Voicing intent says that you are not quite there. I AM places you in the moment, in the now. It is not separate or different or apart. IT IS and it emanates from within you.

(chuckling) We have heard there has been some ridicule, perhaps criticism of our approach to prayer, dear friends. We are not saying that prayer is inappropriate. We say to you, the ones walking into the New Energy, that prayer is no longer needed. Prayer assumes that things are not in the proper balance.

Even now Cauldre chides us! He tells us there are times when he still needs to pray. We honor this. We understand this. As you move into the New Energy you will come to understand the power of the I AM, of the NOW and of the DIVINE MOMENT. You will no longer need to pray to an outside entity or to a spirit that you do not know so well. You will not need to pray to a guide who you have never met and whi is nameless to you! You will not need to do that in the New Energy. It will simply be in the I AM with no intent, rather simply IS-NESS.

We know you are familiar with the I AM concept. It has been difficult for you to integrate into your heart and to bring it forth into reality. In a sense there has been a closed door that has not allowed the true understanding and the true compassion for the I AM to come forward. Based on the very work you have been doing, we are moving to a new vibrational level. As we mentioned, it will be different. It will not come from the same place you used to connect with Tobias, the Crimson Council and the others the other entities you work with. It will not come from the same place as before. Do not look back. It comes from a new place. If you are wondering just where it will come from, we will pause for a moment so you can

sense the presence within you.
I AM in the DIVINE MOMENT.

The New Energy is here. The Divine Energy that emanates from within you is here at this moment. Search no longer for it. Struggle not in your mind but open your being to allow it to come forth.

(chuckling) We have to chuckle here. We are laughing and crying at the same time! You amuse us quite a bit. As we assemble here, as the legions of angels flow into your space, we see something that you do not quite see yet. We see the ones who will be the teachers, the ones who are setting the energy templates of the New Energy. We see the ones who have a light that is beginning to shine brightly within – beginning to glow steady and true. Your light is not flickering; it is not dim like it was a year ago. It is shining strong and bright. We see this light within you growing, but yet dear friends, so many of you do not see it yet. That is why we chuckle. You struggle with it too much!

You have been searching and seeking for all of these lifetimes of yours on Earth. You have been trained to do this. You have gone to classes that teach you to search! You have looked outside of yourself to find what is inside of you. This has been appropriate, but now things are changing. Change is what the Crimson Council is all about. Change is what your human angel group of the Crimson Circle is all about. All of the work that you have done and all of the challenges that you have been through have been to transmute the energy. Change has been part of a process that has ignited th Christ Fire within you. The Christ Fire is coming into being. We tell you that from where we sit for we can see it in you. No matter how much you doubt yourself, we do not. We see it within you.

Oh, this is a blessed moment for us. You are family. You have gone on many adventures and had many experiences. It gives us a special feeling of love and thanks because there are many who will follow behind you. All of the angels of the universe are waiting, waiting their time to cross the chasm. When they do, they will have the knowledge and benefit of the other human angels who crossed into the New Energy before them. Oh yes, indeed we will have to do it ourselves, just like you are having to do it yourself. But we will know there have been those who have persevered, who have given their lives and all of their being, who have given thousands of lifetimes to get to the point where you are. Why do you think we honor you so much for the work you do?

Yes, we like the term "Changeworkers" created by another person. Indeed you ARE the Changeworkers and we honor you for this. There are times when we could just stop right here and sit with you, cry with you and laugh with you. We wish we could show you the big picture of what you have done. It is awesome.

As the energy in this circle is shifting, you will see many changes in and about you. One of the things you will perhaps feel, as we have said to you before, is that WE are channeling YOU. We are connecting with each of you, even if your physical being is not present in this room. We are connecting with you and literally channeling back to your own thoughts, your own experiences. We ask you to feel yourself in the energy of this lesson. Feel yourself in our words.

YOUR imprint is coming through in the words that are spoken by Cauldre. YOUR imprint is in the energy that is coming through. Your energy comes through the thoughts and the feelings and the spirit of Tobias, and it is channeled back to you. Feel yourself in our words. There is a part of you in here. It is easy for us to connect with this. It is YOU.

You have asked us what your spirit feels like. In this lesson you have the opportunity to experience it. Your spirit is coming back at you for WE are truly channeling YOU. This is all very amusing, isn't it?

There is you, there is the Crimson Circle, there are the other humans who are Shaumbra, there are those who are in nonphysical form that gather here today. The circle is getting very crowded now. But in all of this energy and in all of this love that comes forward, you are there. It is no longer separate or different. You are not just listening to some exalted entity who happened to be thrown out of the Bible and who landed in prison. (amused) Feel yourself in the energy. It is here and it is available to you. You have asked to see the mirror of spirit in you. You have asked to feel the Christ Light within you. It is available now in this next evolution of energy and it is here for you.

Dear friends, has it ever occurred to you that most other humans are not doing the extent of internal work you are doing? It does not matter to them so much, for they are still outward looking. Honor them for this, it is appropriate. But has it not occurred to you the tremendous amount of internal work that you are doing and how much time and energy it occupies? It is because you are going through a metamorphosis. You are going through a divine process. And you are going through changes.

There are thoughts you have the first thing in the morning – thoughts of "Who am I?" and "What should I be doing?" and "Where should I be going?" These inner thoughts create important energies that are moving you forward into greater understanding. They are moving All That Is forward. Throughout the day you have thoughts about Self – what you call the other side of self, what you call the doubt of self. Has it not occurred to you that other humans do not have nearly the amount of chatter and internal discussion as you do?

(chuckling) It is not because you have this great desire or need to process. It is not that you need to always be resolving your issues. It is because this is an attribute of Shaumbra, to dig within and then dig more and consider and ponder and think and do more digging! Each time you do this you are making a pathway through a tunnel of consciousness. You are digging the tunnel further and further. That tunnel leads to enlightenment and understanding. That tunnel creates a passageway for your divine vibration and your divine energy to come through.

Do not chastise yourself for the inner work you are doing. It IS making a difference, not only in you, but also in the energy of this planet and in the universe and in the Kingdom from whence you came. Dear friends continue your inner work. Do it with love and honor.

The ones who join us for this lesson are what you would call the leaders, the assemblers, the figureheads of the other councils that work with humans. Oh, indeed there are many councils! The Crimson Council is but one. The Crimson Council works to refine the energies and vibrations of teaching. You are part of this. Your energy makes up the Crimson Circle on Earth. You are the teachers. Not "will be the teachers" but ARE the teachers of the New Energy.

The ones who come in for this lesson represent other councils. There are many, many councils on our side of the veil. There are councils that deal with the healing arts. There are councils that deal with your physical medicine. There are councils even that deal with engineers! There are councils that deal with the everyday issues of human life, for they are needed not only in human form, but also in the angelic realms. There are councils that deal with supplying the proper nutrition to your planet. Indeed they are the ones who work with the farmers, the ones who work with those who process and handle and develop foods, for there is a need to sustain biological life on your Earth.

So while there are human angels who walk on Earth in physical body, there is a corresponding group – a very large group of angels – who work with those specific energy attributes on our side of the veil. When a farmer is tending to his fields, there are angels of the Growing Council who work with the farmer as balancers of energy. The legions of angels are there for very specific reasons, to balance energy, to hold space and to supply a type of love that can only come in when it is requested. It can only come in when it is requested and when you open the doors.

There are those who join us for this lesson from the councils that deal with the balance of your money, of your finances. Finance is an important aspect of life on Earth now. This will change, but now it is important. So there are humans who deal with finances and there are corresponding councils that deal with finances also. For every human trait and attribute – yes indeed, even of the wars, even of your militaries – there is a corresponding council on our side. There is always a one-to-one relationship.

No, you do not belong to only one group or council. The common attribute with the Crimson Circle is that you are all teachers. But you also may be part of other vibrational councils. You might also be involved in an energy group that has to do with moving computer technology forward. You might also be involved in helping to balance your environment. You can be that and you can be a teacher. You can be one of the Crimson Circle as well.

The ones who head these councils come in for this lesson. They sit in the second circle to observe. They add their energy and their love. Why have we invited them? Why have they chosen to be here with you? Because dear friends, they are fascinated with the progress you are making. They come here in awe of the humans who call themselves Shaumbra, who are awakening within. They are in awe of the progress you are making.

It was predicted that if you got past the potential chaos surrounding the millennium period, if you got past the potential destruction and the potential breakdown of systems, then the next major change would come in the year 2012, what you call the end of your Mayan calendar? Many have predicted this to be the time of a quantum leap from the energy of "two" to the energy of "four." A shift from duality to divine balance. And did you know that this year 2012 is not set in concrete? Through your work, the work of Shaumbra and the work of all humans of Earth, this date is moving forward faster and faster. Do not hold out for the year 2012 for a quantum leap of self and then of mankind. It could be sooner!

The ones who gather here now are feeling your energy. They are assessing your energy. They will take this back to their angelic councils on our side of the veil. They will relay what they have seen and felt. They will communicate to the others that things are moving faster on the planet Earth.

They will tell their councils about a group of humans who are doing extensive inner work. The work of Shaumbra is now to a point that it can be taught through books and through classes in order to help other humans who are beginning to walk the path. They will tell their councils of the group of humans who are helping to make change on Earth: The Changeworkers of Shaumbra!

You do not so much believe what we are telling you! You find it difficult to understand when all this time you thought you were just dealing with your emotional problems! (chuckling) What you are really doing is building a tunnel from the old energy to the New Energy. Our visitors are laughing now; they are having a good time with you. They are here to honor the work you are doing. But more importantly, they are here to bring back a message to other celestial councils that something is changing. There is a change in energy that allows a melding that was not possible before.

Oh, indeed there will continue to be challenges in your life. There will continue to be situations of duality that occur all around you. This will not change for quite some time. But you, as the teacher, as Shaumbra, will have a different reaction to it. You will have greater understanding and wisdom. We will talk of this much more, but not today.

We ask you to remember these words, for much of where we are going in upcoming lessons will revolve around this: Dear friends, it is not about you any more. It is not about you! You thought it was, but it is not. We will spend much of our third series dealing with this.

But now, the ones who come from the councils, who are here to meld with you and to learn from you, place their hands upon your shoulder. They kiss you on the forehead and thank you for allowing them to be here. Dear friends, simply acknowledge those who come to be with you. Accept the gifts of energy they bring.

Now, we come to Lesson Ten of the Creator Series. We know the previous lessons have not always been what you thought they would be! (chuckling) Perhaps you thought we would give you a magic chant? Or perhaps you thought we would give you a ceremonial dance? The dance we gave you was hardly ceremonial!

Lesson Ten is the first of the final quadrant of the Creator Series. In these final three lessons we will once again challenge you by asking you to release something that you have held near and dear. We will give you tools, we will give you new methods and new ways of thinking, but we caution you now, it is not what you think it is. But by now you should realize that! (chuckling)

In these past nine lessons we have worked to change the perceptions of who you thought you were. We have worked to help you understand the New Energy and what it is. We have worked to help you understand where you came from and why you are here.

The first three lessons were about "allowing." Allowing and accepting. Accepting all things as they are. Stand behind the short wall. Learn to accept yourself, which is perhaps the most challenging of all the lessons. Learning to accept yourself. That is why we spoke at length about what you are going through; what you have been doing; the internal work you have been doing. You have given yourself grief because you thought you were spending too much time on yourself. We are here to tell you that perception is not accurate! It is about changing something far grander.

Lesson Three was also of accepting, of being in the Divine Moment, of no longer being in the past. Dear friends, the past is the future in many ways. We talked to you about being in the Divine Moment, the Divine Space, not worrying about what has transpired or what will be. It is about being in the Now Moment.

Lessons Four through Six were about releasing. They were about letting go. We talked about placing your issues in the Oven of Grace (Lesson Four). Lesson Four was about releasing, about turning it over to your own Divine Energy. Take it out of your hands and out of your mind and place it in the Divine Processor that is within you. These lessons were about turning it over to your divinity. Then understand that when you do this, you are obviously going to have changes in your life (Lesson Five). These changes are appropriate, so bless them.

As the changes occur and you learn to bless them, be in Divine Balance (Lesson Six). Allow yourself a new balance, not of duality, not of two, but in a divine balance of four. We discussed the four roound marbles. In the past there was a dark element and a light element, and a third element that changed like a chameleon. The third element would take on attributes of the light or dark. But we also said that a fourth element of energy, a fourth marble, would come in and provide a needed balance to take you past duality into the New Energy.

Then in the next three lessons (Lessons Seven through Nine) we discussed how to begin the process of creation. We talked with you about the broad stroke of creation (Lesson Seven), painting with a broad-brush stroke. We asked you to give up intent, specific intent. Simply initiate the process of creation with the broad-brush stroke. This starts a process that takes things out of neutral and begins to move them. Not to the left or not to the right, but it begins to expand the potential outward in all directions.

When initiating the process of being a creator on Earth, an energy is needed for this to manifest. We talked about this in Lesson Eight: Receive the Fruit of the Rose. This lesson was about awakening the passion that has always been yours, but has been dormant for quite some time. This brings forth a divine energy. It is time to integrate with that passion again. It is time to receive it within your being. It does not take much work, you do not need to do ceremony, you do not need to struggle with it, you do not need to pray for 21 nights in a row! You simply receive what is yours.

Then vibrations go out of your New House, out into the world around you. These are vibrations of love, compassion and wisdom that you emanate to others. It a light shining out to them, but there is also a reverse vibration that comes back to you. With the assistance of your runners, this vibration brings back all of the appropriate things to you, to the front door of your house (Lesson Nine). This is part of the creation process. It is being in your New House. It is saying I AM. This process is then fueled by your passion. The vibrations go out into the physical world around you. What comes back are all of the appropriate things. Perhaps you will not immediately recognize them as being appropriate, but they are. What you are creating now, what you are creating by all the work you are doing, is now being brought back in the appropriate way to you.

Now we enter the final series of these lessons (Lessons 10-12), being a creator on Earth. There are three more lessons in this series. We will talk for a moment today of the journey of Jack once again. This will help you understand why things are the way they are, and why you are experiencing certain things in your life at this time.

Then there is something precious we will ask you to release. Perhaps this will be a challenge for you. Perhaps releasing it will be difficult, but when you let go of the old, it then makes way for the new. As you are discovering, you will not find the answers you are looking for in the old ways.

What you are discovering now is that the answers are not in the "old." The answers are not where you found them in the past. You are encountering experiences in your life right now that are examples of this. Someone you knew many years ago suddenly pops back into your life. Or an old illness you thought was gone pops back in. Or an emotional situation you thought was released comes back to you along with the emotional pain. And then you become confused. You wonder why you can't handle the situation that you handled before, and you wonder why it comes back again at this time. Dear friends, the answer is in a different place. It is in the New Energy. The answers for all of the things that come into your life are in the New Energy now.

We will digress for a moment here. The inner challenges you are going through do not relate to past lives, for most of those with the exception of small residue are gone. The challenges you are going through for the most part do not even relate to this lifetime for, as you know, you feel so separated from who you were five years ago and twenty years ago and thirty years ago. It is difficult to even relate to yourself back then. Why? You have changed. You have moved into your next lifetime, even while you are here.

The challenges you are going through now relate back to your original crossing of the Wall of Fire. There was a deep trauma with this. There was deep shaking up of everything that you had ever thought that you were.

When Jack crossed through the Wall of Fire, as we have talked about so often, this was a very traumatic experience for him. When Jack crossed through this wall from the First Creation into the Void, it changed everything. It changed everything. When Jack was in the kingdom all things were one. There was singular purpose, there was singular direction and there was singular Will. All things emanated outwards from the center of the kingdom. This was wonderful, peaceful and loving and it was the way things were in the First Circle, in the First Creation. They were one will. When Jack crossed over through the Wall of Fire into the Void he suddenly had a new attribute. It was called Free Will.

When Jack crossed through he now had the gift of Free Will. It was no longer singular expansion of All That Is. He entered into a new dimensionality. Jack had always been the prince, the son of the king and queen, the one who would one day accept the throne. But now he was experiencing something totally different — Free Will. He did not quite so much know how to handle this. For he always thought he understood his mission, his purpose and his contract in the singular will of the Kingdom. But now, all things were available and all things possible. There was no prescribed path or pattern.

Jack's journey is your journey. Each of you felt what it was like to go from One Will to Free Will. This created many interesting experiences for you. This allowed you to be a free creator. All of this is blessed by Spirit.

Given Free Will – you and Jack and all the other angels and all of the humans – given Free Will you have been able to expand creation in ways never before possible. Do you understand the impact of this? You had singular will – loving indeed, blessed indeed – but it was singular in the original Creation. When you came through the wall you were given Free Will.

When Jack came to Earth and took on biology, he still had Free Will, but now he also had something called the veil. The veil prevented Jack from consciously knowing what transpired from lifetime to lifetime. The veil prevented Jack from understanding the journey that had taken him from the Kingdom into the Void, to help create the energy and the templates of your Universe. Combine these two powerful elements – the veil and Free Will – and there is a very potent energy here. It is one that each of you has been living with.

You have the Free Will to do what you choose. You also have the veil, which keeps you from remembering your experiences. Now, here you are, Shaumbra, coming to the completion of your own circle of lifetimes on Earth. You are coming to the completion of your journey, coming to the final clearings that will allow you to go into the new consciousness.

As we have said before, you do not return Home from here. You continue expanding but there will come the point when the veil is released, when you do have an understanding of your journey, you do have more of a complete understanding of self and why you are here.

In the meantime, here you are going through many changes and challenges in your life. You expected this ascension process to be one way and it is another. It is not what you thought it would be! As you come full circle, dear friends, something interesting happens. There is a step you will take. We channel it back to you in this lesson. You know it is coming, but it must be conveyed from the outside for confirmation. That step is quite simple. Going into the New Energy to be the creator you truly are, you need to step past Free Will into your Divine Will.

Lesson Ten of the Creator Series: Step Into Your Divine Will. It is a simple but potent step. It is one that seems obvious at first, but when you start thinking of it in your human mind, it might frighten you. You are already perceiving, you are being asked to – Cauldre certainly questions us at this point! – you are being asked to release your Free Will and move into Divine Will. Now let us talk for a moment of what the difference is.

Cauldre is saying, "Oh, Tobias, what have you brought forth on this day!?" Hmmm.

Lesson Ten: Step Into Your Divine Will. When you came to Earth with Free Will and duality, it allowed you to see the mirrors of who you were. The Free Will allowed you to see the light and the dark. It allowed you to see up and to see down, but in a sense Free Will with a veil is very limiting, as you have discovered. Many of you have even questioned whether you truly DID have Free Will or if you were simply puppets for the angels or for Spirit. But no, indeed you had Free Will the whole time.

When you move into Divine Will, you transcend the duality and separation that you have carried since the Wall of Fire. You transcend the separation from Spirit you first experienced when you left the Kingdom. When you move into Divine Will, it is about the Divine Will that comes from within you. It is connected and it is integrated with Spirit at the deepest levels of who you are. When you move into Divine Will you transcend the humanness that you have carried with you. You transcend the duality that has been part of you are ever since you have been on Earth. You move past the two into what we call The All.

In the Divine Will there will be solutions that have never been there before. They have not been able to come through Free Will and duality. In the Divine Will there is not so much the consideration for just yourself, but there is a greater compassion and understanding for All That Is.

The Divine Will is not owned outside of yourself. It is contained within. When you release the old Free Will and embrace Divine Will, you make a new connection with Spirit. It is a conscious connection and a conscious understanding that you have not felt for eons of time.

Divine Will is not sitting and waiting for God, for Spirit, to tell you what to do. It is already a part of you. It is an inner understanding that Spirit is within. There are no outside voices. Spirit and God and Divinity and the Christ Consciousness are already within you. Divine Will is listening to this deep, passionate inner voice.

When you begin working with this lesson, you will wonder, "What is this Divine Will?" or, "Is this my crazy brain talking to me once again?" And you may become paralyzed to a degree in making that decision. But we tell you when this happens, simply be in a place of peace and say, "I AM in my Divine Will." Understand that what comes forth is Divine Will.

You are used to the old attributes of Free Will, or "Duality Will." There was a constant battle back and forth in your mind. As you move into Divine Will, new solutions will come to you that are far above what you have experienced before. You won't feel it is the two old voices of your old human self arguing back and forth as happened before quite often. (chuckling) When you step into Divine Will, you will feel and sense and perhaps hear a different answer that comes from The All. But understand– and we emphasize this – that it still comes from within you! If you seek outside of yourself for these answers, if you think that there is an entity who exists outside of you that will now start telling you what to do, you are looking in the wrong place! You are looking in the old energy place. Divine Will comes from within. Divine Will is within you at this moment. As we have told you earlier, and we chuckled about it, we see this light in you but you do not see it yet.

Lesson Ten: Step Into Your Divine Will. Perhaps you will feel awkward about this at first. You will think you must hear from Spirit first, "Is it appropriate to do this or that? What do you say Spirit, what do you say guides? I need the answer from outside." And it will not be there. You will hear nothing if you look there.

When you step into Divine Will – which is very easy, very simple to do – the answer will come to you. The knowingness and the understanding will come from a place within you that you have not experienced up to now. It will be full and it will be rich. You will not have doubt about where it comes from because it come from a place of love. The knowingness will come from the very inner part of you that is indeed Spirit. This won't be a mental exercise. It will be a dynamic feeling that occurs within you.

It is time now to release the thing that you first experienced when crossing through the Wall of Fire. It is time to release the attribute called Free Will. Oh, when you first acquired this it was an incredible toy. It was an incredible toy for an angel who had just gone through the incredible experience of the Wall of Fire. It was frightening as well, for you had never had Free Will. You had had One Expanding Will.

But now you were given power, you were given choice like you had never had before. You took that Free Will and began to play with it in the universe, in the Void. Your Free Will was like having an incredible, awesome Creator's tool kit. You could do things that you had never done before. You could play in the Void, you could make the stars, you could create new energies. You could even battle with other entities! You could not do that in the Kingdom.

This Free Will was an incredible new toy. But it also caused you much grief along the way. Much hardship and much pain. You took the Free Will and went to places that were at the lowest of the low, at the bottom of the bottom, at the most painful of places that all of Creation could have ever imagined. But you were simply playing with the New Energy. Oh, indeed you also took it to wonderful places of love and sharing and compassion in creation of light.

You have had this gift of Free Will ever since it was bestowed on you by Spirit. You have had this gift with you for eons of time now. It has served you well to create something in the Void, to create the universes and the galaxies and the stars. Free Will served you well when you have incarnated on Earth. It allowed you to make the choices between the light and the dark, the white marble and the dark marble.

But now dear friends, it is time to step into your Divine Will. It will be challenging. You will wonder what this thing called Divine Will is - who owns this? Is this Spirit coming back now to once again tell you what to do? Is it your guides or angels who will dictate to you? No, Divine Will comes from within. It is your will but it is on a divine basis that transcends duality. It transcends the human dynamics that you have been used to. It is directly linked to All That Is and to Spirit, but understand that you are Spirit. Divine Will comes from within. It provides answers and solutions and experiences and new powers that you have never experienced before.

It will be challenging. You will want to keep BOTH your Free Will and your Divine Will! (chuckling) You will want the wonderful attributes of Free Will while you take on the new Divine Will. It does not work that way. One must be released before the other can be experienced.

When something comes knocking at your door now and you are now dancing with it – many of you have asked Spirit, "Okay, I'm dancing, but what do I do? When does the song end? Who should lead? What steps should we take?" While you are dancing, take that step into Divine Will.

Let's say you are in one of your everyday situations, a challenging situation perhaps, with a coworker. The coworker has come knocking at your door and you have agreed that it is time to dance. You are now dancing and your coworker is looking at you in amazement and now you wonder, "Spirit, what should I do next, now that I'm dancing, where do we go from here?" Take your step into Divine Will.

What happens then we cannot so much to describe to you. You will move into a new place. You will move beyond duality. You will come to realizations that even we cannot define. You will come to new understandings and new levels of vibration and energy that will make the old energy way of Free Will seem flat. Your old ways will seem unexciting, undynamic and lacking in passion. When you step into Divine Will things expand quickly!

With Divine Will comes the answers, the solutions, and the broader picture. At that moment you will know exactly what to do. You will know what to do with the energy that comes to you. We will talk more of it in our next two lessons. But now we challenge you with this Lesson Ten. Step into your Divine Will. Perhaps it seems simple for some of you. Some of you will say "I am more than happy to do that" but you will find that the attributes of Free Will have been with you since you came into this creation. This energy of Free Will has been with you for eons and you will want to hold on to it at some level within. It will be a challenge to move into Divine Will.

You will want to know exactly what it is before you take that step. Dear friends, you can not possibly define the attributes of Divine Will in the consciousness you currently hold. You must step into it first. Once again we are asking you to cross a chasm on your own, without us being there to take you over. We know you will spend some time thinking of the implications of stepping into Divine Will, for it does mean releasing Free Will. Free Will can be wonderful and fun. I know, for I have experienced it! It is an amazing, amazing energy. The Divine Will is grander, more complete and more fulfilling. You who have been asking, "Spirit, what is it that I should be doing, what of my job, what of my relationship, what do you want me to do now?" We say it is time for you – when you are ready – it is time for you to step into your Divine Will. In Divine Will, knowingness will come to you.

We know there will be much discussion of this lesson. There will be many challenges. There will be ones who accuse us and accuse Cauldre of asking you to give up something that is a gift from God, your Free Will. We will be accused of asking you to give up something that has been the cornerstone of all of your experiences on Earth and when you were in the Void. There will be some indeed that will walk from this group at the very suggestion of it! For they do not understand so much. They do not understand the implications of Divine Will. The Divine Will helps to complete the circle of all your experiences after crossing through the Wall of Fire. It moves you to a new level of understanding.

We love you dearly for the work you do. We love you for continuing to put up with us; for going through the lessons; and for studying them diligently. We love you for the fact that you take each of these lessons, work with them, think about them, and apply them to your lives. We love you for this.

In the next several lessons we will help you to understand how to truly move energy when you are sitting in the position of I AM. I AM is the basic, is the foundation, is the NOW. We will work with you to help you understand how to move energy, how to affect energy, and how to become a true creator.

Those who gather in the second circle on this day are literally and figuratively applauding at this time. They have been called here to feel your reaction to this lesson. This lesson will be one that causes a mental roadblock for many, many people. This lesson will be like a high hurdle for some to overcome. It doesn't require you to do much, it doesn't require hours of practice and studying. It simply requires you to release something that has been close to you and to venture into a new type of energy.

The step is yours to take, dear friends, the step is yours to take by yourself, in your own time, in your own space. If you do not so much understand this now, if it is causing conflict within you, take your time with it. Take your time with it. Throughout this process, and during the time you take that first step into Divine Will, you are never alone. There are legions of entities who are with you. We love you dearly.

And so it is.

Lesson Eleven
Give Thanks To Yourself

And so it is, dear friends, that we gather together in our family of Shaumbra. We gather together in our circle. It seems like only moments ago that we sat here with you discussing your divine will, moving into this new energy that would allow the truth, the hope and the love of who you truly are to come forth. And now we are back, for Lesson Eleven of this Creator Series. We are back together with family.

When we first enter your space, it is difficult at times for us to express our love. The energy here is so sweet! It is difficult for us to even begin to express our love. It is indeed very, very sweet. Here we are in a circle filled with humans who have been on an incredible journey. It seems like an eon of time ago when you left Home. You continue to do this work, to be filled with love in spite of many challenges. You come together at times like this to join with each other – human to human – and to join with the angels who come in now. What a sweet reunion this is! We have much to discuss with you.

Lesson Eleven is one that is quite simple on the surface, but challenging indeed! We cannot wait to reveal this to you. (chuckling) Those who join you for this lesson flood into the second circle. There are many, many who come here and they bear a special energy that we will speak of in a moment.

They now enter the second circle. You, the human, are in the first circle. You are in the circle of honor. The others who come into the second circle are the observers and invited guests. They have a particular reason for being here, associated with this lesson. Feel their energy for it is familiar. It is an energy you know. It bears strong traces of the past.

Know that as you are reading this material, we bring a gift of energy to you. It is here and available to you now as you read this. We bring this to you for the remainder of the time we meld with you, as you absorb this lesson. Receive this energy of love and honor while we are together like this. We impart to you this sacred and blessed energy. We bring this in and you can experience it at your deepest levels. It is our gift to you in this channel that was originally given on the Day of the Father (Father's Day).

I personally thank Cauldre for inviting me here on this special day of the energy of the father. It has been a long time since Cauldre and I have walked together on Earth as father and son. I have never forgotten those times! They have always been special. For I, Tobias, this day is most touching and most emotional. I thank you, my son, in spite of your embarrassment. (chuckling)

Now, let us talk of who comes into your second circle for this lesson. This energy is the one you have known as your father in this lifetime. Perhaps your father is still living, perhaps he has joined us on this side of the veil. Perhaps he has even incarnated and is now your own grandchild! There is an important reason why he is here now. If you cannot feel his energy, if you are looking for the energy of the father you knew in the past, shift slightly. Look in a slightly different place. His energy is not specifically as you remember him when he walked the Earth with you. His energy is different on this side of the veil. He has released and cleared many of the energies that were associated with him when he walked on this Earth. Shift over slightly and you will be able to feel him. It is a "clearer", less confused energy that what you might remember. But he comes in at this time for a very good reason.

We know this hurts some of you to have this visit. We know there were times that were not pleasant. You have gone through much healing in your lifetime because of your father. (very emotional) But he comes in on this day because it is important for him also. It is time for him to move on. It is time to have a deeper understanding of this Father energy. So he comes into your space and is next to you. Accept the love – the unconditional love – he brings.

Perhaps you had a wonderful relationship with your father. Perhaps you admired this energy in your life. From your father, you learned about strength and stability and wisdom and love. There are those who have chosen very loving and very positive relationships with their father.

Perhaps your father still walks the Earth in human body. Indeed, his spirit is with you at this moment as well. He is sitting beside you. The part of him that is the conscious human does so much understand the true relationship between you, but the part that is divine knows and understands the challenges and ultimately the love that has been part of your relationship. Welcome this father of yours who comes in now, even if he still walks the Earth. And understand that beyond what may be apparent to you, there is a greater good and a greater service being done.

If you never knew your biological father, if you never grew up with the energy of this biological father in your life, understand there were reasons for this. By the end of our time with you in this lesson, you will have greater knowingness of why it was this way. But this one who is your biological father – who you may have never met – is still energetically connected to you. That father is here with you now, sitting with you.

This space is now filled with a very strong male energy. It may be difficult for you to handle. Perhaps it brings up resentment and anger and emotions. There are reasons for this. It is part of the reason we come to you now.

Now, dear friends, take this moment that we share together to accept the love and the energy that comes in from the one who you have called father. Take this time to bring in the energy. Take this time to accept the love and energy from the angels and runners who are here to help balance the energy of love and emotion. Breathe it in. Breathe deeply into your entire being even as you read this. There is much love and much goodness that comes to you at this time. You have gone through many challenges since you left Home. There is much honor and love for you.

Now, let us talk for a moment of your journey. Let us talk of why we have invited this energy of "father" into this space, and why it is important as a part of your journey, and why we tie it into Lesson Eleven of the Creator Series.

There are those who have asked for deeper understandings of the metaphor that we used of "Home" when we spoke of the Kingdom. We have spoken specifically and deliberately of the King and the Queen. We have spoken of the story of Jack, the prince. There are those who have asked why it was important that there was a king and a queen. There have been others who have asked why Jack was man and not a woman. It would have been "Jacqueline" in that case. (chuckling) We have waited for this day of the energy of the father to help you understand why.

In the Kingdom, all was One. All was singular. There was a singular expression in the Kingdom. But at some point in this Oneness, in the love and the bliss of Home, Spirit, All That Is, the Eternal One, God, knew that it was time to take an inner look. It was time to come to a greater understanding of why existence existed. It was time for All That Is to take an account of Self. Everything up to that point had been a singular outward expression.

The very moment Spirit contemplated looking within, contemplated taking a look in the mirror at Self, what had been One became Two. God now had the ability to look at Self. What had been a singular energy in the Kingdom now became the King and the Queen. It became what you would call a "male" energy and a "female" energy. And there was a "marriage" between the two. There was still unity, there was still oneness. But now, because Spirit even thought of looking within and contemplating Self, it instantly created a duality. It created two energies that we call the King and the Queen, the Mother and the Father.

For those who walk on earth in the female biology in this lifetime, you will appreciate the fact that in the Kingdom, sitting on the throne, there is a predominant "female" energy. It is not balanced 50/50, male to female. Spirit and All That Is are balanced more to the female aspect. And again, we caution here. We are using terms for the easiest understanding.

The female energy, as you know, is one which births. It is creative. It is filled with love and nurturing. The Kingdom is predominantly nurturing, predominantly creative, predominantly birthing. So therefore we say that the energy of Home is predominantly female.

Isn't it interesting that in your society you refer to God and to Spirit as "Father." It should be "Mother"! It should be Mother. That is why we are speaking of this in the energy of this circle. It is time for a healing to take place. It is time for a change. The new energy that you are moving in to has a dominant "female" energy. It is balanced, but it reverts back to what you knew in the Kingdom.

In the Kingdom, there was Oneness that moved into Two. It was the King and the Queen. The moment they looked each other in the eye, they had the greatest love for each other and for all they had created. The moment they looked each other in the heart, they knew what love was, in ways Spirit never could never understood before. This was the original love story. The King and the Queen, now able to see each other, fell in love. And when they did, the Queen gave birth to a son that we have named Jack. This is the father-mother-child trilogy that you even use as humans on Earth.

This creation of the love of the King and the Queen was male in energy for many reasons. The male energy is generally – and again, we use metaphors and symbols – the male energy goes to journey. It seeks and journeys. Even in the Kingdom, the male energy was one that had the strength and stability and was also the one that journeyed. So the King and the Queen gave birth to a son – one of male energies – so that he could journey on their behalf.

Now literally, was this a male in biology? No. We use terms here to help you understand and teach to others later. The result of the love between the King and the Queen was a son who would be the journeyer. The King and the Queen knew that Jack would one day leave the Kingdom. This was part of the love plan. They knew, even when Jack did not know.

They knew that one day he would cross through this thing we call the "Wall of Fire". He would leave Home. He would leave the First Circle and go into a void where nothing existed. The King and the Queen had no concept and no idea of what existed outside of the First Circle. But their only begotten son was to journey there. In a sense, it frightened them for they did not know what would happen to their own offspring. In another sense they understood the implications of love behind the journey.

Each of you is Jack. Each of you are the journeyers who left the Kingdom, who went beyond – beyond. You went outside All That Is. You still do not so much understand the implications although we have talked of this for quite some time. But dear friends, this was and this is an incredible journey that you and that Jack took. You left All That Is.

We look at you now. You do not even understand the implications of what you have done on behalf of All That Is. You left the Kingdom to discover something for Spirit that could not have been done without you. You who thinks your life is small, you do not understand how big it truly is. You do not yet understand why we come to you in such great honor. Perhaps you will begin to understand now of what you did on behalf of All.

✧ ✧ ✧ ✧

The King and a Queen conceived a son named Jack. Someday Jack would assume the throne. But before Jack could do that, there were things that needed to be experienced. There were things that needed to be expanded and balanced. And yes, oh yes, your own scientists and physicists are beginning to see the path that you took to get here! They are starting to see the beginnings of the creation of your universe. They are beginning to understand the most basic vibrational tones that were sent out when you came flying through the Wall of Fire. They will continue to look at and ponder these things but, dear friends, sooner or later they will understand this was not a single event – a single big bang. Rather, it was an event that took place when all of you who are Jack came through the Wall of Fire and appeared in the Void. It was not a single big bang, it was multiple big bangs that took place when you and all of the others left the Kingdom.

Now let us return to the journey of Jack. The energies of Jack and of all of you have been predominantly male. This male energy was needed to journey outside of the First Circle, the Kingdom. Each of you has carried a strong male energy, even if you are female in biology. It is time to heal that now. It is time for healing. It is time for a rebalancing. As you move into the New Energy, you will have much more of a "female" balance to your being.

Those males who will become fathers of children in the New Energy in the next few years to come – what we call the "clear fathers" for there will not be a lot of old energy attributes – they will have a new strength and balance. These clear fathers will have a closer and stronger relationship of love with their biological children. They will spend more time playing with their children than fathers of the past. They will help to raise them and care for them because they will have a better balance of the male and female within their being.

Even at this moment, your father and their father and their father, join you. The angels who facilitate this energy come in now to work with them and work with you to heal something that has been wounded. It has been in need of healing and balancing ever since you left Home.

Let us talk for a moment of karma, while we are speaking of fathers. You have carried your own soul karma from one lifetime to another. As you know, it sets up challenges for you based on your experiences from the past. As you also know, you can choose to get off the karmic wheel at any time. You can make the conscious choice to get off the karmic wheel at any time. You do not need to go through a prescribed number of lifetimes or a certain amount of suffering to get off your karmic cycle. All it takes is a conscious decision that you're ready for that merry-go-round to stop. That is all! You do not need to go back and clear every lifetime on Earth and times you had before you came to Earth. You do not need to do that! Any time you are ready to get off the karmic wheel you can do it simply by saying it is now time.

Now, for those who have already done this, many things happen as you know. Some things are quite wonderful, yet it sets up a series of changes in your life that are not always easy because you are going through rapid and intense changes. It could affect your body because karma is an energy that is stored within your physical being. Now that you are no longer willing to carry karma it has to find a way out of your body. This can be temporarily painful. It could put you up for a period of time, keep you bedridden. It could cause sores and boils because this old energy is trying to come out. But you are learning well to deal with these things and to release them.

Let us talk of another type of karma. It is an "ancestral karma". It is in the DNA, it is in your biology. It is a "family" karma. We discuss it because your fathers and their fathers and their fathers and theirs are here. They are here now to heal that karma. You have chosen to get off the karmic wheel of your soul. But there is another karma that still lingers. It is the ancestral karma.

This space fills up with many who are simply waiting for you to say it is time to release the ancestral karma. Do you know that within your being, and within the setup of your life, it is not only your soul karma but it also your family karma? It is karma for things that were done five generations ago and ten generations ago and a hundred. It is carried forward in the biology. Indeed you see it with diseases that are prevalent within certain blood lines. If there is a tendency for diabetes in your family, it is carried karmically in your DNA. There are also emotions – ancestral karmic emotions – that are carried within you. There are events that were created by your father's forefathers five hundred and a thousand and two thousand years ago that you are trying to heal in this lifetime of yours. And you wonder why life can be so difficult and challenging? As we have said, it is not just about you anymore.

There are scores of entities who come into this space right now. The fathers that you knew, and the great fathers you did not, are standing in line waiting for this healing to take place.

You needed a male-oriented strength to leave the Kingdom. You needed this. But this male-oriented strength, this energy of the journeyer, was also warrior energy. When you left the Kingdom and entered the Void, indeed you started battling with others. This male energy you have carried with you has been one of structure and discipline. It has been an energy of intellect and not so much heart. It has been one of defending and journeying. You have all carried this with you. It is time on this Day of the Father to heal that and to balance it and to release it. That is what the visitors are here for.

They ask you to release and to heal the ancestral karma that has been part of your blood line. They ask you now, in your heart and your silence, to release this. It will release and heal them also. Be in silence for a moment to feel this energy of the male, this energy of the father, that you brought with you. You have carried it with you ever since you left Home. It wants to be balanced and healed now. The energy of the Father wants to be healed. And in doing so, dear friends, it allows the loving, nurturing, life-giving energy of the Mother to come forward in more balance. If it is appropriate for you to release and heal this, not only the energy of the Father but the energy of your ancestors, do so now.

There is a long line of your ancestors who stand here now. We have said to you before, "It is not about you anymore." Now that you are working in the new energy, you are finding this to be more and more true. It is not about you anymore. You are healing, and have healed, your own past. And now you are healing the pasts of others.

There are even churches that understand this concept. They pray for their ancestors. They pray that their ancestors will join them in Heaven no matter what sins have been done. They understand, to a degree, the energy behind this. They understand that there is ancestral karma.

Oh dear, many changes are taking places here. Many, many changes. (emotional pause)

One of the attributes of a male-oriented energy is that of strong ego. It is not to say that women do not have this also. We would classify the ego as a male-oriented energy. Ego. Dear friends, it was important that Jack took on the male energies. In doing so, the ego was accentuated. This was important and necessary for the long journey that Jack would take.

You have learned well about the ego! It has served you well while you have been in human form, and even before you came here. But you have a feeling that this ego is a bad thing. There are those who have been involved in spiritual work that feel the ego must be killed. They feel the ego must be destroyed in order to move forward. This is not true. The ego only needs to be melded and healed and balanced. This male-oriented energy has served you well.

Ego – derived from your Latin word meaning "I". I-go. I-go. This is what Jack did. He waved good-bye to the King and Queen and said, "I go now." Indeed, the ego was developed when you, when Jack, crossed through the Wall of Fire. It needed to be, because there had never been separation before. This ego was developed and it was important. It created a sense of identity for you.

Your ego was then refined over periods of time. Your ego was intensified when you came to Earth and took on physical body. Your ego was the one thing that you could relate to from the past. Your ego was the one thing that always stayed with you, from the time you went through the Wall of Fire and through your journeys in the Void, until the time you came to Earth. You felt tremendous separation and loss when you left the King and the Queen and the Kingdom. You ego was the constant that came with you. Ego. "I go," said Jack. "I go to the void, I go to an adventure." Ego.

It is interesting that you spend so much time battling your ego. You give it a bad rap. You try to kill it and destroy it. (chuckling) And you have found that you cannot! It is an integral part of you. It is your connection back to Home.

As you move into the New Energy, the ego is transforming. It is changing. You are transforming and changing. Instead of "I go" you are becoming "I Am." I AM. This is the New Energy. This is the new balance of the male and the female, the King and the Queen. Dear friends, be kind and gentle to your ego. It is the father or male-oriented energy within you. Love it and bless it as much as you would love and bless your own biological father in this lifetime, and the fathers who have come before them, and the Father from the Kingdom who helped to birth you.

There is much information to ponder and review. We will tell a short story. We will tell a story of a male, of Shaumbra. It is the story of the one we call James.

James was much like you. He came into this lifetime for a clearing, for a final clearing and completion. James chose a family lineage that he had been with in the past. Allow us to digress here for a moment.

Indeed, when you come into a new body and a new lifetime on Earth, you do choose your family. But you do not just look at the millions and millions of families that are available, and say, "I will take this one or that one." It is not quite that simple. You have an affinity for the blood lineage that you came from. Generally, you will choose to return to a family that you have been with in the past.

There are those who believe that they bounce around from one country to the next, from one race to another. Dear friends, this is not so accurate. You tend to follow patterns. You follow families that you have been part of in the past. Do you know that you could be your own great great great grandfather? (chuckling) This is not so uncommon, for you choose to come back in certain lineages, certain blood lines.

There are stories in your Holy Scriptures that talk of twelve tribes and families of Earth. In a sense, this is accurate and true. From these twelve tribes certain lines have been developed. You have tended to stay within these until the most recent years. Until approximately 50 years ago, it was common to stay within fairly tight blood lines. This is changing now and there are many reasons for this. We do not want to take up so much precious time now discussing this. But understand, you tend to stay within the same family patterns. That is why there is a fascination for your own genealogy. You may show up on your own family tree several times!

Now, James was choosing another lifetime on Earth. He selected a family that he was quite familiar with. Notice the common energy behind the words "family" and "familiar". He came to Earth in this lifetime with a father who was very strict and very stern. His father was coldhearted.

James came into this lifetime with a mother who was loving but weak. Again, if you look at the energy of this lesson, you will understand there is much more here than meets the eye. His father was controlling and demanding and strict. His father gave little love, but gave many rules. James' mother was loving but afraid – afraid of the male energy of the father. She was afraid to truly open her heart. She was weak.

As James grew up and came of age, he realized he wanted to get away from this strict father energy right away. For it was also an energy that required him to go to a church with which he felt no connection. He felt no closeness with this church. For in this church he learned of a stern Father, of a mean Father, of a judgmental Father and a Father who was punishing. He learned that God was this way. God the Father. Vindictive, angry, temperamental, cruel and strict. This is what he learned. He learned it while in the biological family he had chosen, controlled by a strict male energy.

When he came of age, he left quickly. He began a journey of his own for at his soul level he knew that he must heal in this lifetime. He knew he must heal himself, his past, but he also subconsciously knew there was a whole family lineage to heal as well.

Oh, as you know, James tried many different things, many different schools of thought, all of which helped him move to new levels, all of which served him well. But he still had many challenges in his own life. He had challenges of relationships. He did not so much understand how to open his heart to women in his life. He did not know how to relate to the female energy, for what he had seen was weak. The female energy he knew from his mother could barely eke out its love. He was trying to find love in other women, but he did not know how to deal with it.

James finally found a woman who could express love, but yet was strong in her own right. She had a healthy balance of male and female. But James did not want any children. He did not want to subject another human to the type of suffering he went through. So he chose, and his wife agreed, not to have children in this lifetime.

They searched together. They went to many classes. They belonged to many groups, and they learned many things along the way. But yet his troubles continued. He had problems with abundance in his life. He had problems with holding a job. As his relationship with his wife matured, he had problems relating to her, to this female energy. He sought much time alone, off by himself, contemplating, talking to God the Father who he did not so much understand. But it was all he knew. He spent much time talking to God the Father, the one he learned was cruel and angry. But he knew no other relationship with Spirit. It had always been the Father energy.

At some point, after much struggling, James began to read the materials of the Crimson Circle. He connected with the energy of family. He began to understand why he was on Earth in the first place. James began to have new meaning in his life. Oh, indeed it was difficult to let go of many of the old ways. But he began to have new understandings of why he was here.

Some good things began to happen in his life. James was always appreciative and always sat down to give thanks and prayer to God the Father and to the Angels and to his Guides. And then it would seem, as most of you have experienced, that the difficult times would come back once again.

James, who was diligently working on the lessons of the Crimson Circle, went to his job one day and was given a large raise. He was given a large raise, seemingly out of nowhere. He was happy and he thought to himself, "This is truly working now. I'm truly becoming a creator, I am truly learning to manifest, for look what has happened in my life!"

James went home that night, went to his room of meditation, shut the door, lit the candles and the incense, and polished the crystals. (chuckling) He still kept these things in spite of all we have said. James prayed and gave thanks and he said, "Dear Father, thank you for this gift of the raise and this promotion at my job, for now I will have the abundance to pay my bills on time. Now I will have the abundance to buy my dear and loving wife a few things that I have always wanted to give her." James continued, "Dear angels, dear angels, I give thanks to you for arranging this. And oh yes, dear runners, I do not so much understand you yet, but I understand you facilitate my creations. I give thanks to you.

I am happy and I am learning. I'm learning to become a creator. I am creating abundance in my life."

And Spirit, represented by the King and the Queen, and the guides and angels and the runners could all hear this. For they hear all of your words. And they were laughing and they were scratching their heads. And yes, I, Tobias, was there. I too was puzzled and thought, "Why does James give credit to Spirit, to the angels and to the guides, to a God the Father he does not so much understand and that he is even afraid of. Why does James give credit for his accomplishments to these others? Does he think we dole out favors, dole out goodies to Shaumbra, with no particular pattern?"

And we laughed and we were amused and we said, "We must talk to family about this in one of the lessons. It will become one of the most important lessons. We will tell James and we will tell each of you – give thanks to yourself."

Lesson Eleven: Give Thanks to Yourself for what you are creating. It is a simple lesson but it will challenge you. When something good happens in your life tomorrow, you will want to say, "Oh dear God the Father, thank you." Instead, thank yourself!

Lesson Eleven: Give thanks to yourself. There is a reason why this is so important. The energy of thanks to yourself is like a nutrient for your divinity. It is like food and water for the Christ Seed that is growing within you. When you give thanks to yourself, it is an acknowledgment within. When you give thanks to anyone else or anything else – from the King or the Queen, to your guides and angels, to the runners, to Tobias or any others in between – you are literally giving your power away. You are giving it to another.

You are awakening. The energy that the Christ Seed needs, that your divinity needs, is your own love and acknowledgment. Do not give it to us. We do not need it. We love you dearly, but nurture yourself. Give thanks to yourself. It will make your journey much smoother. We do not need it, this thanks, this love, this acknowledgment. Give it back to yourself.

We spoke of ego earlier. The first thing that will happen, when you go to thank yourself, is this male-oriented ego is going to pop up. It will say to you, "I cannot give myself thanks." This is the energy of male ego coming through. It has caused many battles in the Void after you crossed through the Wall of Fire. It has caused battles on Earth. It has caused the misperception of Spirit as a strict and stern and even cruel Father.

When you give thanks to yourself, there will be an immediate fear of your own ego. That is why this lesson is so simple but yet so pertinent.

That is why we chose this Day of the Father to bring up this topic, this Lesson Eleven. They are all interwoven; the energy of father, your ancestral past, the ego, and the ability to honor yourself as spirit.

As easy as this lesson seems, there will be resistance on your part. When you teach it to others, they will resist it. There is a barrier – this male-ego energy that you have tried to suppress and run away from and kill. It is in all of you, male and female. It is in all of you. Honor and acknowledge yourself. Give thanks to yourself. When something good happens in your life – and these will occur more and more often now – when something good happens, thank yourself.

Oh, it will feel strange at first. Take your hand, left or right it does not matter so much. Place it upon your chest – give thanks to yourself. Honor yourself, feel yourself. It will take a bit of work and practice to do this but, dear friends, as you do, you are nurturing and feeding this awakening divinity within you.

If you do not acknowledge your creations, this divinity will begin to wither like a plant on a hot summer day. It needs your love. Your divinity is your true self. It has been in a cocoon for a long, long time. It is who you truly are, and it is coming back to you as a child. It needs your love. It needs the balanced love of the King and the Queen within You.

Oh, there is so much more to this lesson. There is so much more than meets the eye. Dear friends, Lesson Eleven of the Creator Series – one that will catapult you to new levels of a creator – is Give Thanks to YOURSELF. Honor yourself and love yourself. We do not want to hear you thanking us anymore! (chuckling)

Oh, we have thrown out many things that you have held dear, but it is time to move forward. It is time. If we hear you thanking us, we will remind you, in a rather fatherly way, that it is not so appropriate any more. Give thanks to yourself instead.

It will take a bit to get over the old concerns of ego. You will have to work through this. You will have to bring in your own balance of male and female. It will take a bit of work. Some of you will be so challenged by it that perhaps you will even give it up and go back to the old ways. We are challenging you to move beyond the old feelings of the ego, which was filled with the male energy. Move beyond to understand that the ego has served you well. Understand that you are going from the journey, which could be defined as "I GO", to the new energy which is the "I AM."

There are many tears in this space now. They are the tears of your fathers, and the tears of your forefathers. It is time to release the past and move forward in the new understanding of the father energy. You are beginning to understand now that there is not a Father in Heaven as you have been taught in your schools. It is the King and the Queen and the energy is predominantly female, or Queen. The energy of All That Is is predominantly that of birthing and nurturing and loving. Your energy as Jack has been that of a journeyer. It has been that of strength, it has been that of moving forward.

Those who gather in this space shed tears not of sorrow, but of release. They know you are also releasing them, releasing much of the karma that has been ingrained in your own family. Yes there are families here who have had karma of alcohol, karma of incest, karma of emotional imbalance. You, dear friends, chose the most difficult of the difficult by coming into this lifetime to not only heal yourself, to not only heal your past soul lives, but also to heal your own family lineage. There is much healing being done now. It is within you; it is within all who gather here.

Dear friends, do not make it complex. As these changes occur in your life, and as you begin to see the manifestations of the work that you are doing in this Creator Series, give thanks to yourself. Honor yourself. Do not run from this ego. Integrate it.

We love you dearly. We see you, Shaumbra, as ones who will be the teachers to others who cross into the New Energy. This is another way of saying they will cross into their own divinity. They will need human guides. They will need you.

Your students will come to you at a time and they will say, "Dear teacher, I am beginning to have a few good things happening in my life. I am making more money. I have reunited with my biological family who I have been away from for so long. I even have a new romantic relationship." Your student will say, "I give thanks to God for all that is coming into my life."

And you will burst their bubble! You will say, "Do not thank God, do not thank the Father." They will not so much understand. They will think you are putting them through yet another crazy lesson. You will sit with them, as we are sitting with you now, and you will explain to them Lesson Eleven – Give Thanks to Yourself. Acknowledge the awakening of the Christ within. Acknowledge that it is your own divinity creating these things. When you do, it will be like watering and feeding a plant. Then your students will start coming to life.

Your creations will become clearer and stronger and more defined. We know you will be so tempted to thank God, for that is what you have been taught. You will be tempted to lock the door and turn out the light and kneel beside your bed because this is what you have been taught. But dear friends, above all, Give Thanks to Yourself. And remember, Shaumbra, you are never alone.

    And so it is.

✣ ✣ ✣ ✣

"You exist outside of All That Is."

✣ ✣ ✣ ✣

Lesson Twelve
Your New Relationship With Spirit

And so it is, dear friends, we gather together in this space, in this sacred energy, with family. You are clearing the way for something that has been planned for quite some time. You are making room within yourself for this new divinity to come forth into your life.

Dear friends, you are releasing the old energy. You are transitioning from the old into the new. We have been working with you for days and weeks and even months, preparing for this time. It has been the energies of Spirit, of the Kryon, of the Archangel Michael, and of the Crimson Council who work with you. You come now to this point of transition. It is a transition of much significance in your life, a transition of significance for all of those who are in your life as well and for All That Is. Indeed this is a sacred and blessed time.

We always have visitors with us in this classroom of the New Energy. The energy that comes to visit today is that of Home. It is that of Home. They gather in the second circle. You are in the first. They gather all around. It is the remembrance of Home, the Kingdom, where you came from. It has been eons and eons of time since you left – but not really so long ago – since you left on this incredible journey. It is the journey of the angels, from the Kingdom through the Void to this place you call Earth. And now the energies of Home come to visit.

Also gathering in this room in the second circle are the energies of the Kryon and the energies of Archangel Michael. They gather here also. They gather in a type of graduation ceremony for you, a new beginning for you, and a new time for you.

Let us pause for a moment and allow me to tell you who I, Tobias, am and who I have been to you in the past. Indeed I did walk upon Earth. I walked in human body for many, many incarnations. We knew each other in the days of Alt (Atlantis). We worked together. We were searching for our divinity within. We were using technology to discover ourselves, to try to find the hidden divinity within. Oh, we discovered many things! We learned many things. But, dear friends, we did not discover our divinity. When we realized that this was not possible at the time, we chose to leave this phase of Earth. We chose a type of renewal through destruction so that we could begin all over again. We could begin again this search for the divine seed within.

I, Tobias, knew many, many of you then. We worked together, hand-in-hand. We prayed together. We researched together. We laughed together. That is why you know my energy.

There was a time again when we gathered but I was not in human body. We gathered together as family, as Shaumbra. This was 2000 years ago on your planet. You may know my energy from that time. I walked with you in many lifetimes since then, serving as one who loved you, one who held the energy of family for you, one who reassured you. Together with your angels and your personal entourage, we worked together. We had a mission. There was something important to be done on this place of Earth.

I have been working closely with you in this lifetime as well. I, Tobias, and those of the Crimson Council have been working with you in your sleep at night and in your waking states. We know this is a difficult journey of the angels. We know this is a challenging time for you. You are doing something that has not been done before. We will continue to work with you as long as you choose to continue on your path, as long as you continue this journey of the angels.

Who are you? You are the ones who left Home so very, very long ago to take a long journey. You left the comfort of the Kingdom. You left your original family so very long ago. When you left creation and All That Is, you went through the Wall of Fire. As we have said many times before, it shattered you into millions of pieces. When the pieces of you gathered back together again, you were outside of All That Is. You were outside of Home and the Kingdom and All That Is. You were in a void, a nothingness. It was so nothing that not even black existed, not even a vacuum existed.

You woke up in the Void, carrying nothing from Home. In the metaphor it would mean that you had no luggage. You had no belongings. You had no real remembrances. You woke up into nothing. It was part of your new journey. There was a tremendous sense of loneliness and separation and guilt and anger. These feelings, and the desire to return Home have been with you ever since. That is why you cry at night the way you do. We hear you. We understand. The battles in the universe were about trying to find a way back Home. You took energy from other entities and other angels. You fought with them in an effort to take enough of their energy to get back Home. But as you know, it did not work. That is why there were battles. That is why there have been the conflicts, and why you still have conflicts on Earth. Entities are still trying to take energy from one another in order to find their way back Home.

The deep, deep desire to remember Home is why you have so much sadness at times. But, dear friends, with the consciousness you have created, it is now possible for a piece of Home to come here into this very sacred space, to come here to visit you during this lesson. Home comes to you!

We ask each of you to breathe deeply. Breathe the energy of Home into your being, this love, the love of Spirit, of the king and queen, of the original creation. It comes to love you, to thank you and to honor you for the work you have done. You have created something new.

There has only been one creation prior to you leaving Home. As strange as that may seem to you, there had only been one creation. Within that creation, within that Kingdom, everything was one. Everything was a singular expression.

You have helped to create the second creation for Spirit. Yes, you – you, Shaumbra – you, Lightworker – you have done something that Spirit could not have done alone. This is why we honor you. This is why the Kryon washes your feet. We are in awe of who you are.

Now, dear friends, when you left Home, you brought nothing with you except for a tiny, tiny seed that had a protective wrapping around it. It was the seed of divinity. You carried that within your being for all of the days and all of the times that you have journeyed. It has been carefully protected within you. The seed has been carefully concealed within you so that you did not see it and so that others did not see it. It was buried deep within your consciousness.

You have felt something within your being all of this time. You have felt that there was more than what appeared on the surface. It was the presence of this divine seed within. It has kept you going through many of your journeys and travels. This divine seed is still within you, and as you know now, it is beginning to awaken. We use the term seed as a metaphor, but it is an integral part of who you were. It was at the deepest levels of your being, not to be revealed until the appropriate time.

Some 2,500 years ago the vibration of Earth was ready to begin bringing forth this seed of divine consciousness – what we sometimes call the Christ consciousness – from the outer realms and dimensions where it existed. For you know your consciousness does not truly exist within your biology. It exists on levels and planes surrounding you. It is much like your movie projector. The consciousness – the film and the projector – are in one location, and the image is projected onto another. In a sense, you are the image of your consciousness projected into 3D, projected into the body you carry, projected into this Earth you walk upon.

Some 2,500 years ago it became appropriate to begin bringing more of this consciousness to Earth, into your reality. At that time there were families of angels who chose to come in to help facilitate this process. There were individuals who received notoriety for this. There was the one who is called Buddha – Siddhartha – who came in with many, many others. It was not just the Buddha who brought in the consciousness. There were many of the Buddha consciousness who came in at that time.

Then there was a group, the ones we call Shaumbra, who came in 2000 years ago. You came in, knowing it was time to bring this Christ consciousness from the outer realms to Earth. You were the carriers of this energy. Many of you here walked with Yeshua ben Joseph. Many others lived in the surrounding lands at that very time.

Others came in right after the time of Yeshua ben Joseph when the energy was still strong and sharp. You helped to set up the new churches. These churches were the incubators for the Christ consciousness. You are the ones who helped to bring this in. You are the ones who said you would do whatever it took to help bring this Christ consciousness to Earth. You are the ones who have walked the difficult path ever since.

You have known something within you. You have known there was an important mission, that there was important work for you to do. You were the ones who agreed to do it, even in sacrifice of things that would have been pleasing to you as a human.

Dear friends, breathe deeply. Breathe deeply. There has been much work you have done in this lifetime. As you know, things could have not worked out quite so well. There could have been destruction. There could have been termination around the time of your second world war, up through the time of the new millennium. But that did not happen. Here you sit. Here you sit, ready for the next step, ready for the next level.

And what is that next level? It is to bring in your new relationship with Spirit. Up until now it was not fully possible to understand and to truly know God. It was not so easy to understand who you truly were, to see yourself as an angel in the mirror. You have struggled with these issues. Spirit seemed more like an intellectual concept, far and removed from you. At times it seemed like you were placed on Earth, not knowing your purpose, and not knowing your relationship with Spirit. But all of the time, desiring it and longing for it.

That was the old energy, when the veil was thick and strong. You could not so much relate to Spirit. In the New Energy – there is a new relationship with Spirit. It is close, and it is personal. In the New Energy, you are very aware of your relationship with Spirit. There is a deep understanding within you.

In the old energy it was difficult to accept all things as they were. The veil was thick and strong, as was the game of duality. But in the New Energy, it will be easy to accept things, because you will see the grander plan. You will understand the grander vision. You will understand why humans do the things they do, and why you have chosen your path.

In the old energy it was difficult to accept your human self. In a sense, you considered this a punishment for leaving Home. You ended up in a physical body with its aches and its pains and its challenges. In the New Energy, it will be easy to accept your humanness, because you will understand that you are not locked in there. You will understand that it affords you many things, as well. It provides you with many pleasures. It gives you a vehicle for expression of your spirit within.

Dear friends, you are moving into your new relationship with Spirit. In the old energy it was difficult to be in the "now," to be in your Divine Moment. You were thinking of the future and of the past. In your new relationship with Spirit in the New Energy, you will always be in the "now." You will have released the past. The future will only be a potential for you to create. In the New Energy you will be in the "now."

Breathe deeply, dear friends. Breathe deeply of the energy of Home. It is here.

In the old energy it was difficult to be graceful in your creations. You were clumsy and you were not usually aware of what you were doing or of the outcome of your actions. In the New Energy your creations will be graceful, and they will be flowing. It will be like riding the wave, and when one wave is ready to roll over, a new one will be there for you.

In the old energy it was difficult to accept changes. You wanted to hold onto the old because you were secure with it. Even if it was difficult and challenging, you were secure with it. In the New Energy you will understand that change is natural and blessed. You will come to appreciate and even anticipate change, for it is nothing more than the continued expression of your creativity.

Dear friends, breathe deeply. Breathe deeply, this energy of Home that is here with you now.

In the old energy, divine balance was elusive. You had the elements of light and dark, plus the third element that changed back and forth. In the New Energy there is divine balance within you. There is the energy of four that will be stable; it will be secure.

In the old energy you focused on individual creations – small creations. In the New Energy you will create with broad strokes. You will not worry so much if there is a hundred dollars in your checking account. You will not have to worry so much if your car is broken. You will not have to create in small ways. You will create with broad strokes. That is the New Energy. That is your new relationship with Spirit.

Dear friends, once again, breathe in deeply. Breathe in deeply.

In the old energy it was difficult to find your passion. It was difficult to have that deep spiritual passion within. In the New Energy the passion will be with you at all times. It will seek to express itself. It will seek to come forth. It will seek to create with you.

In the old energy, dear friends, you needed to go outside of your spiritual house to create what you needed. In the New Energy, it will come to you. We know this will be difficult for you to understand, to accept, but truly it will come to you. It will come to your front door. Whatever you need will come to you at the appropriate time. Then it is up to you to dance with it. It will be time for you to go to work.

Once again, dear friends, breathe deeply. Breathe deeply. You are entering a time of a new relationship with Spirit.

In the old energy you had Free Will, but in a sense, it was very limited. In the New Energy you have Divine Will which is unlimited. It is all-knowing. It is part of your new relationship with Spirit.

In the old energy you gave thanks to a god and to angels for things in your life when good things happened. But dear friends, in the New Energy you are beginning to understand that it truly comes from within you. It truly comes from within. There comes now for you a new relationship with Spirit. It comes from within you. It is the seed that you have carried from the time you left Home.

Come now your new relationship with Spirit. As simple as this seems, dear friends – as simple as it seems, it will be somewhat challenging to accept and to implement into your life.

Lesson Twelve of the Creator Series: Come now your new relationship with Spirit.

Now specifically, how do you bring this new relationship into your life? How do you manifest it into your being? It is quite simple. It is really quite simple! It is done through breathing. It is done through breathing. As you breathe in – consciously breathe in – become aware of your new relationship with Spirit. Breathe deeply now. Breathe in your new relationship with Spirit. This will feed and nurture the divinity already within you.

Breathe deeply. When it is abundance you choose to create in your life, do not be so specific with it, but rather breathe in abundance, and understand that it is not coming from the outside. It is coming from within you. When you breathe it in you are allowing this awakening divinity, this Christ consciousness within, to now come from the outer realms of who you are into your very being. You allow it to manifest in your life. When you are paying your bills, breathe in abundance. Breathe in abundance. When your body aches and hurts and is in disease, breathe deeply. Breathe in biological balance.

The divinity that is within you is coming forth right now, but it needs a vehicle. It needs a conduit to come in to your reality. It comes into your "now" through breathing.

There are masters who have known this and practiced this for quite some time. But now more than ever, it is truly a tool for you. Up until now it has been difficult, perhaps almost impossible, to bring your divinity deeply within into your human reality. The mass consciousness of Earth would not allow for it to come in easily. That is why it has been so difficult and challenging. That is why there have been those who have sought this for ages of your time. But now, with the higher level of personal and mass consciousness, it is possible to bring this into your life.

Remember at all times, it is you. When your body aches, breathe in health. Your divinity will come forth and manifest in your life and in your body. Breathe in deeply, for this is the vehicle to truly bring the awakening divinity into your life. It is so easy. It is so simple!

When there are relationship problems in your life, do not be specific about what you want to happen, but rather bring in your own divinity through the breath at that time. Breathe in balanced relationships. Do not try to explain what these should look like, but breathe in balanced relationships. When you bring it in this way you connect to their divine being – your divinity to theirs. You shift the level of relationship to a whole new level. You do this by breathing in the balanced relationship.

It is like air to a fire. The conscious breath fans the divine flame within you. It brings it into your reality, into your humanness. It is through the breath that you bring in the new relationship with Spirit. Through the breath you bring the essence of Home into your reality. It is so simple.

When you wonder what it is you should be doing, and you wonder about your own self worth, and you wonder about your mission here now in this New Energy, simply breathe in your own self worth. Breathe it in deeply.

With the conscious breath your divinity is invited into your reality from the outer realms. When you breathe it in, divinity comes in naturally and smoothly. It enters all of who you are. It enters your cells. It enters your human consciousness.

BREATHE in your divinity!

Do not think it in! That is what you have been trying to do up to now. That is what we did together in Alt, in the land of Atlantis. We tried to THINK it in. We tried to bring it in through technology. We tried to discover it with our 3D tools. There have been humans seeking the path of enlightenment who tried to think their way to God, tried to think their divinity into existence. It does not come in through your mind as you now know. Yet you can breathe in your new relationship with Spirit.

Come now the new relationship with Spirit into your life. Your tool for this is the breath. It is so simple, dear friends, but it has not been possible up until now. There have been many changes and shifts on Earth that allow for this now. There have been many things that you have personally released in your life, including past lives, including your ancestral karma. You have released these now. It makes way for the new relationship with Spirit.

When you were planning this lifetime, you knew it held the potential to begin a new relationship with divinity, with Spirit, with yourself. You knew it would be a turning point for you. You agreed to go through whatever it took to be here – even the changes that will occur in the months and years ahead, for the shifts that are necessary. As you consciously breathe, it brings in your divinity. It brings forward your own divinity, your own new relationship with your divinity. Breathing brings it into your life.

We ask you to consciously practice this. Have no agenda with it. Do not intellectualize it. Do not try to think your way into your divinity, for that will hurt! (chuckling) It will not feel so good! Simply breathe it in. This seed of divinity you brought from Home has been waiting for the appropriate time to come forward. And now as you are shifting into the New Energy, it indeed is the right time. It indeed is time to have that new relationship with Spirit. The loneliness and separation you have felt for so long, dear friends, is ready to be filled and it comes from within. It comes from within.

Your guides had to leave. They had to leave your direct energy field so YOU could embrace your own relationship with Spirit. Those who have been with you for ages and ages, lifetime after lifetime, had to withdraw. That is why it has been so challenging and difficult for you. They had to provide you the space to bring forth your own divine seed. It is time for it to shine from within you. Bring this energy into your day-to-day life with the simple breath.

Consciously breathe. Do so now. Breathe in your own divinity. It awakens. We can see your vibration come up several notches as you do this.

Lesson Twelve of the Creator Series: Come now your new relationship with Spirit. It is time. And the simple tool is your breath. We have been waiting for a year to bring this forth. We have been waiting. We have been taking you through a series of lessons to tell you that the Christ consciousness is birthing within you. Divinity is birthing within you. You have helped to bring this energy to this very place of Earth. Now you are helping to birth it within your own self. You bring it into your reality with the simple breath. If you find yourself thinking too much about it, stop. Simply breathe it in. Breathing fans the fire of divinity that is within you.

When you sit with the ones who will call you "teacher," you will tell them of this simple technique of the breath. If you tell them of this without taking them through the other lessons first, they will not believe you and they will not understand. It is important to walk through the lessons one-by-one before you come to this point, in order for the breath to be understood. It is so simple and it is so pure, but yet as you know, the journey of the angels has been long and difficult.

This is a precious moment for us. You do not yet realize the impact of what we share with you. It will come to you in the days ahead when you say to yourself, "Oh, indeed, Tobias told me to breathe in deeply." And then you begin to feel the effects. Remember to consciously breathe in. This will awaken your new relationship with Spirit.

The feeling of loneliness will be replaced with love and fullness. The feelings of separation will be replaced with unity. It will be deep sense of unity with All That Is, a unity with self and Spirit, with human and God. You will learn to breathe abundance into your life, to breathe in new balanced biology, to breathe in the appropriate relationships, and to breathe in the divine angel that you truly are. Come now your new relationship with Spirit. You have earned it.

And so it is.

Questions & Answers

✜ ✜ ✜ ✜

"The Future is the Past Healed"

✜ ✜ ✜ ✜

Questions & Answers

The following are unedited questions asked of Tobias by audience members immediately after the channeled lessons.

QUESTION: Tobias, I am confused about how to allow and let go, knowing that Spirit has no plans for us. How do we create what we need in our lives? In particular, I'm looking for a new work situation. Do I let go and stay in what could be a bad situation or pursue other opportunities, though this does not seem like allowing?

TOBIAS: This is an excellent question. It is a situation that is challenging each of you. Above all, it is about letting go of beliefs and perceptions. It is not about a particular job or a particular situation. It is your beliefs and perceptions that are keeping you in that. Our friend in the canoe (Creator Series, Lesson I) was pulled toward the abyss and he felt himself going over the waterfall. He came to sudden and new realizations about who he truly was. As humans, you fear releasing one thing until you have another firmly in place. You go through the obstacle course of life with the hand on one ring not willing to let go until the other hand is firmly on the new ring. We are challenging to let go of the ring of beliefs you have held onto, let go even the recent beliefs that you have had. We know that for some of you this is frightening. For some you may call Tobias crazy, certainly Cauldre crazy. (much audience laughter) Dear friends, have trust in Self, in your own Divinity. All things that are appropriate will come into play.

You walk along the path, so to speak, not knowing what will appear next, not knowing what your new journey will be. Sometimes you walk in fear, sometimes afraid of losing all things. Do you not understand that buried on path are all of the tools, all of the energies, and all of the abilities you need? You have placed them there before you ever walked the path. It is only through giving up the old beliefs that you will recognize them. They are there. It is much like your pictures and puzzles that have hidden items in them. Remember the pictures in your childhood books? You were asked to find something that was not so obvious. When you changed your perspective and you allowed yourself to see something that was not so obvious, then it appeared. You wondered why you hadn't seen it before. It is much the same in your life. That is why we ask you to remove yourself from the old perceptions of duality.

In the story of Oryan, he finally tired of paddling the canoe. He did not care anymore. He saw no purpose in the old journey of paddling upstream. We are asking you to release, to let go. So many of you have grown weary and are ready to release all, even if it means physical death, even if it means falling into the abyss. Not that you will, dear friends, but it is a fear, an illusion that is there. This is a large step for you, for all of you to take at this time. We understand. We do not take this lightly.

As one Shaumbra said recently, "Trust in yourself, and you will trust in all of the universe." Trust in yourself, and you will trust in all of creation. Trust in yourself, and you will know that all things will come to you appropriately and lovingly. Trusting in yourself is the release, the acceptance and the letting go. You will have those experiences in the next days and weeks of your life to help you come to this understanding.

QUESTION: Tobias, in your Santa Fe channel (New Earth Series, Lesson Eleven) you stated that the Lightworkers will be the first to evolve into the Divine Christ, the New Energy, and there will be no one waiting to greet us. I thought that the man Jesus had gone through his evolution to show us the way. Am I wrong in this understanding?

TOBIAS: With this question the presence of the entity known as Yeshua Ben Joseph (Jesus) comes in. We ask you to feel this. And we will bring forth to you his answer. We ask for a moment to adjust the energies. (pause)

Yeshua says that many of you here in this room and reading this material were with him 2000 years ago. It was a reunion of angels at that time. He says that he told those that gathered in his groups 2000 years ago that he was there to show a way, to bring hope, to bring hope as the main message. At that time, he reminded you that while he would leave Earth, your journey would continue. He came back to this side of the veil while you continued on your journey into the New Energy.

"It is not," he says, "that I went forth. I simply came to be with you, to help unify at the time, to help remind each of you of the journey and the mission. And then I left Earth. Someday you will be there greeting me as I come through into the New Energy. We are family, we are One. Continue your journey, friends. You have made so much progress. We will meet again."

✣ ✣ ✣ ✣

QUESTION: Tobias, is it still appropriate to send white and gold light to other Lightworkers, say in Israel? Is this old or new energy?

TOBIAS: We will not call this old or new. We will simply say that it is time to "stand behind the short wall." In doing so you will come to new understandings of what is happening in the Mideast, and why it is happening. We know you have sent much energy and love to this area. We know this has been done from your heart, for healing. There are others now who pick up the work that you have been doing. It is not like there is a great void left. There are others who will continue this work. But for this group in particular, for the Crimson Circle, it is time for you to gain new understandings, deeper understandings. Pass this torch of peace and love, this torch of holding energy to a critical area of your world. Pass it to a new lightworker, one who has recently awakened, who chooses to use their energies. But now, my friends, it is time for you to begin a new role for deeper understandings. We know it will be difficult for some of you to give up the work you have been doing. But it is time for new understandings.

✣ ✣ ✣ ✣

QUESTION: Tobias, if we have given our intent for things, will they manifest through our allowing? How would you define creation?

TOBIAS: Your intent presupposes that there is a particular path for you. Your intent has been based in an energy of duality. The intent that you have created for yourself in the past was based on old energy ways of creation. It is time now to release all intent for all things. This is difficult concept perhaps, for you have been filled with intent. You have been filled with direction. It is challenging to release all intent. Intent was based on a belief system that you held, whether the belief is about abundance or relationships or love or the way things work. Your intent was funneled through a belief system that no longer serves you.

With the release of intent and the release of belief systems, you will be able to observe how things truly work. You will be able to observe how things are created. When you come to a point of understanding, from a place of peace and a place of New Energy perception, you will then come to understand how creation in the New Energy works.

This not a simple task. It will be difficult. You will curse us out before this is done! (audience laughter)

We come back to the story of the canoe going over the waterfall. There comes a point of releasing everything. Perhaps you will be filled with fear. Perhaps you will be challenged by the potential outcomes of the situation. But there will come a point where you understand the illusion that is being built, the illusion that is at play. You will then understand how the creation process works on a whole and within yourself. With that understanding you will know how to truly cause, truly affect and truly create. You will also have the wisdom to stay outside of a drama or difficult situation. You will have the wisdom to understand when to intervene and when not to. That will be important.

✥ ✥ ✥ ✥

QUESTION: Tobias, what was said in the channel seems to indicate that we've moved from the third dimension to the fourth dimension. Is it true?

TOBIAS: My friends, release your beliefs about dimensions! In the energy that you moving into, these things do not hold true. We have said in previous channels that it is time to put down the books. Don't go back to the old bookshelves for understanding. This is new. This has not been created before. If you hang onto the ring of belief systems of the third and fourth dimensions, it will be a difficult journey for you. And quite frankly, dear friends, we do not even understand these dimensions that you speak of! (audience laughter) These were created by humans to help understand the evolution process. But they do not hold truth from where we sit. It is much more simple but yet much more complex than what has been described as these various dimensions. We do not want to share with you even our perceptions of what we think these dimensions are. And certainly we have our belief systems of these! We do not want to share because we want to keep you open to all new possibilities. So please do not ask us what the real dimensions are. (audience laughter and applause)

QUESTION: Tobias, will you speak about how as channelers we deal with those people that don't believe in you, Kryon, Archangel Michael, etc. and spend their energies questioning.

TOBIAS: First, realize that it does not affect us whether one believes or not. There are many who do not resonate with the messages that are brought forth. But we will take this question to another level as we discussed before. And we have told Cauldre from the early days with him, "Do not make a career out of channeling." Not that he channels poorly (much audience laughter), but that the transmittance of information and energy from those nonhuman entities to a human entity is becoming an old energy way.

There will come a point when Cauldre no longer channels the Crimson Council. When he feels as comfortable bringing up his own divinity, when he finally faces that the God is within him, he will no longer need to channel us. When you finally realize that God IS you, you will no longer need to listen to channels. You will no longer be students. You will be the teachers. There will be no need to channel.

There is a natural distrust of channelers and the messages coming through them. There are many questions that arise, and this is a good thing. This is appropriate. They will not question you when you sit in front of them with your divinity and truth shining strong. There will not be a question of whether this is true or false, whether this is occurring or not. They will know

This is where we are all going. This is where you are going. And this is where Cauldre is going. There will come a day, (a day that he fears, like the canoe falling off the river) when we do not show up for a channel. And on that day he will have to make a decision whether to run out the door or to bring up his own divinity. (audience applause and laughter)

QUESTION: Tobias, we are new to your teachings. Could you briefly explain the absence of our guides that you alluded to? Is this situation the same for all humans?

TOBIAS: It is NOT the same for all humans. It IS the same for those who are moving into the New Energy, who are on the ascension path.

In August 1999, we announced – to the shock of some people – that the guides were beginning to depart. This has been occurring for several years. Some have only recently begun to feel it. When you first came to Earth, there was a need for balance so you did not become totally lost. When you came here, you had "guides" that filled parts of your energy field, part of your etheric field. They were, in a sense, your silver cord, your connection back to Spirit. They were your tether.

Your guides had the responsibility of maintaining a balance, maintaining a connection for you. There has been much misunderstanding in the past of guides and angels. The guides, as you would term them, were the ones who occupied, maintained, and filled a space around you until the time came when you could hold that space on your own. That time began to come within the past several years. Your guides hugged you, kissed you farewell, and they retreated from your energy field. Oh, they still exist. They still linger outside of your direct energy field. They still love you and have concern for you as Shaumbra. But they knew it was time for you to take your own responsibility and your own power. So they left. This caused many difficult feelings including depression, feelings of great loneliness, and overwhelming sadness. It caused a feeling that you had lost somebody close to you, near and dear.

Your guides did not have the responsibility of talking with you, of communicating with you. They held a silent space. They were not the ones who nurtured and talked to you and comforted you. They simply maintained, in the most loving way, a space around you.

There are also angels, as you would call them. There are entities who come and go, depending on your needs, who speak with you, who are like dear friends. But they cannot come in as close to your energy field as your guides could.

There has been misunderstanding about guides and angels. There have been beliefs that the guides or the angels could do things for you. Many believed that they could give you answers, that they could tell you to turn left or to turn right. This has not been so, my friends. This has not been so. There are many angels that come in and speak with you. There are many who come and sit with you and say nothing but send you love. These angels are different from the guides who held the responsibility of your silver cord.

✣ ✣ ✣ ✣

QUESTION: Thank you, Tobias, for being with us. And thank you to Cauldre and Linda for their service. What comments do you have about our upcoming election (November 2000)? I heard a candidate speaking about manifesting the new energy – not in his words. Will this happen and will it be through him as our leader?

TOBIAS: This election process of yours is an excellent opportunity to stand on the other side of the short wall. Stand back instead of taking sides, instead of becoming impassioned about one side of the debate or the other. You will see duality in action. Stand back now and watch. Watch and you will see things that you have never seen before. Stand back, dear friends, and watch the entire power process of humans take place.

(Interjected question from Linda:) How should we vote? No, really, how should we choose to vote?

TOBIAS: In the truest sense it is best NOT to vote in this because you are choosing a side. You are choosing a belief system. We ask you to simply stand back, to accept all that is. (huge audience applause)

✣ ✣ ✣ ✣

QUESTION: Dear Tobias, please hear my confusion about healing versus acceptance. Should I not tend to a toothache, arthritis, or a body disease?

TOBIAS: These are excellent examples of things will be given to you in the days and weeks ahead to truly understand. We are not saying to not treat the toothache or the headache. We are asking that before you do, before you determine that this is not a good thing, to step back for a moment. Don't push healing with your mind. Step back and look at the entire situation. There is a reason for the toothache. There is an energy dynamic behind this imbalance. When you seek to neutralize it, to inhibit the process that is going on, you also do not see the energy dynamics behind it. As you step back on the other side of the short wall, you will see something in that toothache that you never saw before. You will see a way of healing that would have not occurred to you in the old energy.

Yes, there may be a short period of extended pain, but physical pain will be nothing when compared to the insights that you will receive from standing back for a period of time. These are all excellent and real life examples of things that will come to you, whether it is a toothache, whether it is somebody being angry at you, whether it is an election that takes place, whether it is a situation at work. Consciously stand back to see what is truly happening. Release the belief systems about what is right or wrong, good or bad. Stand back. There is a short wall that surrounds your new house. Stand behind it and you will come to understandings of how you can truly be a creator which is nothing like what you would have imagined.

QUESTION: As we moved into the First Circle of creation and exceeded the assignment, why should we want to regress and return to the original circle?

TOBIAS: In between your human lives on Earth, you do not go Home.. You do not go back to the original creation, to the First Circle. You go to an in-between zone where you are met by those in the angelic realms, including many who have also walked Earthly lives. When you first arrive at this heavenly way station, because you have released the physical body and because you feel so much lighter, there is a sense that this is heaven, that this is Home. But my friends, we tell you that it is not. You do not return back Home between Earthly lives. If you did you would not choose to come back to Earth. Also if you returned Home at this time, you would not recognize it. You would not recognize Home as you knew it before you left. This in itself is the subject of a much greater discussion. The very work that you have done as a human has changed the very nature of what you would call Home.

When we first started working with Cauldre, we mentioned that the humans literally created the stars in your universe. He bitterly challenged us about this. He thought that we were speaking in metaphors, and we told him that we were speaking literally. What you see in your physical universe – the new stars that are coming into being and the new discoveries – are things that you are creating, that you are creating through the work that you do here. As Cauldre was looking upon the stars the other night, he asked the question of us, "Is there indeed new life? Is there indeed human type life or any type of life out in the universe?" And our reply to him was, "Not much."

Your universe has certain life forms but none that are as complex as the human. There are – and some will be challenged here – no alien beings flying in little crafts from planet to planet, as you thought. What you are feeling and seeing are activities that took place before you ever came here. There were, in those dimensions, many activities that you are now interpreting as alien beings. But it is really YOU from the past. When you look into your universe, there is very little life form as you would know it.

There is tremendous energy form and structure and activity taking place, things that are not necessarily seen with the human eye. There are tremendous weavings of a new tapestry taking place in the universe. When Cauldre looked into the sky and realized that there was not much out there, he asked why would there be such an expansive universe. Our answer was simple: this is the foundation for the second creation – you are creating it as you go. We apologize for the lengthy answer but found it appropriate to deliver this information.

✧ ✧ ✧ ✧

QUESTION: Tobias, everything people say, including my own words, sounds like BS. Doing things feels like BS. Taking care of my body feels like BS. Can you comment on this? Also we know what Kryon has said about new science and the great stuff Dr. Todd (Ovokaitys) is doing, but again it sounds like BS, feels like BS. What role does science play when everything is a state of mind?

TOBIAS: Quite simply, you are looking outside for the answers, the secret ingredient, or the magic potion that is going to deliver you happiness and joy and peace. As you have discovered, it is not like this. It does not happen like this. You are not feeling a resonance with truth within you because you are looking outside.

You look at outside products. It is time to look within. It is time to accept your own humanness, which many of you have wanted to desperately reject. It is time to trust yourself to provide the "divine moment." It is not us, not the Eternal One, not a golden angel, but your own self. As you trust in self, you will begin to feel those divine moments, and within them there will be a truth that rings loud and clear for you. It is simply your own being saying, "You are looking in the wrong place." Listen to those words from Self, for there is much wisdom there.

✤ ✤ ✤ ✤

QUESTION: Dear Tobias, thank you for being here and sharing with us. My friend feels like she may be a walk-in. Can you talk about walk-ins? Is that what is going on with her or something else.

TOBIAS: Humans devise such clever games! There are very few cases of what you would know as a walk-in. This is not only difficult from a physics standpoint, but it is generally not appropriate from a spiritual standpoint. There are conditions where a human makes great changes in a very short period of time. They feel that they are reborn again within the same lifetime of their physical body. This is what many call a walk-in. There are other cases where there is such extreme denial of the human self that they choose to believe that the old bad person walked out and a new good person walked in.

Dear teachers, you will be working with many imbalances like this in your teaching. We ask you to be discerning with these people. It is time to talk to them about accepting their human self, and to accept all of the things that have transpired in the past. They will hold on tightly to concepts of things such as walk-ins and other things that humans entertain themselves with. Help them to gently and lovingly release that grip, and then to accept all that they are.

✤ ✤ ✤ ✤

QUESTION: Tobias, what can you tell us about "twin flames?"

TOBIAS: We refer you back to the previous answer. You are all that you are. Half of you was not left behind, waiting to reunite with you. ALL THAT YOU ARE AND WILL BECOME IS CONTAINED WITHIN YOUR BEING. Even what you call your Higher Self or True Self is not separate and apart from you. It is all contained within your consciousness and your being.

There are great love stories of humans who have met in the past and have shared very passionate relationships. They come back lifetime after lifetime and feel the flame of their souls. This is what WE call a twin flame. The concept that a part of you is floating around somewhere else – we do not so much understand.

As the new teachers, you are being challenged to accept your human self, to move away from denial, to move away from creating these situations and circumstances. Concepts such as dimensional ladders and twin flames and walk-ins – my friends, be discerning about what is really being said with these things. In the truest sense, yes, we are and always have been One. We are One in many different expressions. So in a sense philosophically, yes, we are all flames together. We are all bright flames that make one beautiful candle.

✥ ✥ ✥ ✥

QUESTION: Tobias, would you give me some information about something I just heard about – the Ashtar Command?

TOBIAS: We refer you back to the last two answers. (much audience laughter)

✥ ✥ ✥ ✥

QUESTION: Tobias, when I was young, I saw the image of Christ for years. I have always wondered about the purpose of the image and what was said to me.

TOBIAS: The purpose of the image was to remind you that you are not alone. The image of the Christ you saw was also a reminder to you of who you truly are – that you carry the Christ seed within you. It was a reminder of the work that you would do throughout the duration of your life. It was a reminder that you have the Christ seed within you, that you would be doing this divine work, and that it would be challenging.

✥ ✥ ✥ ✥

QUESTION: Explain our alien star-seeded parents.

TOBIAS: This is somewhat complex. We ask you not to think of yourselves as being derived from aliens from other planets, particularly porpoises! (much audience laughter) Look at the events that are transpiring in your life now. Look at the fears and blocks that are in your life now. These have their roots in the time before you came to Earth, after you crossed through the Wall of Fire. Those experiences were very intense. The experiences helped make it possible for you to come here in biological form. We ask you not to think of yourselves as beings created by grand aliens from other planets. Think of yourselves as being created by your own True Self, by your own Creator-self through very intense energetic experiences before you came here. You are the parent of yourself.

✤ ✤ ✤ ✤

QUESTION: As our physical bodies change, will this be evident to professionals who might examine our blood or DNA?

TOBIAS: Indeed, not only to those who read your energy, but also to those who look under a microscope. They will be somewhat shocked. They will ask many of you to undergo further testing. This is a good point to bring up here, for there is the potential for this to bring up fear within you that there is something wrong, that there is illness. We remind you to simply live in the divine moment. Let them test, if you so choose. They will see subtle differences, particularly in the cell structure and alignment. They will see changes in your skin and your eyes and your hair. And yes, indeed they will notice differences in your blood, in the balance of red and white cells, and also in the way the blood cells attract new types of cells, particularly the cells which provide healing and prevent illness.

✤ ✤ ✤ ✤

QUESTION: Are there ways to help increase our vibration, such as essential oils, homeopathy, etc.?

TOBIAS: Dear friends, it is already within you. It is within your DNA. It is yours. You already own it. These other things that you speak of – you do not own. It is not to condemn any of these products, for many of them have value. But until you begin the process within, they will have little or no effect on you. You have found this in your life up to now. You take these things, and there is brief and momentary benefit that comes from them, brief and momentary healing, but they are usually not the long term answer. Begin the process within. Begin the alignment within. Then when you take these substances in the future, they will be much more effective. You will also question yourself when you pull out your pocketbook as to whether they are really needed!

✣ ✣ ✣ ✣

QUESTION: Does meditation play a part in the new energy?

TOBIAS: Not as you know it. (chuckling) Cauldre shies away from this discussion and wonders whether things will be thrown at him! (audience laughter) Your meditations have been, for the most part, struggling and difficult. Indeed they helped you get to this point. We ask you to always honor that part of yourself. But as you move into the New Energy, you do not need to sit and meditate daily for a prescribed period of time and fight the thoughts coming through your mind. All you need to do, friends, is to allow and accept All That Is. Accept yourself, and live in the divine moment. You will find that you will desire quiet time to be by yourself, but it will be like a river of wisdom and love flowing through you, rather than a structured meditation. All of these things have served you well, but it is no longer necessary to go back to the old bookshelves. This is indeed the New Energy. When we began this series, we warned that some of this would be difficult and challenging. It would, in a sense, take away everything that has brought you to this point.

QUESTION: What can you tell us about love relationships during these times, especially for single Lightworkers?

TOBIAS: This is one of the most challenging areas, for many of those who are in the spiritual service find themselves alone. We know there is the desire in the heart to share with another. But there is a reason why you have given yourself this quiet time, this time of being alone. It is so that you can truly focus on your ascension process without distraction. Indeed it is not that you are not worthy or capable of love, but you have asked to be in the house by yourself, to go through these processes in order to become a teacher of the new energy.

As you live in the divine moment – oh, they will be attracted to you. They will come to you. They will see the light, and then it will be up to you to discern what is appropriate at that time. We know it is challenging to be on this path alone. It is difficult to see others at the stores, at the parks and at restaurants, enjoying each other's company. But dear friends, you have asked for this time of solitude. We do see this changing, but it is not something you must go out and seek. It will be brought to you in all appropriateness.

✥ ✥ ✥ ✥

QUESTION: A while back you told me to soak in sea salt in the bathtub. Do I need to keep doing that?

TOBIAS: We have often recommended to soak in the bathtub with the sea salt water. There are properties in the salts that will help pull out impurities within the physical body. They will also help pull out stress. This is something that we very much recommend. You are simply allowing these sea salts to help you to release things that are no longer appropriate. You will find this to be very beneficial.

✥ ✥ ✥ ✥

QUESTION: If our old self is dying or leaving and our new self is now here, have we ascended?

TOBIAS: Indeed it is not that the old self has died. The old self has completed its journey, its contract. And now it can be released. There is much honor in this. The term ascension is not one that we use so much, for there are many misunderstandings of this that come from your churches and even from your New Age materials. There is the assumption that when you ascend, you will immediately be healed of all things, that you will know all things, and that you can do all things. But in a sense, yes, indeed you are ascending. You are changing. You are now being able to accept your divinity in this reality. But we only caution you about what you assume ascension is. Again we ask you to understand that things will be quite different than what you have thought. They will be powerful and wonderful but we ask you to hold no assumption of what this ascension process is.

✥ ✥ ✥ ✥

QUESTION: With our vibration drawing all that we need to us as we sit in the "now" moment, how do we work with our runner angels?

TOBIAS: This is an excellent question. There are those on our side of the veil that are here specifically to assist, but they cannot do so until you create the intent and the energy behind this. The runners do not do it for you, but they can facilitate, and they do facilitate the process. This is both in terms of your experience on Earth and also multidimensionally. As you change your own resonance – as you draw to you all things that are appropriate, they, in a sense, are the ones who help get those things to you. They are the ones who on other levels are smoothing the barriers, if there are external barriers that are preventing these things from coming to you, or slowing down how they come to you. The runners, in a sense, are balancers of energy. They work with your energy to help balance, to bring the appropriate things in at the appropriate time. You can request and give intent for them to help, and then you will be more conscious of their assistance, but in a sense, they are also always doing this work.

✧ ✧ ✧ ✧

QUESTION: Tobias, I understand through reading channels from Sananda that we each have 16 parallel physical realities with many opposites to each other. I'm interested to know that in each of these realities are we all the same, i.e. in gender, and do we look the same in each reality as we do in this one?

TOBIAS: If this is what you choose, so be it

✧ ✧ ✧ ✧.

QUESTION: Are we in the process of merging all other realities into one reality and one physical form as we ascend?

TOBIAS: This is difficult to answer due to the human misconceptions about realities and dimensions and ascending. We use this question in particular to remind Shaumbra to live in the divine moment. All of these multilevel, multidimensional, multi-aspect realties – we do not know where you come up with these! There are many, many mansions, but these things you should not so much concern yourself with. They will indeed fragment you. They will fragment your energy.

Now, there are those who are called on as teachers and healers to bring back the fragmented parts that did not exist until you began to imagine them! We ask you to focus on the divine moment, on your being in the divine moment. We also – for Cauldre gets very nervous here – we have spoken that the information given here will not please all. It will not resonate with all, and it is not intended for all. It is indeed the classroom of the new energy, and we will use occasions like this to bring our work together. We will assist in bringing your work back into focus. Why would you want to worry about multidimensional aspects that even we do not understand or see?

We honor and thank you for this question for it gives us the opportunity to speak to your divinity, to your divinity that is present in this room, and in the space you are reading this in now. You will not find the answers to your questions in some complex realities that do not necessarily exist! You will find the answers in your divine moment. Do you understand this?

✧ ✧ ✧ ✧

QUESTION: Tobias, I have cancer, how do I get rid of it?

TOBIAS: It is to honor the cancer, not to get rid of it. Place it in the Oven of Grace. Place it there without agenda and allow grace to find the balance. Cancer, dear friends, is simply imbalance manifested in the cells of your body. It is that simple. Those who work with the new technologies will see this soon. They will understand how to adjust it with the frequencies they work with..

You who ask us this question, there is a more sophisticated treatment available to you today. You do not need to experiment, do not need to have trials. It is available to you today. It is powerful. You are powerful. This imbalance that knocks at your physical body, simply place it in the Oven of Grace. And after you place it in there one day, then place it there another day and another day. Do this with love each day. My dear, there is a tool and a gift in this for you. The gift is that you will one day sit before others who are in disbelief and talk about how you brought balance into your own life. You have chosen this for yourself so that you will be a teacher for others. Use this Oven of Grace, my dear. You will understand.

✧ ✧ ✧ ✧

QUESTION: Speak of the power of prayer.

TOBIAS: In the new energy you will learn to create in a different way. Prayer may be appropriate for those in the old energy. We will work with you to create on new levels. We challenge you to release your old concepts of prayer and intent. They have been valuable tools for bringing you to this place, but it is time to release these. You will go prayer-less. You will create in the Divine Moment.

✤ ✤ ✤ ✤

QUESTION: Tobias, over the past month I have withdrawn more and more from the people in my life. That's OK, but I find myself engaging in constant negative dialoguing with those people in my mind. Lots of chatter, usually doesn't feel good after the fact. I've been balancing it on the hormonal imbalance, but somehow that doesn't seem to be true either. What's going on? Why can't I seem to stay on the other side of the short wall?

TOBIAS: It will take conscious effort on your part to stay on the other side of the short wall. You will continually find yourself pulled back into duality. Right now you are experiencing the energy of the Two Earths moving apart, you are experiencing relationships moving apart that are no longer appropriate. You are hearing chattering in your head, because you are still connected with them in many ways. Know my friends, that as the energy of the new earth moves to new levels, these old chains that connected you to the past will dissolve in love. They will dissolve slowly and surely. You agonize about the chatterings in your mind. Simply understand that is part of the releasing process. When you have these discussions in your mind, simply stand behind the short wall and honor these people, even though they have caused you much friction and challenge in your life. Simply honor them. As you consciously do this, the last vestiges of the old energy will dissolve.

✤ ✤ ✤ ✤

QUESTION: Tobias, is there anything that you would like to relay to me at this time?

TOBIAS: Yes, indeed there is one thing and it is for all of you. In this time you are creating the weavings of the New Energy Earth, for that is why you are here, that is why you are reading this. Dear friends, please keep it simple, please keep it simple. We will remind you of this over and over again. There is the tendency to come up with great conspiracy theories. There is the tendency to come up with realities and dimensions that do not exist. There is a tendency to even come up with fear scenarios. My friends, if you choose empowerment in your life, if you choose to be creators in the New Energy, it would be well to keep it simple. We have walked with you in these past four lessons about very simple steps to help you maintain a focus. These are powerful tools. Your divinity desires to come forth, and it needs your human Self to cooperate.

✢ ✢ ✢ ✢

QUESTION: Dear Tobias, I have two questions about music. First, in a prior Question & Answer session, you alluded to the fact that you have music where you are. Can you tell us anything about what it's like and what it's used for and how it's different from ours? Second, in the classroom of the new spiritual energy on earth, are there any new tools, intents, or powers that a creative, spiritually-minded musician should know about that they could use with that?

TOBIAS: As a creator in the New Energy, and as one who understands the vibrations of music, you have the most awesome opportunity for creation. Your music IS vibration. Allow yourself to experience even more balanced and finer vibrations than ever before and then flow these through your systems, and manifest them in your music. Oh, we see awesome opportunities for you here! Your music will have qualities that will transcend the vibrations you have been working with up to now.

On our side of the veil, we do not usually call it music, and we do not have those here who are proficient in violins and trombones and such (chuckling). We play with vibrations that we create from within ourselves. We will sit with other entities, and we will create tonal or vibrational balances and harmonies. Sometimes we specifically create imbalances for certain effects! Our music here, while beautiful, does not have the depth and the soul of the music that you create on earth. It is difficult to describe this without actually playing our music for you. But in a way, you hear our music when we come in at the beginning of these circles. You hear our vibration, and we are in a way, purring as we come into your space. The next time we gather like this, feel those tones when we first come in.

We deeply enjoy your music, for it literally tell the stories of your lifetimes, of your experiences, of your pasts, of your loves. Oh, it is not words that are stored in what you would call the Akashic records. It is music, it is vibrations, for in those tones are the stories of Earth.

QUESTION: Tobias, you said that gay people have a "clear marble" that does not ever turn light or dark. Is this like a male or female energy? What specific functional benefits does this setup provide?

TOBIAS: This clear marble that we speak of in our metaphor does not take on the full energetic characteristics of the white or the black. It will lean towards one or the other, but will remain more in the gray shades. With other humans, the clear marble will take on the full characteristics and aspects of either the white or the black. The purpose is to have more flexibility, and to have less specific definition to the balance of energy. The purpose is to provide a bridge, in a sense, between light and dark, rather than take on the characteristics of duality. It is also to provide a new balance of the duality of male and female energy. The male/female energy is one of the strongest examples of duality in the second creation. This unusual attribute of the clear marble was specifically chosen by the human angels who you call "gay." We find that such an interesting word – for perhaps there is a certain happiness in not taking on such a strong polarity! They are helping to set the new template that will shatter this old concept of male and female energies.

QUESTION: Please expound further on the simple metaphor of the marbles.

TOBIAS: We use the metaphor of the marbles to help you understand your energy composition and the balance of duality. When you crossed over from the first creation, your oneness was divided it into two. These became light and dark, or positive and negative, or whatever terms you choose to define the polarity.

The third element – what we defined as the clear marble – is much like a chameleon. The clear marble takes on attributes of the white or the black to provide an offset balance of energy. This offset balance of energy then provides the force, friction, and propulsion that are needed for your human experiences. We do not mean this literally, in terms of having "marbles" within you. They simply represent the energy balance of 1/3:2/3 within your being.

We use this example of the marbles to help you understand why you have been feeling certain things in your physical and emotional being. In addition to the white, black and clear marbles, there now comes the fourth element. This is changing your entire energy balance. You are going through many changes in your being.

This fourth element is coming into your human energy composition. Cauldre asks here, "Where does this element come from? Does it come from the First Circle?" And the answer to that is, "No." This is difficult to explain here, but this fourth element is the "child" of the white and the black. It is birthed from the relationship of your white and the black energy balance. It comes from the great love between these two. It is what you would call the Christ child.

Understand that all of these things we speak of are happening within you at this time. There is the birthing of the Christ consciousness within you. That is why you are experiencing the things you are now in your life.

We will spend more time with this concept in our future discussions. We ask each of you here and connecting with us to not over-intellectualize this process. It is very simple. Look at it from its simplest aspect. The fourth element is simply the birthing of the Christ child within you.

✧ ✧ ✧ ✧

QUESTION: Tobias, I am more confused than ever before. Take away old metaphysical ways of thinking. Don't ask anyone. Don't try to create the way you used to. My guides are not available. Just accept and allow. How do I get this task accomplished, i.e., change careers?

TOBIAS: You are trying much too hard! You are looking for answers in all places, other than within your being. For you we specifically suggest a one-week vacation! You need time away from your mind, away from your worries. We have been working with you – and with all the others – on the very deliberate series of steps to help you release the old. This will allow a new balance into your life. Indeed we ask you to be patient, but you struggle much with this. You will tire if you continue these activities.

Again we prescribe a one-week vacation away from others. It is much needed. In this time we will come to work with you. We are addressing the one who wrote the question. We are not asking all of Shaumbra to go take a one-week vacation! (laughter)

✣ ✣ ✣ ✣

QUESTION: Tobias, it is interesting that you refer to a Wall of Fire versus the human understanding of hell. Will you help us understand that?

TOBIAS: Dear friends, it is quite the same. It is no surprise that we use this term of the Wall of Fire. In your religious books, the Wall of Fire is depicted as hell, of being sent to hell for an eternity. Has it not seemed like hell in some cases with your many lifetimes on Earth? When you left Home and went through this Wall of Fire, you knew that you could never return Home. The Home that you left would never be the same because of your work.

We do not mean that you will never reunite with your divine self and with Spirit and All That Is. What is meant in this concept is that all things changed when you went through the Wall of Fire. It is interesting that your own religions have used this concept but changed it to mean something bad, something that does not come from truth. But the symbols and energetic elements are still there.

✣ ✣ ✣ ✣

QUESTION: Tobias, the story of Taylor felt very personal. Was the story of Taylor a metaphor or parable or was Taylor an actual person?

TOBIAS: Taylor is a compilation of many people. It is based on actual experiences of those who are Shaumbra. There have been a few instances when we told a story of a specific person, but in the case of Taylor, it was a compilation.

The stories we share with you should feel familiar. We are simply mirroring back your own experiences. We are putting it in front of you in the form of a story to help you see it more clearly. This information and the energy behind it should feel familiar. It should feel like it comes from you, and it should feel balanced. That is how you will know that this is right place for you.

✣ ✣ ✣ ✣

QUESTION: Is there any chance that there is a special magic pill or shortcut you could share?

TOBIAS: (laughing) This is an amusing question, and we will give you an amusing answer. If you are looking for a shortcut or for a magic pill, our advice to you and all others is to simply stand out of your way. Stand out of your way! There is so much of your intellect that gets involved. But we also see that you truly have fun with this. You truly enjoy playing with this! If you would like a very fast process, stand out of your old human way and allow the changes to come through rapidly and bless them as they do.

QUESTION: It seems that the concept of two worlds is more evident and discomforting. What can we do to handle this better and still live in both?

TOBIAS: Handle this through compassion and understanding. Understand that you are living more and more each day in the New Energy. Understand that there is great honor for those who stay in the old energy. There is the need for those to tether and to balance the old energy. Not all of you can move into the new at one time. This would cause a tremendous energy imbalance. Honor the ones you see along your way who are in the old energy. Bless them and know that one day you will be their teacher. It is time for you to set the example. While it appears that you will be increasing the chasm between the old energy Earth and the new, there will be a bridging of this chasm in the years ahead. You will be the ones who help guide the others across that bridge.

✣ ✣ ✣ ✣

QUESTION: Tobias, can you explain the disappearance of my Oven of Grace?

TOBIAS: Indeed, and this is a profound question. Dear friend, you have simply integrated it! Look around inside your new house. There is not a lot there! When you integrate the elements of your house, they seemingly disappear because they are now within you. As you continue to work with these tools and integrate them, they will be a natural part of your process. They will meld into your being. You will not have to consciously focus on these. You will not have to bring these into your intellectual mind. This will occur naturally. Dear friend, the oven has disappeared because you now own it!

✧ ✧ ✧ ✧

QUESTION: Tobias, I know I have made the decision to stay on earth and go into the New Energy. And I have been doing the things I need to do in order to be healthy. So what if I change my mind? This new energy stuff is not easy. Do I have to consciously kill myself if I choose to leave? (audience laughter)

TOBIAS: Now, this is a good but a difficult question. As all of you know, it is difficult to turn back once you have gained a certain amount of wisdom. There is also within all of you a commitment that was given within the past few years. You were given the choice of returning to our side, but you chose to stay on Earth. In a sense you have said to us, "No matter how much I complain (audience laughter), I will continue with my journey."

We know the pressures are incredibly challenging and you need a type of reprieve. There are times when you can turn off on the wayside, when you can get off of the main highway. You can rest and relax and recharge at this time. You can stay at the wayside as long you want. But what we have noticed with Shaumbra is that you pull over, you open the door for a moment, you get back in and you get back on the journey.

So we tell you in answer to your question – there are waysides, there are rest stops along the way. However, if you choose to no longer continue the journey, you cannot erase what you have learned. You will find it irritating to sit in a space of not moving forward, a space of not continuing to evolve. You will want to get back to your awakening process.

✧ ✧ ✧ ✧

QUESTION: Tobias, did all humans go through the Wall of Fire in order to get here to Earth?

TOBIAS: Indeed, all who are human went through the Wall of Fire. Know that we speak in metaphors for easier understanding; but all who are walking the earth at this time crossed over from the First Circle to get here. And the new ones that will come in must also cross through this Wall of Fire. But it will be different for them because you have paved the way. There was one who spoke earlier tonight (author Ilene Kimsey, Golden Wisdom Beyond the Emerald City) of the Yellow Brick Road and the place of Oz. The Yellow Brick Road is the path that has been paved, and the Emerald City is certainly your Earth. Along this path, you encountered many experiences, including fear, friendship, honor, wisdom, courage, love and many challenges. You created this Yellow Brick Road for the others to follow.

QUESTION: Tobias, can you explain why my interest in things changes so often? I get very passionate about something and then a short time later I no longer have any interest it. I'm thinking of getting a job but I am afraid I will lose interest in it after a short time. What's this all about?

TOBIAS: As we have said in previous discussions [see Tobias channel December 9, 2000], there were periods of time when the clear marble, the third marble, would move very slowly between the black and the white. Then in much longer intervals of time when the black and the white reverse roles. The process of switching roles was slow. As we have said in our discussion last month, this is intensifying now. It is happening very frequently. You will feel this within your being. You will feel rapid change. You will feel hot one day and cold the next. You will feel impassioned one day and disimpassioned the next.

These are all part of the process of the changes that are taking place at the deepest inner levels of your being. As the fourth element comes in to balance the three original, many of you will also feel inner conflict, for the three do not so much want this "foreign" element in. So you will feel great inner turmoil. This may be represented outside of you by the feeling of rejecting people, rejecting things, or feeling you are being rejected. Remember, these are all symbols of what is happening at the deep inner levels inside of you. Understand that changes are taking place. When they become somewhat overwhelming, go into your new house, close the windows, pull the blinds shut, and go into your Inner Room. Go to your Inner

Room and smile and know that all of these changes are appropriate. Know that within you is a Divine Balance, and all things will find their natural level. Just as water seeks its level, so does divinity.

QUESTION: Dear Tobias, recently many of us have experienced very defined distortions in time and space, which included profound dizziness and even nausea. Can you tell us whether some important influx or shift to earth energy may have occurred recently?

TOBIAS: It is – we say this and underline it – an internal thing that is happening to you. Do not look to the sun, do not look to the comets, do not look to the numerology of the day. These are the result of changes occurring within you.

These consciousness shifts will generally occur at appropriate times where you do not have to worry about consequences. It will be when you are standing in a safe space, not while you are driving down the road. There will be a feeling of disconnect or dizziness, or a feeling of spinning or falling even though there is a floor underneath you. When this happens, you are going through consciousness changes. Changes are a key to the entire process that you are going through. These are literal changes but they are also signs that you are changing.

QUESTION: Tobias, you mentioned that our bodies will begin to do all kinds of things the doctors won't be able to explain. Will we be able to regrow organs, limbs and teeth? How long until we begin to experience this?

TOBIAS: The keys of your biology are not set up to do this – yet. We do not see that this is going to happen in your lifetime, in the biology that you are in. On the other hand, dear friends, we do not want to limit your ability as creators! We simply want to help you understand that the keys for doing this are not necessarily in place.

However, if there is enough passion on your part, and there is enough communication with your inner biological and spiritual being, indeed you have the potential to create this. The new ones coming in will begin to have the first of those keys for organ regeneration and rejuvenation. It is one of the things that will distinguish them and will amaze the scientists. However, there are many things you can do with your biology at this time. There is faster healing. There is greater communication between the individual parts cells that can speed the process. And again, much of what you are able to do in your current biology will baffle the doctors who look at you. Much of what you do in your current emotional and spiritual state will baffle even the psychics who look at the old energy ways. When they look at your aura, they will not see one and they will think you are dead! (audience laughter) It is because they are looking in the wrong place. There are many changes you are going through, but what you have spoken of in this question, with the literal regrowth of organs and tissues, will be somewhat challenging to do, but we applaud you for trying. Your efforts will help set the energy for the "keys" that future generations will use.

✧ ✧ ✧ ✧

QUESTION: Tobias, what is the relationship between our self, and our Higher Self and our True Self? I've been accustomed to equating those two terms. Any insights would be welcome.

TOBIAS: Dear, dear friend, you have put your Higher Self and your Divine Self and your True Self outside of your house. They would like to come in now. It is all the same. As we discussed earlier, you are in one room of your house, yet there are many rooms. The many rooms under one roof are what you would call your True Self. Begin to open to the many rooms. It is ALL within you. You think that there is some being out there, a large golden angel that is outside of you. Yet, your divinity is at the smallest level within you and it grows from there. It does not come banging on the door of your house. It illuminates from within your being. The separation that you have placed between yourself and your divinity and Spirit needs to come to an end now. Bring it together within your house.

✧ ✧ ✧ ✧

QUESTION: Tobias, what can I do to assist in my growth ascension taking into consideration that for each of us the journey is slightly different?

TOBIAS: First, spend more time in your New House, the metaphor for all that you are. There are songs, there are tones and harmonies that come from within. You have been wandering the streets outside of your house, looking and searching. You have been traveling the highways and the byways from town to town, looking for these parts of yourself. Bring this inside now. Listen to the vibration.

Also, there is a vibration that sets forth the activity of creation in a more dynamic form. It is a "propelling" vibration. When you are creating, when you are using the broad stroke, there is a vibration. We will attempt to define this in the human sound spectrum. (pause) It is similar to EH-LA-TONE. (struggling to properly channel this tone) It is a vibration of EH-LA- TONE. EH-LA-TONE. This is a vibrational quality that intensifies the creation process. Allow the vibration of EH-LA-TONE to be in your broad stroke. It will propel it, it will add more dynamics to it. This is something that will help initiate the creation energy. It is a vibration that adds more force to it. Work with this vibration. It is like adding an exclamation point to your own creation.

Now we return to your question. Simply listen to the song of your New House. You will be guided appropriately. Then do not be in fear of taking the large brush and creating that first stroke.

✧ ✧ ✧ ✧

QUESTION: About a year ago my brother fell approximately 30 feet from a platform, breaking his pelvis and several vertebrae. He has recovered physically but he now believes two aliens have invaded his physical body as a result of injuries to his etheric body and an operation on his wrist. He also feels that his etheric body is being attacked by alien parasites. In the past year he has contacted a number of healers about his condition and had a number of healings done, so far without success. Can you shed some light on what is going on and what corrective measures are needed to rid him of this condition.

TOBIAS: Dear friend, this accident was a way of jarring and shaking loose some old issues that go way back. The fall literally brought these to the surface. Now you have a situation where old issues have been brought to the surface, because it is time to look at them, to bless them and to heal them. Blaming this on the aliens is giving away your own power. It is giving power to "a lie", or an alien, giving power to something that does not have power over you. We also ask, why would the aliens want to come into your brother's body and live like that? There are many other places they could go! A fruit tree would be a better place for them to live. (audience laughter) Understand that many of the old imbalances from the past come forward now for you to love and to honor and to bless. Then they will go away and you will not be unbalanced. However, if your brother continue to believe that aliens are running his life, we will gladly sit and watch while he plays this game, because we love him unconditionally.

QUESTION: Dear Tobias, recently I showed the video of the December 2000 Tobias channeling to inmates at the federal prison. One of the inmates asks the following question: "Why does Tobias want to come here and be with us? Is he coming because he feels sorry for us poor slobs? Is he going to watch my back? Why does he want to come here?" The inmate became very agitated as he spoke and there were flashes of dull mustard yellow and dull brown in his auric field. Something seemed to bring up an issue of betrayal that had caused him great pain and landed him in the prison. Is there a message for him and others?

TOBIAS: Dear friend, this is such an appropriate question! We will share a story that brings up many emotions. I, Tobias, died in a prison, in a lifetime long, long ago. I was an owner of land, of property. This was not during the lifetime that I went by the name of Tobias, the one where I was thrown out of your scriptures. (audience laughter) It was a lifetime that occurred afterwards. I was an owner of land and there was a person in a position of authority who very much cherished my land. He found a way to have me imprisoned. I was of a middle age and with a family. I was placed in prison to die.

Now, I had much anger with this. I had much feeling of betrayal by Spirit. I could not understand why I would have ever created this for myself as a human. Yet this was one of the most significant lifetimes for me. Prison became a time of quiet and reflection, a time of true connection with Spirit. After going through the initial process of anger and betrayal, I came to understand Spirit and God within me. I died not an unhappy man. I died not in anger. I died having come to a new realization and a new enlightenment. In this lifetime, I chose to free myself from all of the bars that I had put around myself in the past, literally and figuratively.

The one who brings forth these messages, Cauldre, the one I call my son, has also spent time in prison. Not so long ago, but not in this lifetime – thank you. (chuckling) He asked us to put that in. (audience laughter) Now it was not so many lifetimes ago that he spent some time behind the bars for rather reckless activities, which he does not want us to go into. (audience laughter) During this time he came to understand some realities of human conditions and power. He came to understand that there were injustices in your world. These knocked him down a few notches from the high chair that he sat on!

It is appropriate for this energy of the Crimson Circle to find it's way to those who feel trapped and imprisoned, to those who feel unworthy, to those who feel no hope. For the energy of this circle is about hope and truth and love.

There will not be many words we need to say to these ones that are called inmates; we will sit with them, we will ask them to feel a movement of energy. If they are willing to open their beings, we will go to the deepest levels when we gather with them in prison. We will go to the deepest levels to say, "We love you dearly", "We know your are family", "We know your are here for a reason of your soul", "We will sit with you for a while in the greatest of compassion because we have been there."

QUESTION: Do I really belong to this group? And if so, why have I had trouble physically getting here and why have I not experienced all the things others seem to be going through, the pain and the difficulties, etc.?

TOBIAS: First of all, we say that each path is different. Each path is different and for you to say you must be going through a certain set of experiences is not being fair to yourself. It has been difficult for you to get here because you are not so sure you want to be here! You're not so sure you want to be part of the changes that are occurring. You are not so sure if you want to be part of this first wave of humans going into this New Energy. And for this, there is respect and honor, for there are ones who will go first and ones who will go through in the second and third and fourth wave.

Are you family? Indeed! Are you one who we have known before? Indeed, otherwise you would not be attracted to the Crimson Circle. There are those who are given these channels to read and they cannot get past the first line. It is not appropriate for them at this time. There is other work for them to do. Are you family? Indeed you are and you are always welcome here, you are always welcome.

QUESTION: Tobias could you discuss applications of astrology to us as lightworkers at this time?

TOBIAS: It is best dear friends to put down your ways of old astrology at this time – for yourself. For humans who are not walking into the energy of the new earth, astrology is absolutely appropriate for them. For yourselves, you have moved into your new lifetime. How do you chart that? What degrees do you place on the birth of your new Self? It is no longer appropriate to be guided by the stars. We remind you that you created these very stars! You have transcended the need to be structured by the energy of the stars – objects and energies that you placed there!

You are creating the stars that have not been discovered quite yet. You are the ones shaping their energy patterns. Now, we know there are some who will not so much like this remark. We are not condemning astrology by any means. It is still appropriate for most humans, as most humans are still walking in the old energy. For Shaumbra, if you get a reading from the stars or from ones who see energy, they will not understand what is going on with you. They will not see your energy field and they will be shocked — because they are looking in the old place. Your energy field is now in a new place. For those who read your stars and your charts, it will not feel so right to you any more. It will feel like something from the past. And if you choose to let the stars rule you now in your new energy, it will hurt.

QUESTION: Tobias, are you the twin flame of someone who is now a human?

TOBIAS: We previously discussed the concept of "twin flame". Dear friends, there is not a lost part of you or me, in all of creation. If the talk of "twin flame" is meant to express love for two beings who walk together, and the intent is to say they are the same in many ways – they are deeply in love – there is good energy here. However, if the intent of the "twin flame" is to fill in a part of you that you feel is incomplete, you will search the world and the universe in an unhappy journey.

You are complete in yourself! The feeling of being incomplete is the residue of going through the shattering in the Wall of Fire. Is it not amusing to you – the relationship of the words "twin flame" and "Wall of Fire"? (audience laughter) There is not another part of you that is lost. It was just an experience you went through in the Wall of Fire. You and I are complete unto ourselves.

✧ ✧ ✧ ✧

QUESTION: Tobias, children committing what is categorized as adult crimes have been in the headlines recently. What is this and what does the resolution look like?

TOBIAS: It is very simple. Through your news, you are seeing the two earths – the old and the new – at conflict with each other. You are seeing them trying to find resolution and balance.

There are also some cases where the students are trying to resolve old karmic matters in a very quick manner. They do not want to go through lifetime after lifetime balancing karma. So they are attempting to do it very quickly.

In other cases it is the frustration of human mass consciousness wanting to break out of the old energy ways. The students are rebelling against abuse: being picked on, being degraded, about not being accepted for who they are. This is raising anger within them and they are expressing it in these ways.

We have no judgment of these things. We know it is natural and appropriate. We know also that you view these as very negative situations. But dear friends, stand behind the short wall for a moment. Look at what is really happening here. Look at the attention it is bringing to the old ways. It is bringing attention to old ways that need to change now. To you this may appear to be radical, to be violent, but dear friends, we can tell you that these acts have been done in love and they are received in love. It is up to you and the others who see these events, who listen to your news, to take the wisdom from them.

We see these clashes continuing to intensify. They will go beyond your schools. They will intensify until there is an acknowledgment that the old ways, the old institutions and the old hierarchies need to come down. Stand behind the short wall and understand these things are all part of the process of moving from the old energy. Love all of those who are involved in these things.

QUESTION: Tobias, in experiencing this new knowingness of ALL, I find my vision of relationships is completely changed. There is no sense of a need for exclusions of loving one for another. Please speak to the concept of marriage and its place in the new energy.

TOBIAS: (chuckling) Now Cauldre does not always like what we have to say! He worries about those who will throw stones at him and at his house!

In a sense you are very correct in this. We are treading on thin ice here! We will say politically –in deference to Cauldre – that indeed your relationships will change. At its very core, the relationships of a male to a female originate in the old energy. They are based in duality. It is duality to say, "We will commit to each other no matter how happy or miserable we are. We are here to learn of this balance of this thing called duality."

New Energy relationships will be different. You will not feel the need to bind another in the institution of marriage. You will be able to live happily with each other without the old contracts. Or, you may chose to live happily by yourself. You will not need another person to be complete. There will also be some who will live happily together in groups but yet maintain their own individuality.

This may challenge some of you based on your belief systems of what is right and wrong. We ask again that you stand behind the short wall and observe what is truly happening. (chuckling) And Cauldre tells us this was a very political answer to your question! (audience laughter)

QUESTION: Tobias, can you tell us more about Divine Passion. Is it a passion for something in particular? Where does it come from?

TOBIAS: This passion comes from your origins, from the Kingdom of God. It is your birthright. It has followed you up to the time you came to Earth. Divine Passion is something that we will not attempt to define here for, saying this with a wink to you, we know that humans will tend to analyze our words too much. That is why we used a very simple symbol of the Fruit of the

Rose. Receive this within you and the experience will be yours.

In answer to your question, you will have a unique and individual experience with your Divine Passion. We suggest to you not try to intellectualize it, simply experience it.

QUESTION: Tobias, please speak to us about our sexuality.

TOBIAS: Hmmm. (audience laughter) This is another area where you will find changes! As many of you have already found, there is a time of disempassionment in your own sexual drive. This is not caused by age, to answer the one who just thought the question. (audience laughter) Indeed as you move from the old energy into the new, as you go from duality into this new earth, you release many things. In the past you may have been passionate about the making of love, which you call sex. Most of you will go through a period of withdrawal, of wanting to be by yourself, of not wanting to interact with another human in this fashion. You have found that you do not so much care about it and at times it is even less than pleasurable.

In the story of Catherine, she cried for this was something too that had gone from her life. She had enjoyed a strong emotional and strong physical relationship in the past. Now these things were gone and she felt there was something wrong with her. She looked at those who she worked with, those who she knew, and she saw them still caring about things like sex. She saw them still caring about things at work. She saw them still involved in family matters and in family dramas. She wondered what was wrong with her that she did not care so much. Catherine was simply moving from the old energy into the new.

As you receive the Fruit of the Rose, the passion that is your birthright, you will find – and we laugh here – we are cracking up here as you would say – (audience laughter) you will find a new type of sexuality within your being that we are not so much allowed to talk about now. (Cauldre is arguing with Tobias about pursing this subject). That is why we are laughing, for there is great humor in this. It will not be like the old type of making love, the old type of sex that you were used to. This will be something new. Yes, you will be able to experience this with somebody who has not moved into the New Energy because this will be something that comes from within you. So you do not need to go out and find a partner who is only in the New Energy. For as you would say, this would be slim pickings! (outbreak of audience laughter)

QUESTION: Tobias, recently I've chosen to activate my Merkabah. It felt appropriate to do so at this time. Are there any pitfalls, problems or opportunities that might come going through this process while going through this process of working with the new spiritual energies of this group?

TOBIAS: Dear one, we do not mean to wag a finger at you here, but listen to our words. You have an intellectual concept of the Merkabah. The Merkabah is real, but is not what you intellectualize it to be. The Merkabah, as you think of it, is an element of the old energy. It will be difficult to try to activate your Merkabah while you are also trying to walk through the process of these lessons and moving into the New Energy. It is something you do not truly understand.

The concept of the Merkabah is a holdover of the old energy. We suggest that you release this and allow what you consider to be the Merkabah to take the highest order of energy, instead of defining it in your mind. In other words, we ask you to release this concept to its highest good. Now, we understand we have asked you and others to release many of the old ways that you consider to be New Age. (chuckling) Cauldre gets very nervous about this, for he worries that we are attacking all of the old energy ways. We remind you that we are not. These old energy ways have served you well to this point. You will feel the thorn of the rose if you attempt to hold on to old energy ways. If you grasp the rose and attempt to hold on to old energy ways, the thorns will cause you pain. We ask you to receive the Fruit of the Rose and do not try to control it.

This group is among the first to walk into the New Energy. We are challenging you to release the ways of the old, even though you have only known them for a short period of time. The Merkabah is a concept that has its origins in truth, but it has been greatly distorted. In the New Energy, you will not have a thing called a Merkabah that is separate and different from you, and is outside of you. You will have something that comes from within you. You will not have this outer revolving energy field of what you call the Merkabah. Instead you will have something that glows and grows from within. We know we are challenging you and many of the concepts that you hold, but you have agreed to be among the first to walk in this new energy.

✧ ✧ ✧ ✧

QUESTION: Tobias, I've had 4 miscarriages and find myself happily pregnant again. You mentioned previously that many of the new children might come in stillborn but that an energy pathway had been created. Is it true in my case with the miscarriages or was there something else going on? Also, at what point in a pregnancy does a soul choose to become a newborn? Have I been selected by a soul, or is my fetus still up for grabs?

TOBIAS: The miscarriages you speak of were a matter of timing. It was not the appropriate time for the angel to be with you. Your desires to become pregnant and to have a child were very strong. It was not the appropriate time. The child angel that chooses to come in knows when the time of both the earth and your time is appropriate. Your (pausing) — we are speaking here to this angel child — this child-to-be asks you to pay particular attention to your health. You have the tendency to become very stressed. This makes it difficult for the child. We know you are asking if it will be a boy or girl and it is not appropriate to discuss that now. Your stress makes it difficult for this one to come to Earth in a gentle way. You will want to spend much time nurturing yourself. The one who is your mate will give you the care that you need, but you must allow it to be. There are times when you push this away.

There is much that we would like to say here, but some of it is not appropriate at this time. There are dynamics that are being set up for a new type of energy attribute for this child to carry in. There are many who are working to make this possible but it is most important for you, for you dear one, to relax, to breathe deeply, to not stress. Do not put the expectations on yourself that you are doing right now. Release these expectations.

When does the energy of the angel enter the human body? This varies. It generally happens within a day or so after delivery. There are constant connections and communications between the biological cells and the angel baby that is coming in, but the energy of the incoming angel does not actually come in fully until a day or so after delivery. Now there are cases where the energy comes in slowly and does not fully integrate for up to a year after delivery. There are reasons for this. But generally it is shortly after physical birth. There are energetic connections between the cells of the fetus and the angel baby before delivery takes place. These intensify as you get closer to delivery. This is why it is so important for you to release expectations. Know you are being surrounded by love. You are being bathed in love. Accept the help from those on your side. This is a very blessed and sacred and special child that comes forth but this child is also one who may teach you rather challenging lessons of your own.

QUESTION: Tobias, it seems that with all the negative things in the news, people are being forced to explore their dark side, the parts of themselves that have not been consciously explored but indeed dictate their actions. I presume some of these aspects can be healed. Can you comment more on this process and the intensity in the coming months?

TOBIAS: Indeed what you are seeing in your headlines is the conflict between the old energy and the new. There are energies that have been suppressed for a long time that are choosing to be free now. There are also old unresolved karmas that are seeking a balance. In these next few years of time, dear friends, you will see much turmoil around you, but it does not have to be within you. This is the lesson of standing behind the short wall.

As we mentioned many months ago, you will see your stock markets go up and down without apparent logic. This is the attempt to find a balance between the old and the new. These will be the adjustments that are necessary to go on. As we mentioned before, you will continue to see your earthquakes. You will see the shatterings that take place, for even within the Earth is the attempt to transition from the old to the new. As you well know, it is not so easy to release the old and go into the new. There are energies that cry out for attention. There are other elements and energies that do not want to be released. There is even your human ego, as you would call it, which is not so sure it is ready to give up this control.

Each time you look at your headlines and see the shootings in the schools and in your public places, and yes, (emotional) even of the airports – these are difficult things. They tear at your heart. We know. Understand the appropriateness of this and understand that this is simply part of the process. It is, in a way, about understanding the dark side in answer to the question.

Most humans have been taught that there is right and wrong. It is the old duality, the old energy. In the new energies you are finding that there is the

ALL. It is no longer about left, right, or center. It is no longer about the white marble and the dark marble. It is about the "four" that work together.

These will be difficult months to go through if you read your newspaper. You will see much drama and much trauma. Again, dear friends, each of you now is beginning to live in your new house. It is not that you are isolated from these things, but you have deeper understanding. We will continue to talk of these things that happen on your Earth, but each time you see this, understand this is part of the transition into the New Energy. This is the very reason why teachers will be needed, teachers like you. This is why we continue to encourage you on your path. There will be a need for those who are have learned to integrate their divinity, those who have walked in the New Energy. There will be a need for hundreds, and then thousands, and then tens of thousands of teachers of the New Energy of Earth.

QUESTION: Tobias, I've always thought of suicide as a leap of faith. Would you comment on assisted suicide?

TOBIAS: There are those who know it is time to leave. They are not necessarily depressed, for they have gone through that stage. They are not angry, for they have also walked through those emotions. They know it is time to leave but sometimes the physical body does not want to go. The physical body in the old energy has somewhat of a mind of its own, as you have discovered. For those who choose assisted suicide, they know at their core level that it is time to go. They've had plenty of talks with themselves, with Spirit, and the angels. They know it is time. Dear friends, there is no judgment or condemnation on our part for those who choose to leave. There is as much joy and celebration when they return to our side as any others. In their hearts they know it is time to go. In their contracts they have already worked out with the others who come to assist them with this process. It is the thought of the Crimson Council that this should be a sacred and honored time for the human, not a time of shame and guilt.

QUESTION: Tobias, please tell us the story of your sojourn on Earth wherein you died in prison and did not have the fortitude to return. Tell us the lessons you learned, the despair, fear, anger, and desolation. If I could read all of the real experiences of a real angel and the benefit that lifetime was to all of us – if I could read of a personal account of a journey in this dimension, and it was someone we actually knew of, I would have something I could relate to.

TOBIAS: (chuckling) I will summarize, for this is a long story that will be contained in a one of the books that Cauldre will write. (audience laughter) In this lifetime I chose to be imprisoned. At my soul level I was working to break out of the conscious prison which I had placed myself in. I had achieved much that I wanted to as a human in the many lifetimes that I had. The lifetimes in Atlantis were indeed the most powerful, but yet the most traumatic for me. As my final lifetime upon Earth – in that particular cycle – I chose to die in prison in order to truly understand the barriers that I had placed around myself.

I chose to die alone, so that I would have to rely on those powers and those energies from the unseen, rather than from people in the human form. I chose a time of quiet, and although there was much physical suffering and much mental torment, I learned to overcome these things. I learned to go very deep within. It was my first experience with what I now speak to you of as the new house. I found comfort. I found energy, and I found love within myself. It took the walls of a prison for this to happen; otherwise I would have continued my everyday businesses, and continued my relationships. I chose this lifetime in prison as my final lifetime in that cycle. There will be a day when I return, following in your footsteps. There will be a day that I will come to some of you to be my teacher. Ah, we will have some laughs about that! (audience laughter)

✢ ✢ ✢ ✢

QUESTION: Dear Tobias, you have said that many of the New Age beliefs and practices are now old energy. I am currently studying a method of energy healing based on the seven chakra system. You keep saying that we now have only one chakra, so is the healing method I'm studying obsolete or old energy?

TOBIAS: Your chakra healing work is very appropriate for most humans you will work with. The vast, vast, vast majority of humans on Earth continue to work with the seven chakras. It is a small number of humans who are now integrating into the one chakra. The work that you are doing with these seven energy centers is most appropriate. Take these healing arts you are learning and add your own New Energy understanding to them. Beyond what is obvious in the books and the classes that you study are greater understandings. These understandings come from the ALL. In direct answer to your question, in a sense, yes, we would call this old energy, but it is most appropriate, because many of the ones who you will be working with will come from the old energy.

✣ ✣ ✣ ✣

QUESTION: Tobias, what is the validity of current predictions of no meat, fish, and grains in our future?

TOBIAS: Not true. Dear friends, there energies are needed to support life on your planet. These will continue, but they will be refined. When there are crises such as with your beef in England, this causes the scientists and the public and your governments to look at new and more refined ways. This is, in a sense, a transition from the old energy to the new. Something must pop up, or something must fester, or cause a problem for it to be reevaluated. Then humankind moves to the next level. As you learn to stand behind your short wall, you will not pass judgment for any of these things. You will have a greater understanding of why it is happening.

Meats, grains, fruits, and vegetables – it does not matter, dear friends. These are not negative things. These are resources for feeding the biology. As you are in your new house, you create with a broad stroke. You add your passion. Know that the appropriate nutrients will also be brought to you. Know that if it is time for your biology to change its patterns, these will show up at your door. When someone comes to you with what sounds like a silly food or something that you would not normally take into your body, look again. It is being brought to you for important reasons. It would not be so unusual even to – going to extremes here – have a diet of chocolate chip cookies! (audience laughter) Do not be so much in judgment of what is right or wrong for your body. Understand that what comes to your door is brought there in all appropriateness. It is time for you to dance with it.

✣ ✣ ✣ ✣

QUESTION: Tobias, I always felt that I was destined to come into this lifetime to help others during the time of great physical and spiritual change i.e., the great destructions that had been prophesied around the end of the millennium. Since this thankfully did not happen, now I feel lost and useless. Now that I am no longer fulfilling my contract as a Changeworker, what should I be seeking?

TOBIAS: Dear one, this is a most common attribute of Shaumbra throughout the world. Most of you came into this lifetime for completion within yourself, but also to guide and assist, and yes, to teach others during this prophesied time of great chaos. You would be anchors of peace and healing and light in the face of great chaos and turmoil all around you.

Through the work you and all humans have done, these prophesied destructions – the end of the world as many called it – did not occur. You have changed, you transformed things, you moved to the next level. In doing so, indeed the contract that you initially came in with was no longer needed. There became in your life, particularly in the last year or so, a great void. The service work you thought you were being called to, to help others during time of great chaos, to help others cross over, did not occur.

But dear friends, there was a "what-if" clause in your original contract. That "what-if" clause said that if you were to move to the next level without these traumatic things happening, then what would you do? And that is why we sit here with you now. That is the very reason we began these very specific lessons and discussions in past. The date of August 19, 1999 was the predicted date of destruction. This was also the time when we began these discussions in the tepee (see Tobias channel "The Departure of the Guides, August 21, 1999).

We began to work with you on your "what-if" clause. The clause stated that if things DID work out, there would be a need on Earth for teachers, those who had done much internal work, much internal processing and transformation. These would be the ones – and you are the ones – who agreed to go into their next lifetime while staying in body.

Each of you has been given at least one – and in many cases numerous – opportunities to leave this Earth to come to our side. You would return to be angels and runners for those who stayed on Earth. But indeed you chose to stay, to move to the next level.

Now there is a call of the angels that goes out. There is a need for teachers, for the ones who will be crossing over from the old energy to the new. Your work, therefore, is to be human guides. In order to do this, you must first walk the walk yourself. How could you be a teacher if you have not been on the path yourself? How can you guide other humans if you have not crossed the great chasm to your divinity on your own?

The call now is to learn how to release, to allow and to initiate the creation process. And now, to learn to be in Divine Will. These are all things that you are learning. These are all things that you will teach – that you are already teaching. We see many of you are already teaching it to others. Indeed you may change the words to fit them better, to adapt to them. You may describe it in your own way, but you are teaching. This is your calling.

You may work at a place that makes hamburgers – but you can still be a teacher. You may be one who draws pictures and creates joy through artwork – and you are still a teacher. The reason why you are here, the reason why you have affinity with this group and with these lessons, is so you can be the most powerful human guide and teacher to others. There IS work for you to do, do not doubt it!

✧ ✧ ✧ ✧

QUESTION: Tobias, what you ask in the lesson of releasing Free Will for Divine Will is tantamount to selling the soul to the devil. I feel like a wild horse must feel when asked to wear a bridle and saddle. This is a cosmic joke, right?

TOBIAS: This is good! (audience laughter) For this is triggering within you very appropriate reactions and emotions. As we said during the channel, there would be questions about this. We are suggesting that you release a gift given to you by Spirit long, long ago when you first left the Kingdom. You are being asked now to let this go. There will be the thoughts, and feelings that you are now selling yourself out; you are releasing something that was given to you by Spirit. These feelings and emotions will definitely come up.

We cannot answer this directly for you, other than to ask you to feel your own emotions, to feel what this is like. When the time comes and it feels appropriate, you will know. You will step into your Divine Will. You will understand that, in a sense, you are really releasing nothing, that you are moving into something much grander. In a sense, Free Will is truly a subset of Divine Will.

QUESTION: Tobias, please speak to charging money for spiritual gifts.

TOBIAS: (chuckling) What is being asked here is the appropriateness of charging a financial sum for spiritual understandings or classes or lessons. We ask you to feel the energy behind this. Now we will provide our insights.

This is an energy of duality, an old energy. There is within you the deep feelings that the energy of Spirit and money. We do not understand why you do not have equal and balanced respect for these. And now we will add a twist to this. You will be the ones going out to do the teaching. You will need an automobile to drive to your office or to the home of a client. You will need heat and food. Is it not appropriate that you should be compensated for your work? Is it not appropriate that the ones seeking your service should put forth the energy and the effort to balance for what you are doing for them?

The work you do as teachers will be more valuable to them than all the money in their bank. How do you charge for being a human guide and for helping to enlighten others? How do you charge for helping somebody break through the old energy into the new? How do you charge for teaching another how to be a creator of their own being? We ask you, all of you who are Shaumbra, to release this old notion for you will need the balance in the work that you do.

✢ ✢ ✢ ✢

QUESTION: Tobias, is it a good thing to work with those that have passed on?

TOBIAS: In a sense, they are working with you. For the most part they do not need the type of healing work that you believe you should offer to them. They do not – Cauldre challenges us here – but we continue. (audience laughter) They do not even so much need the type of prayer that you do.

Now there is an exception here. That is when they go through their transition heavy with the energy of Earth and of being human. This lasts for anywhere from a period of three days up to several months. You will be able to feel their need to be forgiven and released by you or others that hold them back. They have a need to be told that they are in a good space and an appropriate space. There are those who come to our side who so deeply and firmly believe in judgment that they sit and wait for it. It takes some work on our part and your part to help release them from this. There are those who are in hell even to this day. They have been there for quite some time, for they choose to believe in it, even though there are angels on this side who are working with them to try to break down those old belief systems. But it is difficult when there is an ingrained belief that they belong in this place called hell. It is difficult to get through to them. They think, oddly enough, that the devil is trying to trick them once again – to release the concept of hell.

When another comes to our side, release them. Forgive them if there are unresolved issues. And know that they come back to serve you. They are the ones who join the team of your runners, so do not feel that they need your healing all of the time.

✥ ✥ ✥ ✥

QUESTION: In my experience, the only truly Free Will is the Divine Will because the other choice comes out of old false identity or reaction. Is this true?

TOBIAS: Your perception is – very wise and very accurate. You will learn more about this as you truly transition into Divine Will. In a sense Free Will was an illusion. Free Will was an illusion. Divine Will has always been with you. The illusion was something called Free Will.

This does not mean that you were not free to do whatever you chose to do. But under the guise of Free Will there has always been the current of Divineness. In all of your journeys you have felt separated and alone from Spirit. This has created the illusion of Free Will. In reality, you are never alone. Spirit has always been with you. Spirit has always loved you and supported you. Spirit has always been you.

This has been difficult for you to imagine. Many of you have prayed or intended for an angel or God to appear to you as a "sign" before you take a step into your next level. Many of you have looked at the outer relationship in order to validate something that can only happen on the inside. Indeed you have never been alone, you have never been without Divinity, you have never truly been separated from Spirit.

As we move into our next series – (chuckling) Cauldre says we continue to promote these – we will talk more about how your divinity has always been there. We will talk about how to take your new Divine Will and bring it together for the support and the knowingness of God that you have always sought. We will talk about how to overlay your Divine Will with the support from Spirit, the support from Home that you have longed for all of this time. We will discuss how to truly meld these together.

✧ ✧ ✧ ✧

QUESTION: Tobias, why have I carried such a deep sorrow all my life? It's very disheartening. Is that why I have a hard time feeling my heart? Where is the joy for me? Where do I fit into this bizarre world and universe?

TOBIAS: You have cleared your issues that were based on the karma of your soul. We talked earlier of clearing your ancestral karma. But your core issue, your core sorrow, goes back to when you left Home. It was a traumatic experience. When you crossed through the Wall of Fire, you shattered into billions of pieces. You were in a state of complete fragmentation for what seemed eons of time.

When you left the Wall of Fire, you entered a void. There was nothing. You were cold. You felt you had been banished from the Kingdom. You were separated from Spirit, from your own spiritual parents. You were separated from God. You had never felt anything like this. It was the lowest of feelings. This is what you call the original sin, although it was not a sin. But this feeling of loss and separation would be like that of a young child who is abandoned by its parents, wondering why they are not worthy of love, wondering why they were set out in the cold. You felt you lost the connection of the love between mother and child. You felt you lost the connection of a fatherly love.

You have done much other clearing in this lifetime and now this final core issue comes up. The core issue is the sorrow of leaving Home. It will be a challenge for you, but it will be easier if you understand what created this sorrow in the first place. We have been working with Cauldre and Linda (Benyo) and the doctors on a way to bring Shaumbra back to those issues, to help you look at this time of separation, to help you see it with the same love that we see it (Crimson Circle Intensive - Outside the Circle). Dear friends, we can create the sacred space to help bring you back to the point of leaving Home, in order to help you understand the true love that was involved.

The journey of Shaumbra can be very difficult. You are walking away from old and perhaps somewhat comfortable energies. Moving from the old energy into the new energy often requires separating from things that were close and dear to you, such as jobs, family, loves ones, friends, a home you have lived in for a long time, and even ways of thinking. It is a difficult journey.

When you sit with a student who comes to your door asking for help and asking for guidance, dear friends, you'll look at them and see they are about to embark on a very difficult journey. You will know why they must do themselves. As their teacher, you will want them to understand that the journey is not what they think it will be. Oh, it is indeed wonderful. It is about discovering your divinity once again. But, dear friends, as you know, it is difficult and challenging. This ascension jounrey will be the most difficult thing you have ever done in any of your lifetimes before. In your other lifetimes, you perhaps had challenges, but you never had a challenge at the level you are at right now. You are walking across the Bridge of Swords. You are crossing the chasm from the old energy into the new.

Sitting with your student, you will try to explain that this will be the most challenging journey. You will chuckle as they sit with their bright eyes and big smile, and say to themselves, "Oh, it won't be that difficult, I can do anything." You will chuckle, knowing that it will be the most challenging yet most rewarding thing they have ever experienced.

In direct answer to your question, dear one, you are feeling the pain of the separation. There is healing that is taking place for you. There is healing in the words we speak to you. But there will come a point when you need to face this directly. There will come a point when you face it in your dreams or in your experiences, when you have to face this time of separation. By the way, you are making good progress. Do not give up, but do not struggle so much – the answers will come to you.

✥ ✥ ✥ ✥

QUESTION: Tobias, tell us about sex. What's the energy around it? (audience laughter)

TOBIAS: Hmmm, hmmmm. We will tell a story here and Cauldre does not so much like us sharing. (audience laughter) On our side of the veil we talk much of sex, much as you do. We talk about your sex lives (audience laughter) and yes, there are times dear friends, when we even are available when you are making love like this. Oh, we stand around and smile. (much audience laughter) At times there is such a tremendous symphony of energy that takes place between two people who care about each other. And to the one that asked the question (telepathically) just now, it does not matter to us one bit if it is male and female, or two members of the same sex. What we enjoy is the love that is made between the humans. Oh, it is like your finest music, and we like to watch. (audience laughter) But not in the voyeuristic way you may think. It draws us in and we are amazed at what you are creating. The expressions of love, the feelings of tenderness, all of this, it is amazing.

When All That Is reflected for even a brief moment about "Who Am I?" it instantly created two separate beings, the King and the Queen. They looked each other in the eye and connected in the heart. They loved each other so much that they created an offspring called Jack. You are Jack. The love of Spirit brought you forth. You brought this attribute to Earth in a biological way. When two humans love each other, they can create offspring like Spirit created you. Even when offspring are not created, there is tremendous love and tremendous energy that is created.

The energy that is created through the making of love between two humans does not then go out into the thin air and dissolve or go away. The energy of making love between humans is collected by angels. Then it is delivered in the appropriate manner into the new creation, the new universe that you are creating even at this very moment. This is the most potent of all energies that is used in creating the Second Circle. You started with a void, you are now building a new circle. As we have said, one day the First Creation will move into the Second Creation that you are now building. The most potent energy for this is the energy from humans loving each other. That is why we like to watch! (audience laughter).

Conversely, dear friends, when there is sex and it does not involve love; when there is sex that involves control or abuse of another; when there is dominance from one to the other and there is addiction to this; this also attracts energy. It does not attract the type of angels and entities that you like to work with. It attracts ones that are rather earthbound, ones whose energy you would not like so much. You would call it "dark." They will converge around this controlling type of sex and they will be fed the energy from that also. With that type of sex, an energy is produced that would feed what you would call the dark entities. And do not be so concerned that we will be coming into your bedroom all of the time. (audience laughter)

✥ ✥ ✥ ✥

QUESTION: Tobias, how is an ego formed? I was surprised to hear you say that even inanimate objects have an ego. How does an iron, for example, get an ego?

TOBIAS: These all have energetic identifications, which are somewhat different than an ego. An inanimate object such as a coat hanger, such as a bowl, such as an iron; these all have vibrational patterns. Fingerprints, as it were, of vibration. They do not have the type of spiritual energy that you have. They do not have the ability to be a creator like you do. They do not have the type of free will that you once had (audience laughter) and they do not contain the ability for its own divinity to expand.

But inanimate objects do contain a certain amount of vibration and intelligence. You can easily communicate with them. We sometimes have to scratch our head and wonder why you do not talk to more trees and to more bowls and to more rocks and things. They are very pleasant to talk to! Sometimes more pleasant to talk to than humans. (audience laughter)

All things contain their own type of life force and vibration. They are all connected. You are separate – each one of you is separate and independent – but yet you are all connected in a way. Do not think of these inanimate objects having an ego like yours but think of them having a separate identity. They cannot make the type of decisions that you can, they do not have a spiritual intelligence like you do, and they cannot grow or expand their divinity like you can.

✥ ✥ ✥ ✥

QUESTION: Dear Tobias, I have suffered depression for most of my adult life. I found relief with medication and I'm wondering if the medication inhibits my spiritual growth?

TOBIAS: Now, Cauldre asks us not to give medical advice, but we will ignore him here! (audience laughter) Dear friends, many of you have used these medications for a layer of protection, to get out of the intensity of your own mind. In order to fully move into your divinity you will need to and want to release these drugs. They provide you with a blanket. They provide a barrier that has protected you from the old energy ways of yourself.

You will need to release these to move forward. Now the drugs will continue to carry residue within you for a period of time, unfortunately. When you stop taking them they will not go right away. There is a chemical buildup in your body but more than that, it has caused a somewhat longer term blanket, an emotional blanket, that will take some work to release. There is a layer that will take a lot of love and a lot of attention to release. We suggest to you and to all others who have taken antidepressant drugs and any sort of psychological drugs to find a way to release these. We are not saying they are bad, but they will continue to keep a barrier between you and your divinity.

We would suggest to you to have a support group of Shaumbra that you can talk to for you will go through some difficult and challenging times releasing these. You will be opening parts of your self that you have tried to close off through these drugs. This will be a difficult and challenging time. Have a support group of Shaumbra. If they are not in your area move to an area where they are!

Cauldre can also feel our emotions and knows that we do not so much like these drugs! You are hiding from the problem rather than addressing it. The work of a good new energy facilitator will do much to balance and heal than what these drugs can do. There are core issues that are seeking to come out here. Your doctors and counselors of the New Energy can help address the deep inner issues that are causing the imbalances.

QUESTION: Tobias, there are significant things that can happen to people that just stop taking psychological drugs.

TOBIAS: We understand this. You are speaking in general of those who are still walking in the old energy. We are speaking of those who are walking in the New Energy and are Shaumbra. We understand that this – Cauldre stops us quite often here but we will continue – we understand that there are implications of going off of these medications. But you do not understand yet what type of reaction that a New Energy human will have when they release these medications. The reaction will be quite different than that of a human who is walking in the old energy. Yes, they will need to be under supervision, that is why we said they need a support group. They will need the guidance and counsel of qualified New Energy doctors and facilitators. But, dear friends, you cannot go into the New Energy with a complex chemical that alters the natural and divine processes that are taking place. Period!

✧ ✧ ✧ ✧

QUESTION: Tobias, please discuss more of Shaumbra, of the energy of Shaumbra.

TOBIAS: 2500 years ago and 2000 years ago and 1000 years ago there were major influxes of humans, of angels, who came to Earth carrying special spiritual attributes with them. It was not one person. It was not just Siddhartha. It was not just Yeshua Ben Joseph who came here to awaken divinity. It was an entourage of humans.

There was a group 2000 years ago that was part of this. Dear friends, most of you here and most of you reading this were part of that group. You were not necessarily in this place of Jerusalem at that time, although many were. But you came to Earth at that time to bring an important attribute. You would gather. You would meet. You came up with the name for yourself – Shaumbra. It was, in a sense, a quiet society, a quiet group. You had understandings when you looked each other in the eye that you had come to Earth at that important time to bring something was much needed. You would communicate that there was a gathering to take place by wearing an article of clothing, a shawl, or other apparel of a crimson color. You called yourself Shaumbra. There are agreements that go back to the very times when you came to Earth, of the journey that you would take. Look at each other in the eye now. Do this. Look at each other in the eye. (audience looks into each others eyes) You are family. Look at the love. Look at the divinity. Remember how you agreed to be back together again, even for a brief period of time. Look around. This is Shaumbra. This is family – Shaumbra, meaning the family of Home. We gather here now in this love.

QUESTION: Tobias, how do we achieve ascension in this lifetime?

TOBIAS: By not desiring to achieve ascension in this lifetime! (audience laughter) Dear friends, we hear this so often. We hear your prayers, all of them. We hear your talk. We even hear those curse words of yours, but we do not care so much! (audience laughter) For those who have the desire to leave what somebody just said in their mind this "stinking planet" (audience laughter) and never to come back again, we have very bad news for you: We will sit with you again in another lifetime in groups like this!

You will be in a new body, but we will be telling you the same stories! You left Home eons and eons of time ago, but we add with a wink in our eye, it was not so long ago. Do you know that creation as you know it is really not that old? In a sense, time is going backwards as much as it is going forward. It was not so long ago that you left Home. You left Home, and you came through the Void. You created the stars. You created this universe and your playground. When things did not work out quite so well, you came to this place of Earth, but there was wisdom and divinity behind this decision.

You come to this place of Earth to birth a new type of divinity. That is why you are here. This Earth is a nest, a home. You are birthing a new type of divinity that has never been seen in all of creation. You come here to create the new energy, what we have called the "second creation."

Dear friends, when you ascend, you do not go back Home. Home will eventually come here to you. It will come here. We do not know how to say this so well – you cannot go back Home. You cannot. But Home can come to you. All That Is will expand into where you are. It will come to you.

Ascension means going into the New Energy where your divinity shines in this new place where you have birthed it. It is not about going BACK Home. It is about creating something new for Spirit that could never be done before. You exist outside of All That Is. Oh, Cauldre has challenged us over and over on this, but we continue to say that when you left the Kingdom, you went outside of All That Is. Someday, All That Is will come to you. It will expand. That is the reason why you left the Kingdom in the first place.

Dear friends, you are never alone.

✣ ✣ ✣ ✣

"And So It Is ..."

✣ ✣ ✣ ✣